Call of the Soul

Anne Carroll Decker

 VERITAS PRESS Ltd.

Call of the Soul

©2006 by Anne Carroll Decker

Library of Congress Control Number: 2005910000

ISBN 0-9652504-2-3

Printed in Canada
First Edition 2006

Published by

VERITAS PRESS Ltd.

P.O. Box 270735
West Hartford, CT 06127-0735
VeritasLtd@aol.com

Produced by
PPC BOOKS
Redington Shores, FL

Call of the Soul

Books by Anne Carroll Decker

Songs of the Soul

Circle of the Soul

One

W rite this down and do not question it," the Archangel instructed me. "God is with everyone, now. And they do not realize it. Open up your hearts to Him and let Him be with you so that you can hear Him and understand His ways."

He knows me too well, I thought. It had been several months since the Archangel had come to me delivering the messages recounted in my first two books, *Songs of the Soul* and *Circle of the Soul.* Those books were full of my questions. When he responded I peppered him with more questions, challenging his answers if they didn't satisfy me. Often I ignored the weighty topics he brought up and changed the subject to my own immediate concerns.

After I finished those two books, I had no idea if I would ever see the Archangel again. In the meantime I had suffered a debilitating illness. I was very discouraged and totally preoccupied with my physical problems. Now in December of 1998 he returned.

We were sitting on a large rock overlooking the sea, where we had often met before. Still in my dark mood, I barely noted the grandeur of his presence or the stunning beauty of his purple robes threaded with silver. I paid little attention to the huge import of the words he had just addressed to me.

Without even greeting him I blurted, "Can't we talk of health? It's such an issue in my life."

"Go ahead," he answered.

"Why do we get sick?"

"Because in difficult times you are faced with more forks in the road, more choices to make. In good times you often ignore the purpose of the soul."

"I wasn't."

"Yes you were. You were consumed with telling the story, not living the story."

"Oh," I said, unsure of what that meant.

"Now you will have more compassion for those who are ill, those who are lonely, those who are in need. You will not forget this time, nor will you want to."

"I always forget the bad feelings once they're gone. That's when I break promises to God."

"During this experience you have learned the lesson of compassion for others. You have learned many lessons in the last three years but this was an important one for you."

"But what about my worrying?"

"How has worry served you except to age the mind and make the body infirm?"

"It hasn't, I guess. But I can't let it go."

"You must breathe in the Spirit and take yourself beyond yourself."

"What do you mean?"

"You must get out of your own small world, your own small way. Many people around you are suffering and yet you ignore that."

"Oh gee. I just begin to think I'm living a decent life and then you tell me this."

"It is all right. You are in a school of learning. If you knew it all you wouldn't be here. But in your heart you *do* know it all."

"That doesn't make sense."

"You had all the knowledge once, and then turned from God and draped a cover over it. You became ignorant. Now you struggle to pull off that cover and remember the beauty of being one with God."

"Oh, please help me."

"We do all the time. God is always there. Rest in these words. We once told you to flow like the river, and you find that difficult. You struggle against the tide and weary your mind and body. Surrender. Enjoy each moment that God has given you. It is a gift from Him."

"Please heal me. Please ask God to heal me."

"You are being healed as you write this. Turn to Him and allow His warmth to penetrate, His knowledge to enter, and your body will be healed too."

"Thank you." I was weeping gently so I added, "I should go now."

"Tears cleanse the system. It is all right. Allow the light of God and the blessings we bring to enter your body."

"Thank you."

"Amen."

2

Two

Although I continued to pray, six months passed before the Archangel returned. Again we were at the beach, the cool breezes kissing my face.

"You are healed," he declared.

"Why did I go through such hell? Why did it happen?" I had had a severe liver reaction to an antibiotic I had taken. For weeks I had fevers every night. I was so ill that just going down a flight of stairs exhausted me. Mentally I just about lost it. At first the doctors thought I had hepatitis. Finally they decided I was allergic to the antibiotic, but last week the drug was pulled off the market because it had caused six deaths from liver failure and permanent liver damage in many other people. I was lucky to be alive.

The Archangel's answer startled me. "You are the one who insisted on an earthly body."

"What?"

"You insisted on an earthly body to develop your wisdom to a deeper level."

"What wisdom?"

"You are a teacher and a healer."

"No I'm not," I argued. "I lecture a little but I'm no healer."

"On another plane you are a teacher and a healer and you knew how to help others. You needed more wisdom, wisdom that comes only from experience."

"On what plane? Where was I?"

"Do you think this earth is the only place where God has created love? "

I shrugged.

"Some are more advanced, others less so. So each of you is sent to where you are needed, either for yourself or for others."

"Are you talking about other planets?" This sounded bizarre.

"In centuries past men believed the earth was flat because they could not conceive of it as round. Similarly, because you don't see God's other creations you don't think they exist. Yet God is infinite love, infinite love, and for Him to be such, love must expand through the universe to more creatures, more for whom He has love."

"What about me? Why was I so sick?" My thoughts always returned to a minuscule level, to myself. Here he is speaking of universes and others whom God loves—and I want to know about my own tiny little self. I was ashamed of my behavior, but that didn't stop me.

"You have learned lessons during this illness."

"Yes, that I've become a basket case. I'm afraid to take an aspirin or put anything else into my mouth that might affect my liver."

"No, you have learned to relinquish control of that which is beyond you to God. With a small step you have begun to walk the faith of which you will speak."

I nodded.

"What did you do when you were so ill?"

"I worried."

"And what else?" he prodded.

"I was so sick I couldn't even pray. I felt abandoned by God, by you, by the angels. But I knew something terrible was wrong with me. So I called all the priests, the ministers, the nuns, the churches, the prayer groups I had spoken to, and asked them all to pray for me."

"And you were healed," he said definitively. "The power of a community praying for another is stronger than any weapon, any drug. We have told you this before. But now you can see it. You did not understand it fully. You didn't understand why you were still so ill when people were praying for you. You got angry that you didn't get well immediately. Yet you were not poisoned. A healing took place. It was stronger than the man-made chemicals that supposedly fought infection."

"Are you saying that prayer is stronger than medicine? Some religions believe that and don't let children have any medicine when they're sick. And the children *die*!"

"Prayer is stronger than medicine, of course. But I am not saying not to take medicine when you're ill. Medicine is also a gift from God. He gave man the ability to discover it. The herbs that grow profusely throughout His lands hold many beneficial healing powers for people. But when man fails with his discoveries, God is stronger."

"Why did this happen now?"

"You are a difficult learner, always questioning, always wanting to control life. This time in your life allowed you to grow and to understand more deeply the community of prayer of which you will need to tell others. It is one thing to repeat the messages, but for you to truly teach them you've had to live them and understand them at your soul level. This is why, in your wisdom, you know you must take on these lessons."

"Are you talking about reincarnation? Because I don't believe in that," I said rather adamantly.

"There is only one life, but many lifetimes if you choose. You were all together with God in the beginning, turned away, and will all be together with God again, at the beginning."

"You mean 'the end'?"

"No, the beginning of another level with God. You all will have attained a higher degree of wisdom, so that turning from God will no longer be a possibility for you. You will want all his creatures to return to Him. You will still have free will, but you will choose God; you will choose to return to His love. These messages will begin again for you and for the others. The wisdom from the One will permeate the souls. Amen."

"Amen," I said softly, ready to go scratch these messages onto a pad of paper. I had no computer, just a pencil. As I wrote I remembered everything and the words flowed quickly onto the page. When I was finished I sat quietly, wondering if these messages too would alter my path.

Probably.

Three

Two mornings later I was going upstairs to take a shower when the words came into my head, "Don't postpone your prayer. You must pray now."

I sat down on the couch and closed my eyes. My inner vision was completely covered with black clouds. I stood amidst them calling out for help. "I can't see anything. Get me out of here."

"You are in the darkness, where you have been for months. Darkness is not always 'evil' in your terms. It is an alienation from God, which can bring evil, despondency, lost hope. You have been in this foggy darkness, searching for God, searching for answers."

"Please, help me out."

The clouds parted and I stood on the beach once again. The Archangel waited, sitting on the rock.

"Thank you," I said.

"Thank God," he replied. "He is the one who sent me."

"I always say in my lectures that I don't expect you back, because there is so much to learn in the first and second books—and I've hardly learned a tenth of it. I know what it says, but I don't live it."

"That is true," he replied. "You still have much work to do, but the messages will begin again because there are others who have advanced and need them. These messages will help you understand and live the previous ones even more fully."

I bowed my head in shame. He had given me all these messages of God's love, telling me just to walk in faith, but during my sickness the previous winter I didn't do that. I couldn't see past the horrible illness.

"You are human," he said. "Your body is human. Do not be so hard on yourself. You are here to learn, and with learning come mistakes, errors, and then advancement. If you learned without any of that, the wisdom would never truly take root in your soul. You need to know, once again, that you are a spiritual being in a body, and this body will eventually die and rot away, but you will not. Your soul will soar."

"So again, what's the point of the body?" I asked somewhat flippantly, but deep down really trying to struggle with the question.

"You are here to advance toward God. These messages are here to

6

help people do that, to remember why they have chosen to take this path, why it is a joy to be on earth."

A *joy?* I thought of the torturous deaths in Kosovo, the hatred one religion has for another. "It's not always joyous," I said. "Horrible things are going on as we speak. People's level of anxiety is high all the time, even people who live 'regular' lives."

"You are not here to acquire lands, money or property. People forget this. If this were true, property and material possessions would disappear from the earth as each person died. You take only two things with you when you die."

"Two things?"

"You take wisdom and love, the wisdom and love that you have acquired during your lifetime. Both of these bring you closer to God. That is the purpose for your being here. Nothing else matters."

"Wisdom?"

"Yes. With wisdom you understand the meaning of your lives, the journeys of your souls. With wisdom you learn compassion and caring for those less fortunate, those still in darkness."

"But," I argued, "that can't always work. I'll give you an example. Say a person is born severely brain-damaged, maybe so much so that they are bedridden for years, never speaking, never talking, and because of the damage never thinking. How can that person acquire wisdom and knowledge in his lifetime? Or people in irreversible comas—how do they continue to acquire wisdom? They can't."

"You see only what you want to see," he said softly. "You always speak in your lectures of the bigger picture. You tell people that they look at their lives through binoculars, focusing on what they want to focus on, and when they remove the binoculars, the picture is much more beautiful, much more expansive. It is God's picture."

"Yes," I said. "I've seen it happen. But I can't see how brain-damaged people can acquire wisdom."

"Wisdom is not just learning literature, biology, and so on, although that too can bring you closer to each other and closer to God. But true wisdom is seeing the light, understanding those in darkness, and living compassion. The people of whom you spoke can learn in their bodies love from others, who in turn learn the wisdom of the Holy Spirit, because that is the wisdom of caring, compassion and infinite love. God is infinite love. Those who are cared for by others feel God's love and thus learn it through their souls, while those who care for them learn the meaning of sharing and caring and living God's truth and word as He wanted you to."

"They can learn?"

"Learning is on many levels. Your brain is locked on these people learning. Yes, they can feel love. Infant children know virtually nothing, not math, not biology, not literature, not how to balance a checkbook. But when they are touched and caressed, they absorb the love. This is how they learn to accept love and give love. And with love comes wisdom. With wisdom comes love."

"Oh," I said.

"Do not stop there. Continue. The people who come to this world and cannot move, cannot talk, or are 'impaired' as you call it, may already be filled with wisdom and love, and ready to sacrifice their lives to teach others how to love."

"But what if someone is in a coma for years and people don't show love around that person, and they call her a 'vegetable' and treat her like a thing?"

"It is an opportunity to get closer to God, and people have failed this lesson. They must learn it somewhere at some time before they return home to God. So it is everyone's prayers that allow kindness and compassion to be available. Send it out into the world and it will return in the world. You may never see it return to your life, but it will return to someone's."

"Tell me more about wisdom."

"Christ had wisdom. Wisdom is understanding. His words were 'Forgive them, Father, for they know not what they do.' He understood that darkness is ignorance, that evil is ignorance. Therefore it is important to achieve all the wisdom you can through this life."

"I can think of some computer people who have a lot of wisdom, but they aren't spiritual. They've made major developments in technology. Do they take that wisdom with them?"

"That is knowledge. They have learned, and they have helped or hindered humanity with the knowledge they have acquired. Knowledge and wisdom are different. Knowledge may lead to wisdom, but there are many who acquire wisdom and never have the knowledge of which you speak. You take only two things with you when you die: wisdom and love. Nothing else is important. Once you have achieved true wisdom, love is the only gift you will keep because true wisdom is infinite love. That is the goal. When you were made in the image and likeness of God, you were made in the image and likeness of love. You sinned and turned away. Your path is to return to infinite love, to return to God. Ponder this. Pray on it. You will realize these words are from the Holy Sprit. I am only delivering them for Her."

He put his hand over my liver and made the sign of the cross. "You are healed. Now take this healing and change your life and others'. It was not your time. And you needed to learn, once again, the power of a community praying for each other. You think you have not advanced very much, or learned the messages very well, but do not be so harsh on yourself. In your darkness, when you could not pray, you still called on others to pray for you. That is a huge step toward God and belief in communication with God. It is a living example of the circle of the souls."

He left me, rising into the sky. I stood watching the clouds where he had disappeared. I brushed away tears, trying not to cry.

Why do we put ourselves through so much, when there's a picture we don't even understand?

From the heavens I heard the Archangel call out, "There was a time when you understood it and chose it. God created you with free will, and that free will extends even to choosing the place you have been born, the people you encounter, the lives you live."

I wasn't sure about that. Wouldn't I have chosen a house on the ocean, perfect health for my family and friends, never feeling despondent?

"Tell me," his voice echoed through the skies, "would you send your child to the first grade every year, just because as he got older the grade was so simple for him he received only A's all the time?"

"Of course not. That would be stupid."

"Then think of your life. The struggles put in front of you are *gifts*. You may not see that at the time, and some of you will never see it during your lifetime, but I assure you they are gifts, gifts that you have requested.

"God bless you. Praise His holy works. Amen," he said.

Four

It is late at night, nearly two weeks after I last saw the Archangel. I haven't prayed all day or sat in meditation or even thought about it. I am still consumed with fears about my liver, thinking that every headache is connected to it, that every warm forehead is the fever about to return. My doctor put me on an anti-anxiety medicine, and that made me feel I couldn't cope on my own—and I guess I can't.

This is a low point of my life.

At this late hour, while I'm sitting at the computer knowing that I should have sat and prayed today, the Archangel returns.

"Why have you not sat in the silence?" he asked, not judgmentally, but firmly.

"I don't know," I said. "You tell me beautiful things, and right now I'm in a dark place. I'm having trouble implementing what you say, so I guess I don't want to hear it."

"You are healed," he repeated. "You must get past this and move on to your spiritual life. Your physical body will never function correctly with your worries and your lack of spiritual concern."

"I *am* spiritually concerned. I just am overwhelmed."

"And you look in the wrong places for help."

"The doctors?"

"No, I didn't say that. But foremost you must find your spirituality, and give it time each day. You give your worries half an hour each day, half an hour of negativity and darkness." (The doctor had said I had to postpone all my worries each day to an allotted time. I've tried it today, and it's worked a little.) "You must do the same for the light. Doing it for the darkness is good. It will help you face your fears, tire of them, and move on. But you must also do this for the light, because it will help you face the light, grow and thrive and move on."

"Why is it so hard?"

"Because, as we have said before, humanity finds comfort in the darkness. It is what you know, what you have been programmed to know, and what the Evil One wants you to know. Any kind of fear alienates you from love, from Infinite Love which is God."

"You make it so easy," I said, sad and tired. "It's not as easy as you say."

"During the day you put a stop sign on your worries. When you think of goodness or light, or pray to God, put a green light on the thought. Carry it through. It is a simple exercise but one that will work. Allow God to enter your thoughts and soul and fill you with the light. He will fill your soul with joy and happiness. But you must allow it to be filled, and in order to do this you must empty it of fear. Fear and love cannot exist together."

"Great," I said sarcastically. "Because fear I've got plenty of. My friend, a minister, asked me to write down ten things that help me to fly, and ten things that ground me, and I only wished he had asked me to write ten things that are fearful for me, because I could do that task easily. Fifty things would be a cinch. But I struggled with the others."

"I saw the list. You listed the ocean as both flying and grounding, and you listed prayer as grounding. Go to the ocean, sit, and pray. Go early in the morning and find God waiting for you. He is there. If that will allow you to open the doors without fear blocking you, then do it. You are in a transitional period of your life. Each event leads you to God; each is a lesson. People often complain about their suffering and their tribulations, and we understand that is a human condition, but those are also blessings. They are opportunities to find the light, opportunities to grow as a person. If everything were perfect you would not grow. If you kept your child in the first grade his whole life, after the first year it would be simple for him but eventually he would be bored and stagnant and never grow as an intellect or a person. Yet moving on to a different grade brings fright and apprehension, but then, when that is gone, enlightenment. That is why fear and love cannot exist together. But if used correctly, as a tool, fear, faced and conquered, will bring you back to the light. Do not ignore the fear, or allow it to swallow you. If you do you will become ignorant of the spirit and alienated from God."

"I know that saying, 'Face your fears.' "

"There is truth in it. Tell the others that once fear is faced, it is usually of little consequence."

"Right." Again I was sarcastic. "People are faced with chemotherapy and you say that is of little consequence."

"It is how you face each situation in life that determines the situation."

"What do you mean?"

"Face the fear of the cancer, and then the cancer does not have the power it did to overtake your emotions."

"I don't get it. I don't have cancer but someone reading this might. How does it work?"

"The thoughts that race through people's mind are of pain and suffering and death, and often jealousy that others are healthy. This is acceptable, a normal stage of growth. But in order to conquer this emotionally, you must face the cancer. Talk about it with others. Realize that it does not have power over your soul, over who you really are. Once people realize that, that their achievements are within their souls, not within their bodies, the light will shine. They will grow with astounding leaps and bounds. They will be filled with infinite love."

I didn't think that made much sense. "I don't think I'm at the level yet to really grasp this."

"No," he said sadly, "you are at the level. But you don't want to move on."

"That's not true!" I screamed. "Of course I want to move on. I want to advance spiritually. Why do you think I'm going to the minister and the doctor? Because I want to be stuck?"

"It's what you know, and it's easy to do even if it brings anxiety and displeasure. To move to the next step, to think of God within and around you, to think of yourself as safe within His arms, is not easy for you."

"No, it isn't. Sometimes I don't feel it."

"Because you are not open to feeling it. You, and the others, must open yourselves to God's love. The only way that can be accomplished is to face the fear, empty it, and fill it with compassion and love. Then growth occurs at astounding rates."

"Give me some hints, some way to do this."

"Believe."

"Oh great. A single word. Believe." I breathed the word out slowly, in exasperation and disbelief.

"It is a powerful word. 'Believe' is a powerful verb. Repeat it in prayer. It will encompass so much for you. Believe in letting go of the fear, believe in the love that awaits you, believe that you are in the situation to grow and that God awaits you all the time. When you truly believe this, truly have faith, your view of the world will change."

"It's not too late? The way it's been explained to me is that chemically your brain is altered. If your reaction is, say, immediate fear when you get sick, then that pathway is established and you move directly to that."

"Yes, it is conditioned. Did you ever get into a car and end up at your destination and not even remember driving there? You did it on automatic pilot. Or have you headed toward somewhere that's familiar and ended up there, even when you planned on taking a turn somewhere else?"

"Yes, "I said, still wondering where this was going.

"Well, chemically you have trained your body to go directly to that destination when you get in the car. The car may be a metaphor for sickness, and the destination for the fright. But there are other routes to other destinations. You can take out a map and actively decide to go somewhere else."

"That must be so difficult. Because physically your body responds."

"You wanted that."

"Wanted what?"

"A body. You insisted on it. But now, like so many times before, you're complaining."

"What are you talking about?"

"You keep insisting on certain lessons for your growth, and God allows it because they are the lessons you need. Then, when you're in the middle of them, you forget all of that."

"I don't know what you're talking about." I shook my head.

"Everyone chooses the lessons they need to learn for more wisdom. The problem is, when the lessons are presented humans can accept them or not. They forget they're the lessons they chose themselves. So if they are not accepted and learned, they continue to repeat themselves."

"What's my lesson?"

"Compassion."

"Compassion?" I asked defensively. "I'm a compassionate person, a very compassionate person. I wouldn't have picked that lesson."

"Compassion comes on a variety of levels. You have learned that you are as vulnerable as others, and now suddenly you realize that and begin to have compassion for those you were judging."

"Oh," I said, knowing exactly what he meant. I didn't have to question that part.

"You thought you were stronger, better, more enlightened than the others, and now you see that you too have your steps backwards. So with compassion comes wisdom. But this lesson will repeat itself—"

"OH NO!" I screamed.

"—if you do not face the fear which is engulfing you."

"Will you help me?"

"We will to an extent, but it is your journey. Prayer will allow the fear to leave, because if you truly listen to God—and if you allow it—the fear will have to leave. There is not room for both fear and God in the same breath. Only love and God."

"But wasn't Christ fearful when he knew he was going to be crucified?" I asked.

The angel nodded. "Yes, and he asked, 'Why have you forsaken me?' So for that brief moment, even in Christ's life the fear pushed God from him. The fear made him think God was gone. Yet moments later he dismissed the fear and said, 'Lord, I will do Your will.' Then God can come into your life.

"Your work on this leg of your journey is to push the fear out and bring the love in. Do not be so hard on yourself if it doesn't come easily. Dark times can be opportunities for finding God at a deeper level, if you want to move from the darkness. Even Christ, in his pain and fear, felt abandoned. Yet it was not God who abandoned him but Christ's thoughts that were filled with fear. Remember he was both divine and human. Human nature moves toward fear."

"Isn't fear good sometimes?"

"In the physical sense. If you see a wild bear approaching you fear runs through your body and allows your adrenaline to help you run and avoid death. But if you harbor the fear, get stuck in the fear, the light will not come in. The adrenaline will not kick in, you will not run, and the bear will kill you. So fear must be overcome with light.

"Goodnight. Pray," he said softly, "and remember you are where you're supposed to be at this junction of your journey."

Five

A few days later I knew I needed to quiet my mind and listen, either to the Archangel or to the silence. Both would be healing.

I find that when I give lectures I can block out all distractions in my life, all my worries. I become energized by telling people of God's messages and gifts for them. The other night I gave a lecture in someone's home. She wanted me to tailor part of it to children aged ten to fourteen. Initially I just dismissed her request. I had given over two hundred lectures *the same way* and I didn't think I could start changing it without ruining the impact of the lecture. She called that day and restated her request. I hemmed and hawed. She said, "Pray about it."

I did. It was really quite an easy prayer because I was too tired to get into all the details with God. I just said, "God, if you can help me with this, when the time comes please put the words into my mouth."

I am always concerned about talking too much. The lecture is usually forty-five minutes, which somehow I have found to be the perfect length, long enough to get the story out but short enough so that people don't start squirming in their seats. Adding children's aspects to the lecture could only lengthen it and bore the adults—I was sure of that.

I arrived, on an extremely hot June day. The woman had told her guests to bring lawn chairs and I gave the lecture outside in her backyard. As I spoke I added examples that the children might understand. I always speak about patience, recounting being behind a woman in the express lane at the grocery store (twelve-item limit) who has eighteen items (I know because I have counted each one as she's removed it from her cart) and she's going to purchase part with a credit card and part with a check, and I feel the anger and frustration mounting within my chest and throat. People laugh, but they understand.

But children wouldn't. So I added, "You might not understand that. But you do understand being in the cafeteria line for lunch and someone cuts in front of you. And then another, and then a third."

A young boy held up four fingers. I laughed and said, "Okay, four people cut in front of you. You know the feeling of anger and frustration that builds up." He nodded back.

At the end one of the children came up to me and said, "Usually I feel stressed and worried. But today I feel all clean." I swallowed hard, trying to find a voice to thank him.

On the way home I thought, as I almost always do, Anne, listen to what you say to people. Listen and live it. Each time you say it, you're saying it to yourself too. Remember to sit in the silence and pray.

Six

I've had difficulty praying and meditating lately. I've been overly anxious about small, petty things, and that has unsettled me. I've found that such simple (or perhaps profound) activities as praying, meditating, listening, become lost in my petty obsessions, and I can't sit down and listen to God

Today I tried again. "Tried" probably isn't the word. I just sat. I breathed. I hoped I'd connect. And a pain came into the middle of my forehead.

"It's your third eye," the Archangel's voice said.

"What?" I asked.

"You've had pain there before. It's your third eye."

"First, tell me again what this third eye is."

"It's the eye to your soul. You can close it, and when the information you need is sent to you, the information bounces from it. It cannot enter, because you have closed your third eye. It's an ancient belief but a true one. Recently you have been seeing with only your two physical eyes. But it is the third eye, which sits invisibly in the middle of your forehead, which is the most important."

"But it hurts there so much. Maybe I should take a Tylenol or something."

"That will not change it. You can heal it in a moment."

"I can?"

"Yes. Just allow it to open. Allow the knowledge from the Helper to descend."

"How?" The pain was similar to the hot/cold feeling of an ice cube sitting in the middle of my forehead.

"Ask God to see the information."

"See it?"

"Yes. Visualize it in a physical form."

This is nuts, I thought.

I closed my actual eyes and concentrated on the headache. Then I asked God to "see" the knowledge. A ray of deep bright blue light came into my forehead. My forehead hurt more.

"Open the eye," the Archangel commanded.

I couldn't see this "third eye." All I felt was something banging away at my forehead. The best I could do was to visualize behind the eye, where I opened imaginary shutters, as if standing behind a window.

And the pain disappeared. My mind was filled with blue light.

"Better?" he asked.

I nodded my head. I shut the shutters and the pain began again.

"AH!" he said. "I thought you'd do that! Stop that!"

Stop that? The Archangel never gave me such sharp commands. Was he losing patience with me?

"No, of course not," he replied, apparently reading my mind. "It's just that when you experience something beautiful, you often stop it midstream. We don't understand it. It's as if you'd almost rather have the pain."

I stopped. His words had struck a chord in me. Would I rather have pain than beauty? And if so, why would that be?

I was talking to a friend yesterday about how I grew up in a church where we pounded our chests three times while saying in Latin, "Mea culpa, mea culpa, mea culpa," which means, it's my fault, it's my fault, it's my fault. She looked amazed at first, and then shrugged. She had come from a very puritanical Protestant church and understood, in a different context, the same concept.

We were brought up being not good enough. We were at fault.

I'd been reading a book by the Dalai Lama, who is astounded at the feeling of self-hate that many in Western civilizations feel. He says in Buddhism such a feeling does not exist.

And now I'm back to the pain in my forehead. Why do I choose that rather than the beautiful blue light?

"I don't know why I do," I said, near tears. "Do you?"

"I believe that you, and many others, still do not understand on the deepest level that you are partakers in the divine. Because when you do not understand this, you do not truly believe that happiness and joy are acceptable gifts. You are stuck in a negative circle, a circle of low self-esteem."

"I believe God loves me unconditionally," I told him, although I wondered if I said it with a huge degree of confidence. "I tell people that all the time."

"And when you say it, you believe it," he agreed. "But you believe it for them. Not for you. You believe it wholeheartedly when you talk to the murderers and the drug addicts, but when you drive home you still think that you are so imperfect, how could God love you?"

I didn't reply. He seemed too much on target. He was right. The messages I gave to people about God's unconditional love for them, regardless of what they had done with their lives, I believed wholeheartedly, strongly, with conviction and love. Yet for myself I had a hard time truly believing it. I would constantly remember some small selfish act of mine and harp on it until I was sure I was an awful person.

"We have told you before, and we will tell you again: You are human. Humanity is not perfect. Your souls are divine. They are perfect. They are connected with God. They partake in the divine energy. You are sure to fail if you rely only on your humanity. You will be stuck in a circle of negativity that grows endlessly."

"How do I stop it then?"

"Forgive yourself."

Forgive myself? This was a new concept. We had talked about forgiveness in *Songs of the Soul*, but that was when I couldn't pray for murderers, child molesters or other criminals.

"You must forgive yourself. You must realize that God forgives you immediately, the moment you are conscious of an action, and even when you are not conscious of it."

"I just can't do that."

"It will take practice for you. You need to perform a variety of tasks."

Tasks? Oh great, I thought. He's going to give me jobs to do. "What kind of tasks?"

"Each day you are to relish an aspect of your personality that is joyous and wonderful."

"What?"

"Do that."

"Perhaps that would make me overly confident, cocky. The other extreme."

"No, it will not. It will allow your personality to rest and come into alignment with your soul. It cannot do that while it still lacks self-esteem. In order to grow that self-esteem—"

I interrupted him. "I'll do more things. I'll give more lectures. I'll go back to school and then I'll feel better about my accomplishment."

"No, that is not the answer. If you'd like to go to school for the sake of learning we'd be delighted, because at death you take only two aspects of life with you, wisdom and compassion. But achievements will not eradicate your lack of esteem. What will do that is understanding that your personality is unique to the world, as is everyone's, and that God gave you this personality with its gifts and its flaws in order for you to grow as a soul. What is a joyous aspect of your personality?"

"I have a pretty good sense of humor. You probably wouldn't even know it from our conversations, but I do. Or at least people tell me I do."

He nodded. "We know that and enjoy it. Why did you add 'or at least people tell me I do'? Humor is a gift from God. You have an abundance of it, and sometimes do not use it because the negativity draws you from it. Tomorrow sit and pray and thank God for your humor. Tell everyone to do this task. Each day find an attribute in your personality that is wonderful. Everyone has them; we do not want to hear people say that they do not. Meditate on that. Thank God for it. Embrace it and relish it. Think of times you've helped others with it. Thank your body and mind for housing it. At the end say simply, I am worthy of God's love for me. I am a partaker in the divine. Do that tomorrow." He rose into the sky.

While I was with him the pain in my head had gone away. As he departed it came back full-force.

Seven

I was concerned about the Archangel's words that I was a healer and a teacher at another level and needed to learn compassion on earth. It bothered me. After all, wasn't I compassionate? Hadn't I learned the lesson that we are all one? I knew I was no longer so hard on criminals. When I heard horrendous stories I prayed not only for the victim but also for the perpetrator, and my prayer was real. I meant it. I realized that we are all one, and all capable of evil acts. So, wasn't I compassionate?

I went to see our minister, Henry. Years ago when I wrote *Songs of the Soul*, he was the person I first gave it to. He was the person who helped me spread the messages to others and who reassured me I wasn't crazy. Sitting in his office I told him, "Listen. I have a problem. The angels have returned sometimes and told me I was a teacher and a healer, and I'm here to learn compassion. On top of all that I won't tell anyone except you, because I think it sounds pompous or something."

He smiled. "What's the problem?"

"Well, I might be a teacher in a sort of way. I give lectures, tell my story and hope to get the messages out, so I can go along with that—kind of. But I'm no healer. I don't know anything about medical issues, and when I get sick I can hardly contain my own panic. Even if it's a chest cold, I think it is bronchitis, then pneumonia, then death. So that's not healing." Lastly I added indignantly, "I *am* compassionate."

He shook his head. "You are not only a teacher but also a healer," he said.

I rolled my eyes. Here's a man I respected and he didn't get it. "Henry, I get anxious if someone next to me sneezes. I don't think most doctors get that way."

"You are a spiritual healer," he answered. "They didn't say you were a medical healer; they said healer. To be truly healed, people have to be healed on many levels. You often tell me, off the cuff, stories people relay to you about the impact of *Songs of the Soul*, how the messages have changed and impacted their lives. That is healing."

I let his words sink in. I didn't feel like a healer.

"Well," I countered, still obstinate, "I am compassionate. I don't need to learn compassion. I know compassion. I've learned that. I could think of lots of things I'd need to learn—patience, more love, being selfless—but I *am* compassionate."

Henry shook his head. "You have compassion, but often it's blocked by your judgment. Reread your book. You judge first and then are compassionate. True compassion comes without any judgment."

Did I judge first? I was struggling with anxiety after being so physically sick during the winter. Henry went on: "Pretend that Anne is sitting there in that chair," and he pointed to an empty one nearby. "Tell me what you think of her."

"She should pull herself together," I said flatly, talking about myself. "She's a blessed woman with a wonderful family and while there are so many terrible tragedies in the world she worries over stupid things."

"But when she does worry and have anxiety..."

"Oh, I feel bad for her."

"So there," he said. "I've made my point. You're judgmental first—even of yourself —and then, after the judgment, you have compassion."

My jaw dropped open. He was right. Here I was thinking I had progressed so far, could really believe in the oneness of humanity—but still, even with myself, I was judging before loving.

I prayed and the Archangel met me by the beach. "Can I talk to you about compassion?" I asked.

"Yes. It is important that you do."

"How do I acquire it? Especially when I thought I had it?" I looked down, ashamed at my pride and ashamed at my ineptitude.

"You do have it," he said tenderly, "as do all the others, but you block it with fear, doubt and darkness. When you are truly compassionate, you become the other, you feel for the other, you have not just sympathy but true empathy. And that is a large step for many, because it means breaking down barriers, accepting yourself and others. To have true compassion you first need to see yourself as you are, and then to love that self and esteem it. Some of the most talented and educated people in the world have no self-worth. It comes from within, from your divine soul. And it is there for you to access all the time. But the barriers that you have built, the shells around your souls, keep this compassion from escaping and thus from growing. Your road on earth is to let this compassion grow to huge and infinite size. God has compassion beyond your imagination and your capacity to understand.

Compassion is an aspect of love."

"So fear is blocking me?"

"Don't we tell you all the time that fear and anxiety block you?"

"Yes, but even that bothers me. Because a friend of mine says that her anxiety is a chemical disorder, that she'll have it for life, and that it's not her 'fault.' So how can she unblock it?"

"It is not her 'fault,' as she puts it. There are diseases of the body, among them anxiety disorder, panic disorder, a variety of chemical disorders. But still it holds true that when you are anxious, you are not in the state of peace God wants you to be in. Anxiety and fears pull you from God. If medicines help alleviate her anxiety, then that is a gift from God. But when people are anxious it is harder for them to draw closer to God, because the problems of fear block them.

"Fear blocks love. Period.

"Any method to get past fear allows love to enter. If that method is medicine, so be it. If it is meditation and prayer, quiet time, sports (which often help to dissipate anxiety)—all of these will help you find calmness."

"I like listening to the ocean."

He smiled. "We know. That is why we often meet here. The sounds of the ocean help calm you and unblock the fears. Then you are willing to listen to the messages."

"Let's get back to compassion."

"Yes. For you, first you must learn compassion for yourself. In your lectures you talk about loving yourself, and you are correct. But you personally are not living it, nor are many other people. You are impatient and difficult with yourselves. Pretend, as Henry suggested, to see yourself as a stranger. Tell others to do this. Evaluate that person. Talk about all the good things that person has done, and then the low points. If you see yourself objectively, you will see much more good than bad. Then your self-love will grow."

"Listen," I said. "As a Christian I was brought up with original sin."

"You all turned from God," the Archangel said somberly.

"But even as a little girl I was at Mass pounding my chest three times and saying 'mea culpa, mea culpa, mea culpa'—it's my fault, it's my fault, it's my fault. We'd go to confession every Saturday, and Friday night and all of Saturday morning I'd lament over what horrible things I did as a seven-year-old. How can anyone brought up like that have self-love?"

"It is important to separate the person from the act. That is where many religions, many people, have lost their direction. You are human, and you have turned from God, bringing darkness, fear, and doubt upon yourselves. But your souls are made in the image and likeness of God. They are partakers in the divine energy of God. They are whole and perfect. So your self-love, your self-esteem must come from that. You must access that."

"And then won't I become proud and haughty?"

"No," he said, quite simply. "That could not happen, because the love from your soul is pure love. It is not exaggerated or pompous. It is pure, and you will feel it like spring water rushing over you on a warm day. It can never exceed and go beyond pure love to pride. Pride is of the darkness. Everything that comes from partaking in the divinity of God is only of the light, and it cannot be turned to negativity."

"Tell me how to do it."

"Begin with yourself. You have compassion, but it is buried sometimes. You've come a long way, as have many, but you have many more steps to take on this journey. Each day in prayer ask the Holy Sprit to allow you to see God within you, to see the wholeness of your being, the beauty of the love He has planted within you. Pray that the judgment and fears and doubts that block you will fade away. Prayer will allow this to happen. You often forget the power of prayer, and many of you do not pray for yourselves. You pray for others but not for yourselves. God wants this to be joyous."

Joyous? I stopped him there. "I think you have that wrong. My friend's husband is forty-four, they have two children, three and five, and he's just been diagnosed with bone cancer. How can you say God wants this to be joyous? Why did God give this to him and his beautiful family, when other people who are serial killers or child molesters are perfectly healthy?"

He shook his head again. "Again, you are judging one against the other."

"Well, isn't that natural? He is a wonderful family man. It doesn't seem fair."

"God created this world, and please keep in mind, the beauty of humanity is that He gave you all free will. You can do as you wish. There have been many factors that have brought on this disease, but I assure you, this is an opportunity for your friend and his family to grow spiritually. That is the only reason that all of you are here, to grow spiritually, acquire wisdom and love, and move on toward God. Once you realize this, and truly believe and live it, the road becomes joyous."

"When I was so sick last winter with my liver problem, and the fevers came, the chills, and I couldn't get out of bed, I wasn't joyous. I could barely pray. I was angry with God."

"And you missed the opportunity to grow closer to Him."

"I what?"

"You missed the opportunity to grow closer to God during that time."

I swallowed hard. "I'm sorry."

"Do not be sorry. You are learning, slowly, the lessons you need to learn. You did learn many from that experience. You learned the power of prayer, and that in itself was a huge lesson. But the peace that comes from giving your anxieties to God still eludes you. So first learn compassion for yourself and others, and that will help you bring peace into your body. While you are still harsh on yourself and others, the peace cannot exist. The energies are different. You need the energy of love to surround and enter you."

"Will this ever happen?"

"Oh yes, of course," he said, almost gleefully, "as long as you continue to stay on your journey. Continue to ask for help from us, and pray to God the Almighty to bless you and your understanding of this time on earth.

"This is enough for tonight. You have done well—do not think you have not. Do not concern yourself with 'missed opportunities.' God gives you hundreds of opportunities each day. Many are missed, but they are abundant. Sometimes you are not capable of receiving and acting on all of them. Once you start recognizing them, and have the peace of the Lord within you, the opportunities and lessons accelerate, and your ability to learn and acquire wisdom grows at astonishing rates."

"Are all 'opportunities' things like sickness? Because if they are, I'm not sure I want them."

He laughed. "No, many are small occurrences that happen every day. Some are monumental, such as your friend's right now, but others are as small as a kind word to a stranger. But realize that every day each of you encounters hundreds of ways to become closer to God and unlock the wisdom of your souls. As you learn and pray, you will take advantage of more of these opportunities each day.

"Flow with the energy of God. Pray to accept His gifts, and give homage to Him every day. Amen."

"Amen," I said, watching him disappear into the night sky. I wondered when the sun had set. The stars above me glittered and twinkled. Did such bright light exist within my soul, and had I darkened it with my shell of fear?

His voice called from the heavens. "The light within you is brighter than all of these stars," he said. "It is the light of God."

Later at the kitchen sink I was still mulling over the compassion exercises. How else could I learn compassion?

"Take out a gem each day," the Voice said.

"Each day?"

"Don't you tell people the gifts of God are abundant and everlasting?"

"Yes."

"Well then, each day in prayer take out a gem. Hold it, look at the color, and ask the Lord your God to help you accept the gift He wants for you that particular day. You may receive the same one many days in a row, or you may not. But contemplate the gift, hold it and feel the energy, and once it has been accepted, if you know its meaning, think of how it will help you in particular to learn compassion. Others need to know what their gift is and how to learn what they need to learn. Some will be different—for some it will be forgiveness, for others the ending of jealousy and envy, but for you at this period it is compassion. The gems will help you and the others to acquire and hold your gifts. Amen."

Eight

Okay, I picked a stone. It's light yellow, with all kinds of bubbles within the glass.

"Yes," the Archangel said. Today he was wearing bright crimson robes, the sleeves embroidered in gold. The embroidery appeared to be words written in a language I didn't recognize. "Tell me what it means to you."

"Yellow means warmth to me, but there are a lot of bubbles in it."

"Are you judging the stone?" he asked.

"I guess I am."

"Even the gifts of God you judge. Do you think perfect means without flaws?"

"Well, of course," I said.

He shook his head. "Perfect is how God sees you, in your wholeness, in your beauty. People with sickness, people with malignancies, people with malformations are still perfect and whole to God."

"Oh," I said.

"And that stone you picked—you did not feel its warmth, hold it to the light, see the reflections it causes, the beauty it has? Hold it."

I held it up to the light. It seemed prettier than the first time. The shades in the yellow seemed to change. But still there were the bubbles inside the glass.

"If those bubbles were not there," the Archangel said, "it would have no character, no prisms. Can you understand that?"

"Yes."

"And such is it with you. What you consider 'imperfections' are vehicles of change and beauty. It can be whole in its differences, not imperfect. You see it as imperfection; we see it as beauty."

"Oh."

"Now use that same concept with yourself, and have others use it with themselves. Take your flaws and see how they can make you whole."

"I'm lacking compassion," I stated flatly.

"Not lacking it, but rather not using it," he corrected me. "You have it within your soul. You're just not using it as you should be. It does not come to the forefront."

"Okay, well, whatever. That's one of my flaws."

"That's one of your bubbles," he said, smiling. "Take that 'bubble' and see how it can change you. To understand your wholeness you need to understand all of yourselves. You need to look within yourselves, see your fears, face them, and take that energy and make it work for goodness and love. That is where wholeness begins. What you see as a flaw is a challenge, an opportunity, to face the Lord and develop what is within you. It is beautiful."

"Can I take another one?"

"No. One for each day is enough. But you can ponder this and you can find the answers within you."

"I'm impatient a lot."

"So we know."

"Isn't that an imperfection?"

"No, it is a condition. Stop talking about perfect versus imperfect. All of you are perfect in God's eyes. What you do may sometimes be imperfect, such as sin and turning from God. But even impatience can help you in your wholeness."

"Give me an example. I don't understand."

"Impatience is wanting something or someone *now*. There is no time with God. 'Now' does not exist in the way you think of it. So impatience has no meaning in our world."

"But it does in mine. If I have to get something done by Thursday it has to get done, and if someone doesn't do their part, my impatience and intolerance grow."

"We understand this. Those are earthly, daily concerns. We are not concerned with your hurrying to make a dentist appointment or getting your television show on today versus tomorrow. We are concerned with the impatience of your soul."

"My soul? My soul is impatient?"

"Yes. You want to know everything *now*, and you don't understand that now is all times. We cannot begin to explain that to you today because you will not understand it, and it is not terribly important that you do at this juncture. Just remember that impatience is, once again, a judgment, a judgment against yourself or your brothers. Being impatient to learn lessons, being impatient with yourself, is not a flaw, but working with it, acknowledging it, will bring you closer to wisdom and wholeness, and then the impatience will fall away. Then you will realize that for your soul all time is God's time. You will understand that impatience and patience have no meaning when time is infinite."

"This is getting very hard for me to understand."

"Then just remember and try to absorb this: These flaws that you see are not flaws. They are like the bubbles in the glass. They are aspects of your personality that will bring you to wholeness if you use them correctly, if you acknowledge them, if you face your impatience with yourself and your neighbor and realize it has no importance. You need only be patient in God's time, and then impatience will fall away. But acknowledging it will bring you closer to wholeness and compassion, compassion for the bubbles in the stone, compassion for the bubbles within yourself and your neighbors. Those bubbles will eventually bring beauty and wholeness. The stone without the bubbles would be 'perfect' in your eyes, yet with no individuality, with no character.

"As you face these bubbles, embrace them, understand them and move toward God in love and compassion. The flaws you think you have will be tools to help you learn, and once you have learned to use them and have mastered this, the bubbles will disintegrate and burst, and you will move on."

"I'll need to read this again, because I don't know if it makes sense."

"Embrace what you view as 'flaws,' and work with them. They are there to help you understand your wholeness. With love, I leave you to pray and to hold onto your gem. Hold onto the gift of warmth and love, and embrace the 'imperfections' that you see, because if used correctly they too are beautiful gifts to help you grow toward God."

"But what if I don't use them?"

"Then they become blockages of fear. Many do that. They get stuck with these blockages and do not grow. You must understand them—see them and embrace them as learning tools. As children outgrow their childhood toys, soon you too will outgrow some of these bubbles."

"Flaws?"

"Parts of the whole that make you who you are, parts which are there to help you learn love and compassion."

Nine

I pick a blue stone. For whatever reasons blue stones always bring me tranquility. They make me think of the Blessed Mother, of calming seas, of peace.

I desperately want peace in my life, but I have trouble stilling my mind.

The Archangel appears. "Can we talk about death?" I ask.

"That was not what I had planned for you yet, but we can," he said, with a slight crease in his forehead.

"A famous young couple was suddenly killed in an airplane crash. A friend, a wonderful man with two young babies, is diagnosed with a deadly form of cancer. A friend's friend was killed saving two children from drowning; he was 40 with two children of his own. I've heard all of this in the last week and it seems overwhelming. Explain something. Tell me something comforting. And don't tell me they were here for their soul's work and their soul's work is done."

He smiled. "But you know that is true."

"No I don't," I said emphatically, "because you see young people die, and even older people, who have given so much and have so much more to give. My friend died of an aneurysm last year. She was 58. She worked all the time with the homeless, gave huge amounts of money to charity, and was helping to raise her grandchildren to be wonderful young people. Now she's gone. Her work was not done!!!"

He sighed. "In your opinion her work was not done. But in hers, and her Father's, it was completed. You are here for soul work only. When that work has been achieved, you move on."

"She had more to achieve."

"No, she didn't. She did all that she could while she was here. She showed love, she learned compassion, she gave of herself. She took with her more wisdom and love than when she came to the earth. That is your purpose, moving yourselves and each other closer to God. The only things you can take with you are wisdom and love."

"Well, okay, then maybe it makes a little sense from that viewpoint. But what about the people who haven't learned their lessons? What about the horrible criminal who is a murderer and drug addict and gets killed on the street? He hasn't learned wisdom or love. He hasn't done all he can to move closer to God. So if we follow your argument he should still be around, trying to learn those lessons."

"You are given a pathway at birth, a pathway with many roads, many forks, many potential journeys. Some of them lead nowhere, and you need to return to the beginning. This is what happens when you take the wrong roads. You are sent back to the beginning. You have lost the opportunity to move ahead to God and acquire the wisdom and love you need. So you will not progress because your choices have been the wrong ones. But even in those wrong choices, you may have helped someone else."

"Give me a break. A serial killer gets shot, and he helps someone else?"

"All things become good with God."

"Explain." I crossed my arms in front of my body in a defiant stance.

"The surviving family members now have the opportunity to do one of two things: to turn to God or to turn toward darkness. This becomes an opportunity, another path in their map that they can choose. Remember, God gives all of you free will. His plan is larger than your plans. But through tragedy many of you realize the brevity of life, the sacredness of life, and have the chance to live life full of joy. The reminder of a young person's sickness or death may help someone else, maybe a thousand miles away, learn the lesson through that experience."

"So a serial killer murders someone and is shot—tell me again the scenario. Because I don't think I get it, or understand it, or more important, like it."

"He has been given free will from God. He has made the wrong choices on his map of life. He could have taken other routes, other paths, but did not. So in this darkness his life ends because of his choices, because of the darkness. He is shot. He has given out negativity and then received it. But with God all crisis, all chaos can end in good."

"A family loses a child and that ends in good?"

"The family may become strengthened through this tragedy. They may take the road of compassion and courage. They may move closer to God and spirituality. They may realize that the body is fleeting but the soul has returned to God. They may also help others going through similar times, giving comfort to other families. In some drastic cases they may turn and see that the criminals who have done this are in

31

darkness. They may be in the mental darkness of a disease, or they may be in spiritual darkness. But in any case true Christians will also understand that the 'criminal' knows not what he does. All of this may bring the victim's family the wisdom they need to acquire, the love and compassion they are here to receive, if they choose that route."

"If?"

"Yes. Again free will comes into play. Opportunities surround you all the time to bring you closer to God. Even when evil strikes God can bring goodness from it, but without God evil will prevail. That is the choice you have."

"So get back to this death thing. There are two reasons we die. One, we've done all the soul work we can do, or, two, we've made all the wrong soul choices and we're not going to progress." I was trying desperately to sort this out in my mind.

"Yes. "

"And God makes this decision? How does He know that in the second case the person won't progress? How does he know that in the first case the person won't do something wonderful?"

"God doesn't make that choice; you have on your soul level. The soul makes that choice. It knows where it needs to be for learning, and it knows if you've achieved your learning here on earth or will advance no further. In both cases, the case of the wonderful person and the case of the person who chose wrong, both souls know they will not progress any more on this earth."

"And we're in charge of this? That just doesn't make sense. My friend was looking forward to spending time with her grandchildren, giving them love, helping the poor."

"You do not understand the bigger picture, but your soul does. God has a large and divine plan for each of you, and your soul is connected to that plan. When the soul realizes that the learning has stopped, it moves from the earth. Period. That's it. When Christ had finished his work on the earth it was time for him to depart. He was sent back to help his followers understand that. He was sent back to give the message of eternal life, for had he not returned the message would not have continued. He was also sent back to show that his deeds on earth were to serve as an example to others. But his death completed *his* earthly mission. He returned only to help others on their earthly mission, but he couldn't have done that without his death and resurrection.

"The soul is connected to the divine. The soul listens to the divine plan of God. You have choices and free will, as does the soul, but the soul listens intently to God's plans. The soul is drawn to God. The soul is perfect and divine, while the human is still struggling with the pathways home. But you will return home to God, because the soul and its divine wisdom will guide you. Pray each day to the Holy Spirit. Pray to Her to allow you to gain wisdom and understanding, to gain compassion and love for yourselves and your neighbors.

"Go. Do not weep for the dead. They are with the Lord. The body is merely a shell for the soul. The soul has left and is with the magnificence of God if it so chooses. Amen."

"Wait! What do you mean, if it so chooses?"

"Remember what we told you earlier. You have free will. Your free will can choose whether to face God or to turn from Him. Most face Him, but some still turn from Him."

"But if the soul is connected to God, doesn't it just want to go home?"

"Yes, the soul does. The soul is your connection to God, but you also have an individuality that is a wonderful gift from God that accompanies the soul. That makes it unique. The soul, on the other levels, cannot override that individual free will. Therefore, if in life you have turned from God, in death you have the same choices. It saddens the soul, because more work must be accomplished, but it is still possible. Turning from God in the afterlife is hell. But it is your choice."

"Oh. What about the normal everyday people? Not special, not really holy, but not evil?"

"Almost all turn toward God. Their soul convinces them to connect to the Almighty. But evil is lurking, and if people are accustomed to evil, the soul cannot convince them. But the soul can tell them when their journey on earth is over. The soul is the life-giving breath of the body. When the soul, the connection to God, decides to leave, the body dies. It is not the heart or the brain or any other part of the body that is the most essential life-giving force. It is the soul. Amen."

Ten

As I sat in my living room holding the stone I had picked, the Archangel appeared. "Surround yourself with prayer and light," he commanded. "The messages today are important. We do not want evil to infiltrate."

"Tell me what is so important," I said, my eyes riveted on his blue robes. I had never seen nor could I describe the richness of the royal and silver.

"You have been talking about miracles. Your friend has cancer and you are asking for a cure, for a miracle."

"Yes, of course."

"Do you not know that God works miracles every day, all the time? And that prayer brings such miracles?"

"You mean he'll be cured?"

The Archangel stopped and sat down beside the rock on which I was sitting. "I do not know. I do know that God wishes us to comfort him, and that people need to realize that God wants people comforted during difficult times."

"That's nice," I said rather flippantly. "But we're praying for a cure. We want him healed. He has a very aggressive cancer of the bone and he's only forty-four. We're praying for miracles."

"Only God knows the end results, but we have told you before, the soul makes these decisions of life and death. The soul is connected to the divine, to God, and when someone's time has come, the soul, the life-giving force of the body, leaves. You keep praying for miracles, but you don't see the miracles that occur."

"Like what, in this situation?"

"I cannot divulge people's private journeys. That is not for you to know, unless they share it with you. But I can say that healing is often on the spiritual level, not the body's level. That is what the journey is all about, the spiritual level. None of you truly grasp this. You are always concerned with the body, with the material, with the earthly. The only reason you are here is the soul and its journey."

"If that's true then why aren't we sent down with just souls, or floating around some 'spiritual' school with no bodies, with no material or earthly worries?"

He smiled. "Because the soul knows on its deepest level that for you to return to God you must relinquish what you tried to acquire in the first place. Adam and Eve did not turn from God to the earthly alone. All of you did as one, and now your path home has to be the realization that the earthly holds no holiness, no real peace, and that only your soul's journey can bring you back to God."

"I don't get it."

"The lessons you learn in this body—a journey, by the way, which you insisted on taking—are of the utmost importance for your soul. Understanding that the physical, the material, the flesh is not of importance and *cannot bring true happiness* is one of the most important and valuable lessons that you can learn. Once you learn that, you quickly accelerate and learn love and wisdom and compassion, because you are brought closer to God. You left God for possessions, and you will return to Him when you realize they don't bring happiness."

"How long does that take?" I said. "Because I understand they don't bring happiness."

"No," he said, smiling. "You, and most of you, do not really understand that. Even if material possessions do not call to you, health or bodily concerns do."

"Of course."

"And then you must realize again that the body is just a part of the earth. It will turn to dust and become one with the earth, while the soul will become one with the others and with God."

"But how can I, or my friend, or anyone with a major sickness, keep this obscure, profound idea in mind? How can his wife, who has two babies, even think it? She has to work, take care of the children and take care of her husband. How can she not be swallowed up with fear for the body?"

"Through prayer."

"That simply?"

"Yes, that simply. God's peace can descend on everyone."

"But what about people with mental illness? I don't mean just worry and anxiety, but I mean real mental illnesses, like schizophrenia, say. You can't tell me that they are even capable of prayer in their darkest moments. How can you say all this?"

"But are not the ones surrounding them capable of prayer?"

"Sure, but it's a mental illness—it's not something that can be cured by prayer. It's chemical. It's serious and it's constant."

He sighed. "Your doctors have much to discover, but it is for them to discover it. Yet today there are medicines that allow people to live an easier life."

"That's not enough. They're strong medicines. Some of these people hear voices telling them to kill."

"And you think that is solely chemical?"

"Yes."

"Part of it is, and part of it is evil."

"Don't tell those sick people that it's evil."

"The voices which spur them on are chemical, but the actions which they take are encouraged by Satan."

"So, what have you told me? They can't pray because they're sick, and their actions are evil. This is a horrible thing to write in a book to comfort people."

"Oh no. It is comforting that there are medicines to help with some of the chemicals, but the truly comforting thing for these people in anguish to know is that there are people and angels surrounding them and praying for them. People who are prayed for will find peace, not necessarily a 'cure' as you call it, but a healing."

"A spiritual healing?"

"Yes."

"And what purpose does a life like that serve? A life of torment and mental anguish?"

"Oh," he said joyously, "they may have chosen that path for a self-less reason. They may have chosen to suffer in order that others around them learn compassion and love, learn the importance of prayer and community."

"Who would make such a choice?"

"Many souls who are advanced and want to help others."

"So you are saying that some people who are suffering greatly may be suffering by their own choice? A choice that came before birth?"

"Yes."

"All of them?"

"No, some are suffering for their own advancement, to learn the skills they are lacking for themselves. But you cannot dismiss the millions who are suffering to help others on their spiritual path. They saw the routes others could take without them, and they offered to come here and help their neighbors and their loved ones advance."

"Is this reincarnation?"

"I know you do not want to believe in it, and it is not necessary to believe in it. But before you were born you were with God. All of you chose to turn from God. He in His goodness and mercy allows you to return home. But you must want to come back home on your own, not by His choice. So before your birth you are offered a variety of life maps, life plans. You chose the one that will help you, or your loved one, advance toward the most important goal, returning home to God. That is all you are here for, to acquire wisdom and love. The wisdom allows you to see that you need to return home, and the love is the vehicle for that. With that knowledge, the wisdom of the Holy Spirit is poured forth over you and fills you with Her compassion and understanding. With that, you see more clearly. I urge all of your readers to pray each day to the Holy Spirit for wisdom. With wisdom come love, compassion, empathy, understanding of the map homeward and the need to return to God. Then a peace beyond your understanding will overcome you, and even in the depths of your despair it will stay with you."

Eleven

I again picked a blue stone from the bowl. I choose a stone with my eyes closed, as a gift God wants me to have. I've realized that although the bowl holds many different colors, all the stones I've recently chosen are either yellow or blue. Today's blue seems especially appropriate. Blue always calms me, centers me, and makes me relax; I think of the Blessed Mother, the ocean, and just serenity in general.

It's a gift I readily accept, but don't always hold tightly.

The Archangel greets me at the ocean. "You have been given blue each time to remind you of your obligation."

"My obligation?" I asked.

"Yes. You are always concerned about fulfilling your journey on earth, constantly wondering what your journey is. Even as a small child you had this question."

I nod. I remembered those feelings well.

"Even as we watched you as a child, we realized that you, like many others, need to know your journeys. You come with the blueprint at your birth, but as the child grows the blueprint disintegrates, and free will and the material begin to steer some in the wrong directions."

"You mean we know our purpose as a small child?"

"Of course. You knew it before you were born, you knew it in the womb when you were knitted, and you knew it on the subconscious soul level as a baby. But then the human condition begins to intrude and many of you lose your direction."

"Well, what's mine?" I asked.

He shook his head. "Oh, it is not for me to tell you."

"Well then, how do we ever know what we're here for?"

"You pray, you meditate, you connect with the divine, and the answers appear to you. You ask specifically for your life's goal, and when it is again revealed to you, you will recognize it as being correct, as being pure and of God."

"When I picked up the blue stone, I heard the words, 'You are to heal people of their anxieties.' But how could I do that? I'm anxious myself. I'm hardly the right person to help others with anxiety."

"Who would be better?" he asked. "When you come through this and learn to truly connect with God, you will understand more about anxiety and calmness than you have ever understood. You will be able to empathize and *teach* others what you have learned. What a gift that will be, what an extension of God's hand that will be."

"Me?"

"We have told you before that you are a teacher and a healer. In your limited human capacity you keep thinking that healing is a physical task. But we speak mostly of spiritual healing because when the spirit is whole, connected to its divine source and a partaker in the divine energy, it will turn from anxiety and darkness and move toward its purpose, its purpose of love and wisdom."

"And how can I help people do that?"

"You can help others on many different levels, but your struggles, your hopes, your dark times will allow others to relate to your experiences, and your faith in God will come forth and give others comfort. But to truly understand the *how* of it, you must pray to God for directions for opening your heart and your soul to His way. Oftentimes many of you believe you have the way, but only Christ was the example of the way, the truth and the light. He gave unselfishly. He gave his life, dedicating his work to others. That is the most important task of everyone's life, to follow that example. The example of Christ is the way to salvation. To truly understand this you must face the truth and the light. The truth is that you are here as spiritual beings who have turned from God but want to return to paradise. In turning from God you also turned from the light. You need only to turn back and this light shines with wisdom, understanding and compassion.

"Each of you has a magnificent task on this earth. All of you came knowing your tasks, *all* of you, even those who are mentally challenged, those who are in comas, those who are handicapped or brain-damaged. All the while you are alive your soul still knows that you are capable of this magnificent task."

"In a coma?"

"Those in comas may be suffering for those who surround them. They may be in that position to teach another soul caring, or patience, or the brevity of life and the importance of love. Their suffering may be a gift to someone else, or to many others."

"But when you're in the deep darkness of that, it's so hard to understand." I shook my head. "It's so hard to understand why someone is born brain-damaged."

"The soul is still giving life to that person. That person still has spiritual work to do, still has a magnificent task to complete before its return to the Father."

"This is hard to understand, because sometimes the parents become exhausted, bitter, envious of other children." How could this angel even begin to know what these earthly feelings were like?

He shook his head and lowered his voice to barely a whisper. "That is free will. That is what God gave you, but when people do such things, although it is understandable and human, they are diverging from their souls' pure and light-filled purpose. Many of you have seen people burdened with hardships turn those hardships into miracles, not in a physical sense, but in taking on that task and learning love and giving to others in similar situations."

I thought of a famous family who had a retarded daughter, and one of the family members then went on to help others on a national scale.

"It is following your soul's purpose. Pray to God to remember your soul's purpose, and ask all the others to pray to the Holy Sprit to remember theirs. Then all of you must pray for guidance and perseverance to follow that purpose. Other things will call to you—darkness, comfort, materialism—but none of them are part of the soul's purpose. When you realize your purpose and commit to it with God's hand nearby, the light will shine and everything will become clear. For those readers who do not understand true happiness, I am here to tell them, when you remember your soul's purpose, and then live it with God's guidance, you will achieve happiness."

I sat back. "Happiness?"

"Yes, happiness. You all run around looking for it, searching for it, but rarely do you think that your soul holds the key to it. But each of you has within your grasp *true* happiness on a level you cannot really understand right now. Go, pray, and ask God to *re-reveal* your purpose on earth and how to achieve it. Everyone has one, one that is *magnificent*. Not to achieve it during this life is a tragedy of large proportions."

Twelve

I keep wondering about this map we have before we're born, and the Archangel's words that some of us follow the plans we made before our birth but others stray. And in either case, either when we've achieved our lesson or when our soul knows that we will not achieve it, our soul and God, together, call us back home.

It seemed a little strange to me. At Mass on Sunday, while I sat thinking and wondering about it, the priest read the second Scripture reading, Romans 8:28-30:

Brothers and sisters:
We know that all things work for good for those who love God,
who are called according to His purpose.
For those He foreknew He also predestined
to be conformed to the image of His Son,
so that he might be the firstborn
among many brothers and sisters.
And those He predestined He also called;
and those He called He also justified;
and those He justified He also glorified.

As I heard those words my ears perked up. I did not have the passage in front of me, but immediately after the service I looked it up. And I sat down in wonderment. Was I reading this Holy Scripture wrongly? But it seemed to me that indeed we "are called according to His purpose," and that we are brothers and sisters in Christ, and must, in order to follow His plan, follow the image of Christ. And "those He predestined He also called."

I wondered, was this predestination but with free choice? If that was the case, then it's not really predestination.

The Archangel appeared by the sea. He sat on the rock, and immediately I was by his side. The day was lovely, warm and hazy, one that reminds you of the last days of August. But it was July. Usually on such days the beach is filled with people, but we were alone.

"You are never alone, "he said, and suddenly I saw the crowds on the sands.

"Do they see us?"

"No," he laughed (a rare occurrence for him). "They are not concerned today with the spiritual. The heat, the sun, the water have them concerned only with their day here. Someone who is really trying may be able to see me—but not you. Your path, your struggles are not for others to see unless you make the choice to share them. That is part of your own free will. But I can allow others to see me, if I so wish."

I breathed in the salt air, relishing the warm sun. But then, just like those around me, I wondered about the heat. "I'm not going to get burnt here today, am I? I don't have sunscreen."

"When you are with a messenger of God, no action will result in harm."

Oh good, I thought. Then I too laughed. "Gee, you must think sometimes that I'm a difficult case. Here I am with you, you such a willing teacher of the divine and the spiritual, and I'm concerned with burning my face and getting skin cancer."

"We know you and understand you. It is not of concern to us."

"Oh," I said.

"You read the passage from the Mass on Sunday?" he asked, bringing us back to the topic.

I noticed that the crowds were no longer visible to me. The beach once again looked empty.

"They are there, but you find it a distraction," he said, reading my mind. "I have just made the beach more tranquil for you."

"Thank you," I replied. "To answer your question, yes, I read Romans 8:28. Does it validate what you told me the other day?"

"Yes. 'All things work for good for those who love God.' That was your question last week, when you asked how people who shot people and then were themselves murdered could possibly have any good impact on the world. I answered that the families of those victims, with their free will, can choose God and change the lives of others. Or they can choose darkness and bitterness, and when they do that, they move from their original pre-birth plan."

"Let's talk about that again. The Scripture reading talked about predestination. Explain that to me. If we're predestined, why bother?"

He smiled again, and I was beginning to realize that it was a smile of love, patience, and even (could it be?) humor. Usually he was so formidable—an angel with an agenda, and nothing moved him from that plan.

42

"Only God knows the ultimate destination, the ultimate choice each of you will make, and the hour of your death. We do not. Even your soul does not, until it consults with the Divine Maker. Then the decision is made together, and the soul departs from the body. But the map of your life is predestined, because God 'foreknew' you and allowed you to choose what lessons and maps you needed to take onto this earth. But once on earth, you have the free will He gave you, and you may choose rightly or wrongly. Yet God, in His ultimate wisdom, knows the final outcome. Only He."

"Then why do we bother?"

"Because you turned away from God before, and now this is your opportunity to return to Him. You will not return to Him of your free will until you learn the lessons that connect you to God. Those are lessons of love, compassion, peace and understanding, and the need for wisdom from the Holy Sprit. So God gives you these opportunities, again and again, until you realize your soul's map, realize that you are here for a greater purpose, a magnificent purpose.

"You must tell everyone that *each person on this earth* is connected to the divine through the partaker in the divine, the individual soul. And all people, no matter how low their self-esteem or intellect, no matter how they berate themselves or how they feel about themselves or their neighbors—every single person came to this earth with a divine and *holy* plan. You must remind them, as these words do, that the holy plan is available to everyone. Everyone has it embedded in the soul. The key to understanding this plan, to remembering it, is prayer.

"Do not let the children wander from the plan. Do not let the adults direct the children away from the plan. In their young years children can connect to it even more quickly, but then the adults lead them astray."

"I have another question then." While listening to him I had been watching small waves break onto the sands, becoming almost mesmerized by their ebb and flow. "I was thinking that this might be all right, that maybe our soul decides with God when to return home. But there are also accidents in the world. Take a woman who is walking into a convenience store and suddenly sees a robbery, and she's shot. She's in the wrong place at the wrong time. Nothing more. If she had been stuck in traffic, she would have lived. Or sometimes you see three young people die in an accident. How can you tell me that all three were supposed to go that day? What's the difference between an accident and your soul's choosing?"

"There are no accidents when it comes to the death of the body. The timing of that woman, that she was in that store at that specific hour, was not an accident. Her soul made the decision to leave. If she were supposed to have stayed on earth longer, she either would have been caught in traffic or not been fatally wounded."

"You mean her soul made that choice to be facing an evil person with a gun?"

"A person," he corrected me, "who is a child of God, yet was doing an evil thing. Remember to differentiate that, and not to judge. And yes, her soul chose that moment. She may have chosen it for her own development—she may have reached a point on earth where her soul decided that to be with God would better help her continue her learning. Or she may have chosen death for the sake of someone else."

"What?"

"I know you can't see this, but perhaps she chose it to help the murderer."

"*Help him?* Let's take the example further. She leaves two young children. How can that help anyone?"

"We'll take it one by one," he said. "The murderer may be incarcerated for this crime, may finally find remorse and remember that all things can turn to goodness with God. Again, she may be giving that murderer a second chance to find his spiritual life."

"And her children?"

"I understand that you cannot see this clearly." His tone was soft, without judgment.

"You bet I can't."

"But you are not seeing on the spiritual level. She can help her children from above. The loss of a mother is a devastating experience. It can either, again with free will, help the child turn closer to a spiritual life—if the adults lead the child that way—or turn the children from God. So that mother has left her children an opportunity to grow closer to the spiritual."

"It seems outrageous," I said. "If she had lived, she could have brought them to church, given them her wisdom, helped them grow spiritually."

"You are right. That is the role of many mothers. But somehow she decided that their opportunities were stronger in this case, or she just realized that the murderer's need for redemption was the most important spiritual issue at that time. She chose, like Christ, to give up her life for another."

"And what if that murderer doesn't accept redemption? Then she chose for nothing."

"Not for nothing, but not for the intended purpose of the souls. And then more lessons will be given the criminals, more sacrifices may be made by others, to help that soul along."

"I'm tired."

"We understand. Go, pray and take in the peace that is the Lord's. Love the Lord. And let these messages be known. Amen."

"Amen," I said softly, watching him rise into the hazy sky.

As I turned to climb down from the rock I saw the throngs of people on the beach. No one took notice of me as I made my way along the shoreline, my feet sandy in the warm lazy surf. I felt peaceful but overwhelmed, as if life had so many answers and I still didn't even understand the correct questions to ask.

I had been pondering them for a long time. Just recently I found a poem I wrote when I was twelve or thirteen, in which I saw myself as an old woman lamenting that my purpose in life remained unfulfilled.

Tranquility is beyond my reach,
the old woman cries.
My life is over, I am old
and I don't know what
my purpose here was. I
took a journey, my mission
unaccomplished, for I knew
not the goal I wanted.

Reading this poem now, I have the same worries, the same misgivings. I ask this young, inner child of mine: Why did you write about such a thing at so young an age? And I receive an answer:

I am not young. I am older than the ages, and it has been a concern of mine for eternity. Now it is time for you to realize this on a conscious level, to face it, to understand it, and to DO IT.

You're 13. What are you talking about?

My young body is 13, but the soul from which this thought came is ancient, ageless. It is the soul that talked to me and talked to you. The soul is who we are.

As a young child I was concerned with many childish things, but when I sat in prayer, or to write, I listened to the soul. For years you have been blocking out the soul. But now, if you are to really grow in wisdom, you must face this message you wrote decades ago. You must go past the fear and pray to realize the goal.

Realize the goal? Tell me what the goal is, and then I'll realize it.

The soul knows the goal. Each time you sit in the morning quietness and pray beforehand, you connect with the soul. The soul is a partaker in the divine God. And all answers are available.

Do not disregard this poem, but use it always to remind you that you have this lifetime to face your goal. With prayer you know what it is.

The child's voice grew stronger. *You have always known it. You are a teacher and a healer, but a reluctant one on this earth. This reluctance sometimes causes you to ignore the opportunities, the gifts with which God has surrounded you. But eventually you must face them.*

Softly she said, *Your goal is to be enveloped in wisdom from the Holy Spirit, to learn compassion. Then you will be the healer and the teacher that you truly are. All of this is accomplished through your connection to God. Do not fear it; embrace it and use it, and it will guide you.*

Then I will not have to read that poem again to you in your later years. You will have accomplished what you need to do to help others, and in doing so you will have truly grown and connected and listened to your soul's plan for you.

Do not let fear of material burdens stop you; do not let anxiety stop you. When you connect with the divine, all is understood. Your goal today, as it was yesterday and as it ever was, even as a child, is to be of God and use that to bring others to Him.

Later on that day I was doing laundry.

"You're not talking about reincarnation, are you?" I challenged the Archangel. "Because it goes against the Church's teachings, and it goes against what I want to believe. It isn't what Christ told the 'good thief' that day."

"Nor did he tell the 'bad thief' that he was doomed to hell for eternity. He said to God, 'Forgive them for they know not what they do.' "

"I've always understood that our conception was the beginning of us. Period."

"When God has a thought, it is a creation. God has known of your existence from the beginning of time. Therefore He has 'thought' of you and created you from the beginning."

"And reincarnation?"

"Why is this so important to people? Your soul has been making decisions on many hundreds of levels for years. But it is this life *now* that is such a gift to you, such an opportunity for your soul. Concentrate only on this and realize God's gift in allowing you to return home to Him. This is a vehicle home, if you use the pathway, the map, and listen to your soul's guidance and pray to the Holy Spirit. Amen."

Hours later I hadn't stopped thinking about the Archangel's words.

"I'm still concerned with this example of the mother being shot down at a 7-11," I said aloud to the air. "You said perhaps her soul knew that by leaving now, she was either ready herself or was helping the criminal to move closer to God in some way. I don't like that answer, because I threw in two little children who will have to grow up without their mother."

His voice was strong and firm within my mind. "The soul knows only its destination and the destination of others. What you still have not learned is that you are here only for its journey. To use that mother as an example, if her soul realized in that convenience store that her work would be done by helping that criminal in some way to face his mistakes, then the soul would leave for that purpose alone."

"And the children? What of the children's souls?" Even to me the question sounded shrill.

"What you still must learn is that *no one soul is more important than another.*"

"Even to the mother? I can't believe that."

"In paradise there is no mother or father, no husband or wife. You are just one with God."

"Then we won't see our family."

"Did I say that? No, you are together and you know and love one another, but the roles you took here are no longer the roles you have in paradise. Yet you are still with those whom you love. Amen."

Thirteen

Day after day I keep picking the same stones, either yellow or blue. The bowl is filled with dozens of different colored stones, but I get the same ones.

"You will receive the same gifts until you take them and embrace them," the Archangel said as he arrived at the beach.

"I have taken them," I said defiantly. "I take them and hold them and try to understand what they mean to me."

"You know what gifts God is giving you."

"I think the blue is serenity, at least for me, and the yellow seems to say happiness."

"And why do you not embrace both?"

"I do," I said. Geez.

"You have become better, yet still you are not completely flowing with the current of the river. Once you, and everyone, can do that, can flow with the spirit of the wisdom, your life will be free and happy."

"It's so much easier for you to say. You don't know what we're all going through down here. It's not just fun and games, you know."

Rarely did he laugh, but now his laughter was full, deep, rich. "Please tell the others that your reactions to life are what you become."

"What?"

"Your reactions to life are what you become. If you react to life with fear and apprehension, then you will become and absorb fear and apprehension. All of you will face difficult and sometimes devastating times in your life. It is how you react to these times that will mold and build you and allow you to follow your life's chosen path. You have a choice in every matter that you face, a choice of how to act. That is your free will."

"I don't always choose very well, do I?"

"No," he said, not judgmentally but with quiet truth.

"When I was so sick with my liver disease, I broke down. I became obsessed with being sick and with death."

"It is a pattern of panic that you have learned."

"But how is it possible to break it?"

"You must use other patterns to break it. It is your reaction that is

48

doing this to your body. Someone else may have the same illness, the same circumstance, and yet not react with the same panic."

"I think it's chemical now."

"It is chemical now. But that can be changed. Regardless of what you have learned, or what the medical doctors tell you, it can be changed. New patterns can be rerouted in the brain. But it takes time, practice and patience with yourself. We see you walking and training your German shepherd puppy each day. You do it with love and yet firmness. You are training him to go the right way, to do the right thing, to 'come' when there is traffic, and so on. You are more patient with him than you are with yourself."

I didn't answer him because I didn't know what to say. I had almost blurted out, "But I love him." I had stopped myself because I knew that meant that somewhere, deep down, I'd also be saying "I love *him*, but..."

"Not yourself?" the Archangel filled in. "You have traveled so far that now it is time to love yourself. It is the missing peace." (As I typed that I kept the word "peace" as it was given to me, because it seemed so right. "Piece" should have been the correct spelling, but somehow "peace" fit even better.)

"You tell people they are connected with God, and yet you have a difficult time discovering that for yourself."

I admitted that he knew me too well.

"This is your goal, to understand God's love and caring for you *always*, and then when you fully absorb that, you as a teacher and a healer will do wondrous things for others. But until you understand that yourself, others will not truly understand it either. Many, many people all over the world struggle with the same feelings you struggle with. That is one of the reasons you were chosen. You are an example to others because others can relate to your struggles."

"Oh, great. You picked me for my imperfections."

Again he laughed.

"It's not that funny," I said.

"No, it is how you see it. But you were picked because of your perfections, your ordinary perfections. We see them as perfections because they will lead you, and others, back to God. As the Scriptures say, as the passage you wrote yesterday says, all good comes from God. As for those reactions that come from fear, when you change them by embracing them, and learn to get past them, they will become perfections because they will help others with the same quest, others who have the same concerns."

"Can we talk of other things? I don't want to keep talking about me. If this ever gets published, why would anyone want to hear this?"

"Because you are all one," he said strongly. The sea air was blowing my hair behind me. I inhaled deeply. "And because you are one, you face the same concerns, you face the same reactions, and sometimes seeing someone else move in the right direction gives you courage to do the same."

"It won't be boring?"

"Again, if you all realized your true potential, nothing about anyone on earth would be boring. Your potentials are beyond your imagination. You are connected to the divine source, to the God of all the heavens and all the earths. You are an outlet for His love, His power, His understanding, His compassion. His power is greater than the universes combined—there is no word for it in your language. And you, each of you, have access to His power through prayer to the Holy Spirit. Christ left the Holy Spirit with you. Christ came to show you the way, the truth and the light. Yet when you do not follow the way, still he does not desert you because the Spirit is there to guide you back to it. You need only to tap into this source, and your lives will change."

"Give me an example," I said.

"Many of you know about the saints. Some of you know modern saints, who may have been canonized by the Church or who may not even be of the Church. They are those people who unselfishly give their lives, their emotions, themselves—and the proof that they are connected with God is that they do all this in *joy*. Their faces radiate a peace from God. Their faces radiate a piece of Him Who created the world."

"I'd like that."

"It is accessible as the gifts He gives all of you. Just pray to the Spirit, read these messages, and realize that not to use your potential, not to connect with God, not to learn and listen to the Holy Spirit, is a loss of the gifts, a loss of this life on earth. Because Christ was human he had the choice not to sacrifice his life for his brothers and sisters. It was still a choice for him, but he connected to the divine and realized his full potential. Many of you have not connected, so you pass up all of your opportunities for greatness in the Lord, out of fear or out of ignorance. Christ asked his Father to 'take away the cup,' but then he said, 'Your will be done.' Many of you ask the Father to take away the cup and truly do not want His will to be done. Many others do not even pray or talk to God. They ignore the cup and flee.

"All of you have within you, in this life, the destiny of greatness, the destiny that God preordained for you, the ability to be who He wants you to be in this world and the hereafter, but you allow the cup to pass. You let the opportunity pass because of fear, because you think you are not capable of greatness. But God is within you, so greatness is simple. You need only to believe.

"Believe in God, believe in the great destiny He has preordained for each and every soul on earth. And then make the conscious—and this is very important—the conscious decision to accept it and be a part of His plan.

"Do this through prayer. Amen."

Fourteen

I picked a blue stone again, but this time a much lighter blue, not as dark and deep. Before I picked the gem I prayed that God would surround me and ease the fears that block me from Him—my material worries, my dread of sickness, etc.—and let only His energy and peace abide within me so that I could do the Job I was planted here on earth for. (Again, for whatever reason, I capitalized "Job," and I noticed that it is the name of the biblical character Job. I know he suffered much but never gave up on God. Job lost all material possessions, got sick, lost his family, and still had steadfast faith. Because of that faith he was again rewarded. It's interesting that I typed Job. Perhaps Job's job is my job: to relinquish everything to God and just have faith.)

The Archangel appears on the rock by the beach. I find myself sitting next to him without having had to run or walk toward him. I dismiss that thought from my mind and smile at him.

"Good morning," I say.

"We are here to talk of God's love for each of you."

"Okay. Tell me about that."

"God's love is beyond your grasp, beyond your imagination, but it is with you each minute, each day."

"I know you've said that before," I answered, "but it still seems so hard to always believe. When I see people suffering so much, people so sick, so poor, children molested by their fathers or strangers.... On the news just this morning, a young woman was found decapitated in a national park. When I hear that and then hear you, it seems conflicting."

"This is humanity's largest challenge, to understand God's love for you but also to understand that He gave each of you free will and that evil does exist in the world. He allows people to make their own choices; if He didn't, you would not be a part of Him. He has free will and therefore wanted you to have it too. His choices are His alone, as are yours. Yet His choices are always in the name of love, always in the name of creation. Unfortunately human nature's choices are not always in the name of love. Evil is present—and rising—and the only way to counteract this force is through prayer, because prayer allows God to enter your lives on a deeper level. Prayer allows the piece of God to become larger. It connects you with the divine."

"You sound like a politician," I said. "Explain to me where God was when that woman was decapitated. She was young and attractive, and someone just did that to her."

"God was within her, and we were around her. But we cannot stop the other person's actions in every case."

"What do you mean, in every case?"

"Again, the soul's and God's infinite and majestic plan is greater than what you see at the moment. What occurred was evil. Yet the man had the choice and chose the wrong path. What you do not know is whether the young girl's soul agreed to leave the earth at that time, in order to help another person's soul. That is not for you to know, and it is not even for me to know, but in many cases that is the decision the soul and God make together. Each person's spiritual growth is personal, between that person and God. Yet we know that the souls as they partake in the Divinity always make the right choice."

"The man didn't make the right choice," I said.

"He was not consulting with his soul. He was consulting with the evil that surrounds him. At some point the soul will break through his shell. It will either make the decision to leave this earth because it cannot progress on the path he has chosen, or it will break through to him and let him see God's love for him."

"I'm not sure that makes sense."

"It is hard for you to grasp, because many in the world are telling you that everything is good and evil does not exist. I am here to tell you, and to tell you strongly, that evil does exist, and how it works on the most profound level is to allow the personality to ignore the soul. When you ignore your soul, you ignore the part of God that resides within you, and then everything else becomes simple tasks for evil to accomplish."

"It sounds like your soul is your conscience."

"Your soul is not your conscience, because your conscience is a part of your personality, but your soul can talk to your conscience. Your soul is directing your spiritual life. When evil invades it makes the shell surrounding the soul impenetrable, and the personality of the human ignores its connection to God. When this happens evil takes over, and it grows and abounds.

"It is imperative that you tell people that evil exists, and that the soul is the connection and the partaker in the divine. Evil's job in this world is to shut down your communication with your soul. You communicate with your soul through prayer, through meditation, through good and kind words, through selfless acts. All of this allows the soul to grow and to direct your path to the one you had originally chosen before birth. But evil interferes."

"Well then, where is our free will?"

"Oh," he said, "that is the choice. You can choose evil, or you can choose to listen to the goodness, purity and wisdom of your soul. It is easier on other levels, where there are no temptations such as riches or illness or drugs. But here on this level the quest of the soul is to allow its divine path to be followed. Evil obstructs the pathway with materialism, with greed, and as it grows it shows the person only earthly desires, while each day the soul struggles to reach the person's true destiny."

"Well, if someone is in such a dark place, is that when the soul takes them home? If the person can't get out of it themselves?"

"Yes, if no one is praying for the soul."

"What do you mean? "

"If people are praying for, say, the man who decapitated the young woman, and praying earnestly and feverishly and constantly, never giving up on God's plan, then if the person has an opening to allow such prayer to come into his being, his life can be changed by those prayers for him."

"I'm not sure this all makes sense."

"It will to you, and to the others, as you reread and discuss this. This is new to you, a new concept. But it is true. It needs to be told now so that each of you can realize the importance of following God's plans for you, plans your soul made with God before you arrived here.

"God is infinite and His love for you is infinite. He wants you to return home to Him, but only freely. He wants you to eagerly rush to Him. In doing so you embrace love, compassion, kindness, and you turn your back on evil, because when you turn toward evil you block the light from your lives.

"Do not think that only the most hardened criminals have blocked God from their lives. Many of you do it each day, on different levels. When you do not fully live your life, when you envy your neighbor, when you speak ill of someone, you have turned from true love, true compassion, and have turned—although not totally—away from God."

"Oh," I interrupted, "it's such an insurmountable task not to do some of those 'small' things, like getting mad at your boss and hoping he loses his job—stuff like that."

"Pray for him, and then you will no longer have those dynamics with him. It is that *simple*. You have heard people talk of it. They have tried it after reading *Songs of the Soul*. Remember the amazing stories?"

"Yes," I said humbly. "People found their interaction with others had changed dramatically after they prayed for them. They noticed that people who would be cold or distant or difficult suddenly no longer were. Was it their reaction to those people? Was it that they didn't put up the same defenses?"

"It was partly that, but always partly the power and strength of prayer. It travels with incredible energy, because it is the energy of God, and causes major changes to occur on the earth. Major changes."

"I am tired."

"We know. Continue to pray, to contact us. Your time is now."

"Now? "

"Yes. Accept it and embrace it. Finally face the journey you had planned, and then you will never regret your life here on earth."

"That sounds so beautiful," I said tearfully.

"It is," he said somberly. "To embrace your destiny and to bring yourself and others closer to God is true beauty. It is the Way Christ spoke of. Amen."

He rose into the warm hazy summer sky. I looked at the deserted beach and suddenly it was filled with people wading in the ocean, floating, swimming over waves. I climbed down from the rock and began walking, until my mind returned me home.

Fifteen

Again I pick a yellow stone, and I wonder if I haven't been accepting and keeping the happiness that I think this color means for me. Each day, though, I have been embracing happiness, trying to avoid worry, and trying to enjoy each moment of the day. Yesterday a friend and I went to a summer theater by the shore, where we had a lovely lunch and saw a wonderful play. I truly enjoyed the day. Before I accepted the invitation, my first thought had been not to go because I should try to write the book proposal for the sequel that the book consultant said needed to be done. And before this summer I would have either felt guilty going to the play or not gone at all. But yesterday I just went, enjoying being healthy enough to go, enjoying the summer and the gifts it offers in its own particular season.

So why did I pick the gift of happiness again?

"It is a reminder," the Archangel said. Again we were sitting by the ocean. I had noticed from our previous encounters that many times when he met me at the ocean it was for my individual growth, not for the community's growth.

"A reminder?" I asked.

"Yes. As a reformed alcoholic needs to say each day, 'Today I will not drink,' and to take each day at a time and not worry about tomorrow, so many of you must remind yourselves to embrace happiness."

"Explain," I said, fidgeting on the rock. It was warm against my skin, and I tugged at my long shorts to try to keep its heat from burning my legs. Although the sun overhead was strong, I no longer worried about getting sunburned since the angel had said I was protected while he was with me.

"You, and others, take the gift of happiness, embrace it for the moment, and then drop it."

"Why?"

"Because many of you have grown up with guilt, with worry, with suffering, and you do not realize that happiness is a state of mind, a state you can choose just as the alcoholic can choose not to drink for that day. God gives you the gift each day, for you to embrace or reject. You are learning to take it for the day, but eventually the goal is that you will no longer drop the gift but learn to embrace it so much that it becomes a living and breathing part of you. At that point the stone will not be given to you anymore because you will have become one with the gem's gift."

"Let's get back to something you said. You mentioned that many of us have grown up with guilt, worry and suffering. But Christ suffered. He suffered tremendously. He suffered when a dear friend denied him, he suffered when people didn't listen to him, he suffered when he was betrayed in the garden, and he suffered mentally the night before his death when he knew what the next day would bring. And of course the most horrible suffering was when he was tortured and died on the cross."

The Archangel shook his head. "No, that was not the most horrible suffering for Christ. He understood his path, and although he was human and did not want to physically suffer, the most difficult suffering for him was seeing people turn away from God. His most difficult suffering was seeing people turn toward evil and turn away from the light. That was the suffering that truly penetrated his body and soul. Being on the cross, although it was physical suffering, was in many ways joyous for him because he knew that with his physical death he was redeeming the sheep. He knew he was teaching the ignorant and those in darkness the true meaning of being a spiritual being—willing to give up your life for others, willing to give up your life for even your enemies. And that is what he did. He gave up his life for those who hated and despised him. When the soldiers saw his death, and saw the earth rock and the skies cry, they realized he was the Son of Man and they realized that he gave up his life for them. Because he was bringing that to pass, Christ was joyous even in his most extreme physical suffering."

"But then what about the mental and spiritual suffering he went through before his death? He asked that God take away the cup from him if it were His will."

"Yes, he suffered. It is a part of life. Suffering is a human condition, but it is not the condition that God wants you in all the time. That is what many of you do not understand. Christ turned his suffering into joy. It was his reaction to the suffering. He hung on the cross, physically tortured, but mentally at peace—he was in joy, he was in happiness knowing what this accomplishment would mean to the world. And so this too is for you to learn, that suffering will occur in the world, that evil will try to overcome goodness in the world, but all of this can be turned to *joy* with God's divine intervention and God's strength. It is not your strength; it is the soul's strength that comes from God. And you will realize that all things occur for a purpose, that all suffering can have a joyful purpose, but you must see this pathway or you will not understand. To see it you must realize that it is always your choice. Your free will can bring you to joy or it can keep you in the depths of suffering. In those depths, if you so choose, evil and the devil conquer part of you. If Christ had chosen not to give up his life, he would have avoided the physical suffering but he would have had spiritual suffering, and his destiny, his redemption of the world, would never have happened. It was his choice to make on this earth, and his choice alone. Yet in communicating with God he understood that he had come to the earth to teach love, compassion and the Way. If he had not accomplished that, the spiritual suffering would have overcome him, and he would not have redeemed the world. He was God and he was human.

"And you are human and God resides within you. You are partakers in the divine energy of God. You too have these choices, yet you do not see them as clearly, nor do you remember your destination as clearly as Christ did. Christ knew his spiritual destination from birth. So do you, but in your attraction to the world you lose it. Christ, in his love for God, his attraction to God, continued to follow it from infancy. He never lost sight of it, and because of that, even though he suffered, he had the piece of God, the peace of God, with him. Even in his suffering he made choices. Those choices brought him peace, and his surrender to the Father's will brought him joy, and following his pathway brought the Way, the Truth and the Light to the earth."

"I need to reread this, because I think there's something really important here."

Somberly he said, "There is: that this free will God gave all of you as a gift goes much deeper than choosing right from wrong. It is also your free will that allows you to communicate with your divinity, and that allows you to choose how to react to suffering and how to react to others. You can choose to react in a way that will bring you peace and joy. It is immensely important that you realize this. When you face suffering, you are being offered an opportunity to choose joy."

"But Christ saw the bigger picture," I argued. "He knew that being crucified would redeem us, he knew that being betrayed and tortured would follow God's plan for us to learn true love, true compassion, and teach us to love our enemies. He knew all this during his suffering, and he was God, so didn't that make it easier for him to understand that there would be joy in the final outcome? But with us, when we suffer with cancer or bankruptcy or divorce or horrible and evil things that happen to good people all the time, thousands of times an hour throughout the world, how can we see the plan?"

He nodded. "That is the difficult task for you here. That is the difficult task for all of you to learn. I have told you before—and you sometimes dismiss it as being 'too simple, too easy'—that with prayer you begin to understand and see the plan for your life. Sometimes you see the plan for just that day, and other times you see it for the long term. When you do see it, when you can learn, and step aside and freely choose to partake in the divine, the joy will come. When you say the powerful words that Christ said, 'Your will be done,' and truly mean it, you allow your plan for your soul to develop. You give your soul the permission to follow its divine plan, and that divine plan will bring joy from all situations. All situations. Because when you are in contact with God, when you are one with God, joy is all that there can possibly be."

"I'll reread this later because I'm sure I'll have more questions. But I'm overwhelmed."

"We understand. This is difficult and new to you. But we urge you all to pray, because in prayer you are given insight and wisdom, and with those gifts you use your free will to return to God, to make the right choices. And eventually, with this wisdom, you remember why you have come to this earth. You remember your spiritual destination and its work. Amen."

Sixteen

I picked a blue stone again so I know I must still be anxious and worried, concerned about things that really do not merit my concern. When my mother turned seventy she said, "Everything I worried about never came to pass." I think of that often, but I still can't inhale it and allow it to become a part of me. So that's probably why I continue to get the blue stones. Sometimes they are a different shade but mostly they are deep blue, as if I need the deep blue of the sea and the sky to calm me, to make me one with God.

I close my eyes in prayer and the Archangel greets me. We are not by the sea but in a beautiful mountain range. Although it is still summer, in the far distance I can see that some of the mountains are snowcapped. Ours is lower and it is warm and green, with a pool of fresh water nearby.

"You have concerns?" he asks.

"Yes. Yesterday a man killed twelve people in a wild rampage, and then when the police chased him and found him, he killed himself. I can't understand how the soul is called home when someone commits suicide. It doesn't go with what I've been taught, with the commandment against murder."

"Yes," he said. "We had not gotten there, but suicide is a very complex issue. For those who are mentally ill, the act is still the act of the soul. Because their personalities are not healthy and their souls know this, God calls them home. It is not an affront to God for these people. And most people who do this are in the deepest, darkest place in their lives. Their souls need to go back to God for guidance, reassurance and love. They will learn their lessons on different levels."

"And there are others?"

He was quiet. "Are you ready for this answer?"

"I don't know," I said. "I guess it depends on what you're going to tell me. I guess you know, probably more than I, if I'm ready for it or not."

"In a few cases, and it is not for anyone to judge which cases are which, the person who has chosen evil overrides the soul and its connection to God. Evil, and murder, has become that person's choice."

"So in that case the soul is not called home to God? The person and God have not made the choice together? It is not God saying, this is your time?"

"No," he said. "It is evil working. But keep in mind that these are not the majority of the suicide cases. Most are people who have been lost, who are in darkness, but are ill. The soul communicates with God, and there is no judgment."

"But still there are other cases?"

"God has given you a gift of life. That life is for you to follow to your destination, your pathway home. We have talked about how people with free will are allowed, once they are on earth, either to continue toward their preplanned destination or to choose not to. For those who choose not to, when their soul knows that no other growth is available for them, it communicates with God and returns home. But when suicide springs from evil, when the healthy, unimpaired personality decides to destroy its life—and I stress this kind is very rare—it is not allowing the soul to make the choice. And this is sad, because they have affronted the gift of life."

"Well, I was brought up that if people murdered, themselves or anyone else, they'd go to hell."

"The hell is the absence of God. Each person makes that choice after death, to be with God or to turn from Him. God is love. God is infinite love, and would never punish. But evil can lure people away from God, even in the afterlife."

"This sounds kind of scary."

"Do not be scared when you do the work of God. Do not be scared that evil is around you. Yet it is around everyone. It lurks, it lures, and wants to be one with each of you. But when you face the light, face God, and allow God and your soul to work together in the divinity that is ever-present, you will be protected and loved, and although evil will still lure you, you will find God's strength."

"Does the soul know when death will occur?"

"Only God in His fullness knows the time or the hour. But the soul knows mighty wisdom; it is connected to God and the Holy Spirit and lives and breathes to return home to Him."

"If that's the case," I said, my mind racing, "if the soul just wants to return home to God, why do any of us turn to evil?"

"Because the soul is divine and knows the beauty of the Lord but the human body is easily corrupted and easily swayed, and each of you, having this free will, can choose. And sometimes evil so overtakes you that you no longer realize that the beauty of God resides within you and is one with you."

"Like your free will is overridden?" I was trying to sort this out aloud.

He smiled. "Yes. So prayer, every day, communicating with God and the divine, asking the Holy Spirit for wisdom, is so important in this day and age, because this love becomes an armor against temptation and evil. Even Christ, in the desert, was faced with temptations from Satan. Christ, who was the Son of Man, the Son of God, prayed to resist temptation. Prayer is so powerful and so great. This is an example to all of you to resist the temptation that lurks every day. Many times these temptations are not large and foreboding, like Satan visiting with great riches. They are small temptations, gradually succumbed to, and then eventually you are in the darkness."

"Oh, little things that you know aren't really right?"

"Yes. Small lies, arguments, turning from your responsibility, and each time, you shrug them off, all of you, as if to say, oh well, we're all human. But when they continue to compound, you no longer have the same resistance to them. You have immunized yourself to these evils, and then you begin to accept them eagerly."

I looked down and pushed off my sneakers, letting my feet touch the high grass. I felt very sad. "Do you know," I said, so ashamed, "there was that horrible shooting of twelve people yesterday on the news, and I thought, oh no, another shooting. But then after a few minutes I changed channels. I even said to my husband, I can't believe it but I think I'm getting desensitized to these horrors. And I felt awful. When the news brings horrendous things day after day after day, murders and rapes and robberies, then somehow they don't have the impact they once had."

"That is evil working slowly. When you feel that way, which is what happens when something is commonplace, you become accepting. But we urge you, the next time something horrendous happens, fall onto your knees, pray to God and ask for the angels to assist. Pray that the victims will be safely cared for, and that the perpetrators will be filled with God's love. If you do that, evil's strength diminishes. All of you can change the world. When you fall onto your knees you are reacting, and your reaction will no longer be one of desensitization. The prayer will allow you to realize the horror of the crime, and most important, the need for powerful and unending prayer."

"There's so much here. So much I don't understand."

"Tell the others that this wisdom which eludes you is within your soul and is a part of your connection to God. Prayer will open it up. Prayer will allow you all blessings and abundance, because you will find that peace which eludes you. You will find your true destination, and so many of you are aching for that. Unless you know your true spiritual destination, your lives become empty and sad, and you fill them with materialism or greed or liquor or drugs—whatever weakness you are most drawn to. Evil wants you not to pray, because Satan knows how strong the power of prayer is, and that with that communication with God, you will turn from the temptations, you will find your soul's destination, and you will return home to God. And that will crush Satan."

"I have to go now. I'm tired and overwhelmed. I don't think I understand even half of what you are saying."

"You understand more, and the community will help you understand and learn it better. But realize that these messages are not just for you. They are for the world."

"Well, you'd better get them out into the world," I said flippantly.

"They will be. Do not be concerned."

I found myself alone on the mountain, wondering how I would return home. Then I let the worry disappear, and I was back in my family room.

Lord, let me understand the plan for my life. Let all of us understand our soul's destination and undertaking in this world. Help us to see it, help us to understand it and live it. Do not let us be caught up in only the things we see. Let us understand the things which we do not see, but know exist.

Amen.

Seventeen

I picked the most unusual stone today. It's mostly clear, but with a section of blue.

Am I becoming more serene? I wondered.

"Yes," the Archangel answered. We were back by the small pond on the mountaintop, and the fresh mountain air was brilliant and clean as I inhaled it.

"You are beginning to understand one of your lessons. Today you need only half of what you needed yesterday in calmness and serenity, because now you are practicing and inhaling the calmness and the peace/piece of God."

"Does that mean each time I'll get less?"

He laughed. "No, not necessarily. At some point it will, when this peace resides within you and you cannot topple it with worries and concerns. With time, you will be able to feel and breathe in God's strength. Then you will have fully accepted the gift and understood it, and at that point God will give you other gifts. But for now, we know you are on the path of this understanding, but you will regress at times and accelerate at times, all within the course of fully embracing it. Eventually, at some point in the future, according to your plan, it will be one with you."

"My plan?"

"Yes. To fully understand compassion, which is why you are here, you also need to understand anxiety and understand how to find the calmness and peace of God. When you find that within yourself, you will be able to find it within others, and you will be able to help others find it for themselves."

"Is this just me, or is this for everyone?"

"This is for you at this time, but many people around the world have the same struggles you have. So this lesson is for those souls too."

"Oh."

"You are tired today," he said, "and when you are tired we don't like to give you too many lessons, because they tend to overwhelm you."

"Thank you. I was up during the night with cramps, and then got them again this morning, so you're right, I didn't get the best night's sleep."

"Tell the others that to be open to God, to be open to your destination, the stress and tiredness must be taken care of. You must sit in peace, awake and refreshed."

"But I know people who wake up in the middle of the night and hear God talk to them."

He laughed. "Isn't that perfect timing for them? They have rested, there is quiet, there are no distractions, and they have no other choice but to listen to God's voice, or the voice of His messengers, the angels."

"People get scared when that happens," I said.

"You understand that. When these messages began years ago, you were terrified. All through the Old and New Testaments, throughout all the religious scriptures of the world, we tell the people, 'Do not fear.' It is a human reaction. But the fruits of our words will show from Whom they came. When people return home to God, return to each other and embrace each other like the one they are, they are living the fruits of His messages. The winds of the Spirit bring them to wholeness and the Lord."

"Well, I don't feel *that* tired," I said. "Is there something else you'd like to talk of today?"

He smiled.

"Not for today," he said. "Rest. Become one with yourself. Enjoy your day and continue to pray throughout it. Continue to speak to God, to invoke His aid, to worship Him and ask Him constantly throughout the day for His love to settle on those who need it the most."

"Those who need it the most?"

"Those in darkness. From your home, from your cars, from wherever you are, you can change someone's life through prayer. Ask for those who are most in darkness to be open to God's love and understanding. Miracles will occur, and horrendous crimes will be stopped, all through your compassion and love for one another, for those less fortunate, those in darkness, those who are tempted by the darkness that has become comfortable for them.

"So for today my message from the Lord is this: Pray for one another—small tiny prayers, large breathless prayers. Do it while you do the dishes, do it while you fold the laundry. And when you do this, peace will come to you and your own worries and concerns will fall aside. You cannot fill your mind with your own worries when you are praying for others. It is a wondrous tool, a wondrous gift of God.

"Now go enjoy this day He has given you, and understand that each day is a gift. Amen."

Eighteen

Today I pick an entirely different stone, one I never even realized was in the bowl. It's a deep coral color with an almost metallic shine to it. It's oval, not round, and looks as if it would cover a third of my finger if it were set in a ring.

I have no idea what gift of God this gem signifies for me. Before I chose it I asked God to give me the gift He wanted me to have today, and also to give me the strength to accept it.

I close my eyes in prayer, and for the first time since these new messages began, the Archangel and I are on a rock overlooking the city, where we had met before. I had realized that messages the Archangel gave me here were intended for the community. The day is foggy, and darkness will soon set in. The Archangel sits quietly next to me, his clasped hands holding a string of beads.

"Are they rosary beads?" I ask.

"Similar," he answered. "They are beads that we often hold, and rarely show to others, as a reminder to pray constantly."

"May I see them?"

"Yes, that is the purpose." He handed them to me. They were unlike a rosary, which I carry in my purse, in that the beads were continuous, without breaks. The beads were not beautiful gems but ordinary rocks, like stones you would find on a gravel driveway, and very smooth.

"They are smooth from our fingers constantly moving over them." Reaching into his pocket he pulled out another set, ten beads on a simple rope tied in a circle, with a simple wooden cross hanging from it. The stones were not smooth, but rough and jagged. Handing them to me he said, "Here. Remember these in prayer. Hold them within your mind, and remember that your mind has the power to erase the jagged edges and make the stones smooth. Constant prayer changes the shape and feel of everything, even the most common objects of the world."

I held his beads in my right hand and the jagged beads in my left. As I looked more closely at his beads, I saw beautiful colors emanating from the ordinary rocks. They sparkled and shone, almost like crystals moving in sunlight.

The other set just lay limp in my hand.

66

"When you pray constantly, and constantly think of the Lord, the beads will change, as will everyone's life. These beads have smoothed out from constant wear, from our hands caressing them in our rituals of prayer."

He pointed to the ordinary, jagged set. "And the same will occur with these."

"It would take me forever to get these smooth just from using them in prayer," I said. I rubbed my index finger and thumb against one of the rough stones. "I could live to be a hundred and I couldn't get this smooth."

"Of course you could. Not only your physical touch but also your mental praying changes the condition of things. Your physical touch will rub it and change it, but it is the power of prayer that changes the ordinary into the miraculous. This is important for everyone to know. The ordinary can become the miraculous."

"What you're really saying is to pray constantly."

"Yes, that is the message, and still many of you do not do it."

"But life gets in the way," I said, not trying to be flippant.

"No," he corrected me, almost sternly. "Life is a prayer, if you live your life as a prayer. Life cannot get in the way, as you put it, but only enhance your communication with the Lord if you choose that path. Each task in life can be joyous and return you to the Lord. Each task done in His name will bring you closer to His messages, closer to your own purpose. But that is where many of you do not follow your path. You see the tasks of life as mundane, tiring, or repetitive. You do not see that every ordinary task of life has a meaning for you, that each deed can—if you so choose—become a prayer, can become a communication with Our Lord."

"Okay." I said. "Give me an example."

"You make oatmeal every day, and sometimes you feel you're in a rut."

I smiled. What a small thing for him to observe, but he's right. When you make oatmeal 365 mornings a year, you do begin to feel as if you're in a rut.

"Tomorrow, as you make the oatmeal for your husband, make it slowly and with care. Do not pour in the milk and mix in the bananas as if it were a chore."

"But—"

"Listen," he said. "Pray as you do it. Bless the oatmeal. Ask God to allow the nutrients to feed your husband, give him strength through the day, allow him with this nutrition to do good for others during the day. You will see amazing results."

I must have looked skeptical. "Amazing results from oatmeal?"

"From anything. You think making oatmeal is an insignificant task. But you can take that task and make it significant, and lives will change, lives will be blessed. Try it tomorrow. You will see the energy of prayer change pathways of lives toward God's destination, which is yours. Amen."

Nineteen

Today I light a sage candle and pray in the living room. I am feeling hopeless, as if the joy that the Archangel says God is willing to pour forth has bypassed me. I struggle with finding this inner peace of which he speaks, and I think I never will.

After praying and beseeching the Lord for this peace, this ability to look within and find comfort, I pick my gem for the day. It is not the blue or yellow I so often get, nor is it the coral one I picked yesterday. Today's stone is totally clear. As I hold it to the light I feel God has given me the ability to see clearly, if only I accept it. I place the stone on a quotation a friend recently e-mailed me, and each letter is magnified as I push the stone slowly over it.

Here is the e-mail:

William Hutchinson Murray, the leader of the Scottish Himalayan Expedition team that scaled Everest in 1951, urges the dreamer in you to take a leap of faith:

"Concerning all acts of initiative (and creation), there is one elementary truth, the ignorance of which kills countless ideas and splendid plans; that the moment one definitely commits oneself, then Providence moves too. All sorts of things occur to help one that would never otherwise have occurred. A whole stream of events issue from the decision, raising in one's favor a manner of unforeseen incidents and meetings and material assistance which no man could have dreamed would have come his way."

I sit quietly, realizing on some level that the gem I picked today is a clear magnifying glass for this wonderful quote, and that it is, in a subtle way, God's hand pushing and encouraging me to delve deeper within myself and also reach out to others. Then doors will open, doors I never imagined would open. I remember so clearly driving in a torrential storm to Massachusetts one evening last summer, complaining to God all the way. For the entire two-hour drive I gripped the steering wheel, barely able to see through the rain and fog.

The chain store I was heading toward had changed community coordinators after I had been booked. When I arrived at the massive store, my poster had both my name and the name of the book wrong. I looked around for *Songs of the Soul* on the tables in the front (which is part of the publicity for speakers) but the book was not there. Table space is extremely expensive for publishing firms, and I could never afford the thousands of dollars it costs. But for an author's lecture the coordinator puts the book in the front of the store for anywhere from a week to a month in order to get people to attend.

My book was in the back of the store, as far back as you could get. The store was a superstore, with chairs everywhere, but the new coordinator had put me in book Siberia. A few chairs had been set up, and one lone woman sat reading my book, almost at the last chapters.

My first thought was, I've driven all the way here in a torrential storm to do God's work, and this woman has read the entire book in the store, bent the cover, and probably won't buy it. (Books with bent covers are always returned to the publisher because they are not in "saleable condition.") I was tired, discouraged, and certainly not looking forward to the long dark drive back to Connecticut.

Eventually a good-sized group arrived, about twenty people, and I began my lecture. The woman in the front row, holding my book, began to cry as I spoke. I was used to that; many times people cry during my lectures. At first I had been upset by it, sure I was disturbing people or pushing them off an edge, but I have come to believe they are being touched by the Holy Spirit, because one of the signs of the Holy Spirit is tears.

At the end of my lecture the woman came up to me. She said curtly, the chip on her shoulder evident, "I haven't talked to God in twenty years, nor entered a church."

"Mmmmm," I replied. I'm never there to judge, just to talk of my experience, and hopefully help others on their paths.

"My car broke down today," she said, pointing out a large window to a repair shop next door. "I had to wait three hours."

"Yes?"

"I came here because I had nowhere else to go. Do you see how big this store is?"

"It's huge," I replied. Besides the obligatory coffee shop it had sections with couches and stages for children's shows, rooms for history, and more.

"Because of the storm, or whatever, there wasn't a single seat available in this entire store, except one, this one in front of your book back here, tucked away in the farthest corner of the store."

I smiled. I had a feeling I knew where this was going.

"And today, reading this book has changed my life. My car was ready hours ago, but I stayed for your lecture. I had picked up your book wondering who had the audacity to title a book *Songs of the Soul*. And when I started, I just kept reading."

I nodded.

"Thank you," she said softly. "I've been searching in all the wrong places."

That evening she exchanged phone numbers with a total stranger in the audience to start a prayer group.

As we left the store together she said, "I don't think it was any accident that my car broke down today."

And I smiled. "No. I'm sure it was planned for quite a while."

On the way home I was humbled. The rain had stopped and the stars had begun to shine, as if showing me the direction home. Although it was late and I still had a long drive ahead of me, I was no longer tired. "I'm sorry, God," I said. "If the reason for this whole evening was for that one woman, I understand. Thank you for the opportunity to help her."

And I brushed away a tear.

"You must remember those times," the Archangel said to me this morning in prayer. "You have forgotten the power of the words God has given us to give to you. You must remember these powerful stories in order to keep going. You read the quote from Murray and you believe it on one level, but then you close the door. Open your heart to our messages, and everything else will open. Everything wonderful will become magnified. Tell this to the others. Let them understand that when you give your life to God and allow Him to direct you in your decisions, your soul will flourish. The armor will crack, and you will follow the plan you chose before your birth. And in this you will find true joy."

"Well," I said, "maybe you could help me here. I'm struggling to write the prologue and epilogue of the second book. You know I cannot self-publish a book again. It is too much for me, both materially and physically. I managed the whole process, from the printing to the packaging to getting the distributors, the speaking engagements—over two hundred—and the accounting. If you really want me to spread these messages, I need to be able to just do that. Only that."

"And you shall," he said. "Do not worry about the future. These messages are not for you alone. They are for the world, and the world will hear them. Prior to that time, if a publisher had bought *Songs*, you would not have been the speaker and believer in the messages that you now are. People need authenticity on many different levels in order to believe. If a large publisher, or even a small one, had automatically picked up your book, and you had not had to struggle so hard in order to get out the messages, people would not realize your authenticity as much. But now that will no longer be an issue."

"But if some large firm had published it, then perhaps many more people would have read it."

"No, because you were not ready to be the messenger then. So in essence the book would not have changed as many people's lives if you had not had to publish and promote it yourself. But do not worry now. Everything will be taken care of by the Lord. You need not even think about this. It is in His hands, if you give it to Him. And lives will change, prayer will grow, and God will walk with you. All of the opportunities that you need, as that quote so aptly says, will become available. And the world will change through these messages."

"Thank you," I said earnestly. "I really need to hear that. Some days I'm not sure what I'm doing with my life. I write, I give talks, I lose tons of money in the process, and sometimes this affects my self-confidence."

"You are doing His work. There is no greater work. You are open to the messages. Tell the others the importance of their lives is to live them on the spiritual level in their physical bodies."

"What do you mean?"

"When you are in touch with the spiritual, as you are now, you are filled with joy, aren't you?"

"Yes," I said, recognizing that writing down these messages brought me joy, brought me peace. But afterwards I usually lost it.

"This is a level you can learn to live on all the time. This is the level of being and living to your highest degree. It is the level that Christ lived on, constantly realizing his purpose on the earth. Other religions tell of the same level, and it is important to respect them. The Buddha lived on a level of spirituality in his physical body. When you connect there, you truly live in joy."

"But didn't he say living was suffering, or something like that?"

He smiled at my lack of religious education. "But he lived in joy, because he understood that transcending suffering brought joy, and that life lived on only one level would be only suffering. But life lived on a spiritual level would be joyous."

"I'll have to check that out," I said.

"Do that," he replied. "We saw you pray over the oatmeal today. How did you feel?"

"Foolish," I replied. "I put my hand over the oatmeal and thanked God for the food. I didn't feel foolish about that part, because that's like saying a prayer before dinner. But I felt foolish as I continued and asked the food to nourish my husband, to give him health and joy throughout the day, and to have him realize that it was made with love and kindness. As I chopped the bananas I felt they were wonderful and healthful and a gift from God."

"And?" he asked with a twinkle in his eye.

"It changed this morning from being drudgery to being a joy. While I did it I felt at peace."

"Yes," he said simply.

"But then," I argued, "I lost that feeling within ten minutes. Something happened, and I got that panicky feeling and lost that peace I had."

"It is a practice," he said. "But it is a practice available to everyone and available all the time. It is for all of you to access and take. And as your gem told you today, it is a clear path and one that will magnify as you walk it. It is a clear and discernible path for everyone. When you feel out of touch, scared at the reality of a physical and material world, pray and thank God for your blessings, no matter how small they may seem at that time."

"Even the oatmeal?"

"Yes. What God wants all of you to know is that small things that do not bring you pleasure, which become drudgeries for you, will eventually tire you and wear you out, and you will not listen to your soul. But if you can take those 'drudgeries' and turn them into acts of love, acts of ritual, acts of necessity for living, and give thanks for them, bless them, you will find a piece of God while you do it."

"A piece or a peace?"

He smiled. "They are the same. Go, love one another and practice what we have taught you today. It is God's will. Do it with the laundry, do it with the grocery shopping, do it with whatever you do not care to do, or have tired of doing. Ask for God's blessing throughout the day, and you will find this peace, this piece of God."

He began to rise, and then stopped. "I know you tell people to keep their stones with them in a place of honor. I am reminding you today,

73

especially, to keep the clear stone with you. It will remind you that your destination is clearly chosen, your path is not hidden, and with God's assistance everything good will become magnified. Amen."

"Amen," I said softly, watching him rise. I looked around. I hadn't even noticed where we were, so intent was I on his words. I had assumed we were at the beach, or in the city, but as I looked I saw it was dark. In the far distance I saw an ancient graveyard, and a shiver of fear ran through my body.

"Do not fear," he said. "It is just a reminder to you that the physical body goes from dust to dust. The important task is the task of the soul. You have this life to live your soul's chosen destiny."

"Help me," I begged, "in finding what my destiny truly is."

"You know it," he said. "Go and carry it out. Amen."

Amen, I typed.

Twenty

Have I given all my cares to God? No, I think. I've picked another gem, this one clear but with a foggy streak of blue in it. I try to understand its significance. Yesterday's gem was clear with no color at all, and I felt as if everything blessed was magnified. Was I falling backwards? Or was I misinterpreting the meaning?

"You have not 'fallen backwards,' as you say," the Archangel said quietly. We were sitting by the pool of water overlooking the mountains. "Everyone moves forward and backwards on their forward path. But, as I have told you before, if you are facing God, you are always moving toward Him, even if it is unbeknownst to you."

"But what about this gem?"

"What does it tell you?" he asked.

"That God tries to give me peace and I fog it up."

The Archangel laughed. "Many of you do that. You see the gift, but you create a mist, a fog, to hide it. Remember, and tell the others, that each gift, even the gift of calmness and serenity, brings with it responsibilities. Humankind sees this with their soul, and often turns from it."

"What kind of responsibility could come from being calm and at peace?"

"Having the peace of God within you, having a piece of God with you, will bring responsibilities in that you will need to share that with others. You will need to tell others how to achieve it. This is true with all the abundant gifts God gives us. You may be able to see the gift, touch the gift, but not accept it, and that can be for a variety of reasons. You may be fearful of the responsibilities, fearful of the change, and unwilling to step out in faith. You are all capable of creating a fog surrounding the gifts. Initially many of you do not even see these gems, these abundant and everlasting gifts of the Lord. But even when you do see them, you are sometimes unwilling to accept them. So you cloud them with your protestations, you cloud them with your fears, and you feel comfortable in the darkness that envelops you."

"Gosh," I said sadly, "I sound horrible. God wants to give me wonderful gifts, and I accept some, and then others I just ignore."

"It is a path that takes knowledge from the Holy Spirit to travel.

That knowledge will enable you to accept freely the gifts God wants you to embrace. You will no longer hold onto the fear of the darkness."

"What do you mean?"

"Darkness creates fear, and many of you live in that place. All your lives you live in fear, and that is such a loss, such a tragedy. In faith you turn toward God and relinquish that fear."

"That's so easy for you to say. How can you say that if you've never had a human body? You don't know what it entails to clothe it, feed it, keep it healthy—and send the kids to school. When we get sick fear can override everything."

"And everything can become a wonderful gift from God, if it is accepted in that manner."

"We've had this conversation before," I said, "and I still have a lot of doubts about that." To me, the Archangel just didn't really understand this earthly trial.

"Tell me an example. Tell me a doubt. "

"Okay. Someone has struggled with psychiatric illness and depression for years. Her entire family has, and some have committed suicide. Now explain what could possibly be good about any of that heartache, because I see nothing good in it at all. Then I see people who are greedy and acquire more and more wealth, and they never seem to get sick in any way."

The Archangel turned his head away from me and didn't answer for a while.

"You cannot see God's picture."

"I don't want that answer. I want an answer I can understand. How can I spread these messages without an answer I can understand? Tell me how all this mental illness and sickness in a wonderful family is part of God's picture!"

"God created you to be with Him and be in joy. All of you turned away. In doing so you decided as a whole, as one, that you were wrong. Your lives without God were hungry and desolate, and you begged to return to Him. But God, in His wisdom, realized that you needed to beg not out of necessity, and not out of missing Him, but out of wisdom. You needed to know *why* you missed this Eternal Love so very much. And so He gave you the lessons of learning. He gave you the Holy Spirit. And each of you, in conjunction with the whole, took on tasks that allow you to grow as a one, to return as a one, to the Holy One."

"That still doesn't really answer this—"

"Some of you who have taken on enormous suffering have taken it on for your own wisdom, or for the wisdom of the whole. It may be a learning process for you, or you may already know this lesson from the Holy Spirit, and are suffering for the betterment of others, so that others will learn compassion and love and be able to return home to God as the One."

"But that doesn't help me with the greedy guy who leads a charmed life, a guy who doesn't seem to care for anyone or anything but his bank account. He never gets sick, and seems really happy. Or it doesn't help me with the people who just are regular, are nice, and they too seem to have no problems."

"First let me explain something. Listen to me, and do not ask this again. You are here not to judge. That is one of your lessons, and you are struggling to learn it. You cannot judge your brothers and sisters, nor can you envy them. The lessons on earth should be joyful, but when you do not keep your face toward the Lord, you create suffering. We will take the example of this imaginary person who is greedy and happy."

"Good," I said, thinking he was finally getting to the point.

"Have you ever thought that perhaps he has chosen the wrong path in his destination?"

"No," I said firmly. "Definitely not."

"Well, I am here to tell you that perhaps he has. Those you see who appear safe and secure are oftentimes the souls who are in the deepest darkness. And it may be that the family who is suffering the pain is suffering in order to give the pain to God, in joy, for another's growth."

"But what if that guy doesn't grow? How does it seem fair that a family in India is starving and without a decent home while others live in hundred-million-dollar houses?"

"You are not seeing clearly," he said. "Take out your stone you picked today."

"It's too foggy. I don't like it," I said, shaking my head.

"Learn to embrace the fog, and then you will walk through it. What I am saying to you—and listen to this and believe it because it is a gift from God that this is being revealed—is that no soul is greater than another, but many are more advanced on the pathway home than others. Those who are more advanced have willingly sacrificed comfort to help others. Sometimes that help comes through their offering their suffering in joy to God. That is like a prayer, and it helps their neighbor move toward God, even though their neighbor might not know it. Or such a strong prayer may help them bring the person back to his original destiny. His destiny may be to live in a large home, but that is not his spiritual growth. Spiritual growth is the most important aspect of your lives here. You must grow spiritually or your soul will leave this earth. If you have grown all you need to with these lessons, you move on. And if you have taken the wrong path, you move on."

"So you're saying that some families suffer either for their own growth or maybe for someone else's growth?"

"Yes. Some souls come to earth willing to sacrifice their own comforts for this short time to help others move closer to God. This may occur when people interacting with them learn compassion, empathy and love. Or it may happen by their offering their suffering to God for the mistakes of others, because on another level you know you are one, and so you are willing to sacrifice your lives for your brothers' and sisters' salvation, as Christ sacrificed his life for yours."

"I wish I could 'just get it,'" I said mistily. I brushed a tear from my cheek. I felt so alone, even though he sat near me. I felt so ignorant and selfish sometimes, and so dense. I didn't understand the bigger picture, and when he revealed part of it to me in bits and pieces, I still questioned.

"On this other level," I said, "what do we know?"

"You know that you must learn, as a whole and with free will, the lessons that the Holy Spirit wants you to know in your hearts. Because when you freely learn these, then you will move toward God and rest with Him in eternal light and salvation. But when you turned from Him, you wanted to come back only because you did not like the darkness, the evil. Now you must be within the darkness and understand freely why you want to be with the Lord. When you return as a whole, you will never leave the Lord again. You will have understood in your hearts, learned in your souls, the need for the love, the compassion, the empathy of a God Who is everlasting and eternally loving. And you will take that knowledge, gathered as you grew spiritually from the beginning of time, and go spread it to others."

"What others?" I asked. "If we've all returned to God, whom would we go talk to?"

"God is infinite love. God has creations beyond your imagination. When people love children, if it's possible they have more than one because they have abundant love to give. God's love is hugely abundant. Across the universe there are creations struggling with the same struggle you as a one have struggled with. And when you return, you will help them."

"They too turned from God?"

"Some did, and they need to return from the darkness. Others didn't, and are helping more move closer to God."

"You're talking about people on other planets?" I asked, dumbfounded. Because it's bad enough I've written about angels, I think to myself, but now people are really going to think I've gone over the edge with extra-terrestrials.

He laughed. "You are the most difficult soul at times! Just because you do not see on this earth, you do not believe. God is infinite love. His love does not stop here at this earth. It continues throughout a universe you cannot fathom. But some of His creations are on levels you are not able to understand yet."

"Yet?"

"At some point you will. When you pass from this earth you understand more."

"I don't want to pass yet," I said, getting a little scared.

"Oh, you won't. These words need to be spread. They need to help others and ease their minds, and enable them to understand that their purpose on this earth is to love, to embrace one another, to realize that all of you are one, and to pray. Prayer brings knowledge from God and the Holy Spirit. Christ prayed constantly, and so must you all. Make each action a prayer, and the energy around that action will become blessed. And things will change.

"Amen."

Twenty-One

I pick a blue stone again, this time a solid sky blue, shiny and metallic. I find myself on the mountain with the Archangel.

"Blue again," I said. "Solid and shiny. Am I not accepting the gifts?"

"The gifts are abundant and everlasting. If you feel that the gem you picked today was for serenity, God will pour serenity over you through the day. Do not be caught up in the colors of the stones or what they mean for you as a lifelong purpose. Choose them with joy and see what gift God has for you."

"But I thought that maybe I'm going backwards, in that before I had less blue...am I now more anxious?"

"Do not over-analyze the gifts of God. If this is the gift God gives you today, it is a gift to be embraced and learned from. Some days you will not need serenity; you will need hope, or compassion, or clarity."

"I always need serenity," I said.

"So does everyone."

"No," I argued. "I was thinking about this and praying about this before we met today. Some of this book will not speak to people, because some people do not worry, do not have anxiety."

He laughed. "They may not worry, but they have fear. And anxiety and fear work on similar biological and mental levels."

"What do you mean? Fear of what?"

"Fear of loneliness, aging, illness, fear of lack of money, fear of not being loved. They may not worry, but this fear still blocks them from the peace of God they need for their soul."

"I don't know. I think you're talking about the things—-"

"No." He shook his head. "Picture someone who does not worry, but I tell you they have concerns. They have prayer lists, they have needs that are not met, and because of this they often have a fear which blocks them."

"So fear and anxiety are different?" I asked.

"On some levels they are. Fear in many cases can be stronger, but it has both a holy and a dark purpose."

"What do you mean?"

"Fear when you see a car coming at you makes you get out of its way. It can save your life. In contrast, anxiety might make a person scared, for no reason, that a car may swerve toward him."

"So fear is good?"

"Only in the way it was given to you from God. But because fear has saved people on occasion, they have taken the useful purpose of fear and brought it into parts of their lives for which it serves no purpose. People put up barriers against their neighbors in fear, fear of getting too close, fear of hurt, fear of discouragement. Loneliness and lack of community are the result."

"And biologically fear and anxiety are the same?"

"They travel the same pathways; both were given as gifts. Anxiousness as a gift was eagerness, excitability, but then humankind took it and brought it to the dark spectrum."

"Then what if people read these messages and do not have anxiety or fear?"

"They have learned the lesson of peace; they have grasped the peace of God. Fear will block you from accepting gifts. Fear will say, 'I am unworthy.' Fear will say, 'I understand where I am now; I cannot accept change.' Fear will stop you from moving on to that next step. God wants His children to be joyous on the pathway home, to find delight in the journey of the soul, but fear will block that and keep you in the material and physical. Even those who do not worry oftentimes struggle with fear. Fear is a barrier. Sometimes it is for protection, for defense, but it becomes isolation from others. Fear uses many excuses, and grows to become a blockade around your physical, mental and spiritual elements."

Hmm, I thought. Did I do that too?

"You are learning to drop the fear," he said, not in a congratulatory manner but just matter-of-factly. "Tell the others that to drop the fear you must realize your pathway is glorious. To leave the fear behind you must take that step toward God with hope and delight. Then the fear, which has turned negative, will ebb away. It will fall away. You have been reluctant, as many are, to walk blindly in faith, to trust the Lord in all His wonderment."

"I know people who wouldn't think they have 'fear.' They are outgoing, friendly, and..."

"And what?" he asked. "Do they tell you their fears? Their concerns?"

"I thought they did."

"People oftentimes block out their fears, deny them, and when they do this the fears stay as a wall around their beings. To be totally free of fears, you must face them, realize they are nothing but negative emotions (when not used for God's purpose) and move onward to God. Unfortunately people carry many fears with them, fears that they don't even know they have. So we urge you to tell them to work with the stones. Pick the stones and write what they feel about the stones, the gems from God."

"I know that many people will think that's odd, or New Age or something." The stones were nothing but small different-colored glass gems, extremely inexpensive, that are often used to fill part of a vase and hold flowers. On the shelves of craft stores or toy stores they are certainly not considered "holy" in any sense.

"Tell them, as you have before, there is nothing magical or wrong with sitting in prayer and taking a gem from God. These stones, which are in reality nothing but glass from a factory, will become symbols of the gifts of God that surround you. When people pray, and ask for the gift *God wants them to have*, they are, in that act alone, giving up control of their lives and asking for God's direction. That in itself is powerful; it is a magnificent step toward Our Lord."

"What if they take a gem and don't understand it? I've done that. I pick a color and hold it and wonder what the heck it means."

"And always, if you sit and pray about it, you will understand it. Perhaps not that day, perhaps not that month, but you will, as you take the gift and hold it."

"How does that work?"

"By holding the gem you will realize God has abundant gifts for you. You will pray, you will be open to Him, and your soul will connect with the Divine Source. Your soul will partake in His knowledge, His wisdom, His guidance, and you will begin to see more clearly the pathway that your soul needs to travel. This will happen through prayer and patience. We also ask that people keep these gifts in a place where they can be seen, and each time they see them to connect with the divine, remembering what it is that gem symbolizes for them. This is a holy ritual, a way for people to connect with the divine within them and around them. And then, if they feel so inclined, they should write something of it down."

"Even if it's nothing?"

"Yes, each day, even if it's nothing—just that single sentence. But we urge them to listen to God's whispers to them, and by the end of the year the 'nothing' will have turned into something magnificent."

"It's a way for people to pray?"

"It's a way for people to pray, to realize that God has infinite gifts for them, and to connect with the divine within them and around them. When they do this consistently, they will understand their purpose on this earth. It will open up the knowledge that they have sealed within their souls. And they will recognize it."

"Recognize it?"

"Yes, as if to say, 'Oh, of course. That is how I return back to God. How could I have been so mistaken?'"

"It sounds beautiful and simple."

"It is. You have begun it on a larger scale, but we would like everyone to do it—on a small or large scale. It will simply return them home with directions and love."

"And this is holy?"

"How can holding a gem which symbolizes the gifts of God, how can praying and asking for God's guidance and direction, be anything but holy? Many people can do this without the physical gem, but the glass stone a person holds is a helper, to bring that person closer to God. Go. Live today with joy. Pray for your brothers and sisters that they too will find joy in this day."

"Please take care of my friends," I say. "My friend's husband was getting a second opinion on his cancer at a Boston hospital today."

The Archangel bent over me, and lightly touched my face with his cheek. "You have grown tremendously, and God is pleased."

I was dumbfounded. "Why would you say that now? I've always wanted people to pray for my sick friends."

He nodded. "But now more than ever you understand the true power of prayer. You believe it more than ever before, and you empathize with those who are struggling much more than you ever did before. You are following your destiny, and are not as reluctant as at other times.

"God is pleased.

"Praise Him.

"Amen."

Twenty-Two

Blue again, I laugh! I look at all the whites, the blacks, the greens, the oranges, the ambers and violets in the bowl, and it seems I pick only blue.

"You need to breathe more deeply. We have taught you that, but you do not always listen to us," the Archangel said.

We were back on the rock by the beach. As I climbed up the rock the crowds on the beach disappeared, and once again we had the expansive land to ourselves.

"Breathe more deeply?"

"Yes. The body is so constructed that on its own, if given the chance, it can cleanse itself of anxiety and fear. Breathing, as many of the ancients knew, is a vital technique to help you to cleanse your body of toxins. Look at a baby sleeping, a small spirit in a tiny physical body. The baby breathes quietly, rhythmically, and deeply through her stomach."

"Through her stomach?"

"Watch the child's stomach. It will move up and down as she breathes. Watch an adult in a business meeting, and all you will see is the chest either moving up or down or not moving at all—shallow breaths that barely give the body oxygen. Without this oxygen the body finds it difficult to relax and find its original state of relaxation, the state it had as a baby."

"How did we lose that?"

"Many ways. When you began to talk, you hurriedly tried to communicate and lost touch with the breath. Or in your haste to worry, you lost touch with your body's mechanism. Many of you are told to be rigid, polite, and quiet while growing up, and quiet has been interpreted as taking shallow breaths, which are toxic to your physical selves."

"If you run and exercise, in most cases your body will try to revert to its original pathway. You will breathe deeply and your stomach will move up and down, not only your chest. This will bring in the air you need to cleanse the blood, energize the body, and heal the mind."

"Sounds so easy," I said.

"You have seen it work," he answered matter-of-factly.

And of course I had, I thought. I had finally returned to Tae Kwon Do after almost a year's absence. During that time, of course, I was very sick, but I also noticed that because I wasn't exercising my asthma was returning. I dragged myself back, as many of us do, knowing that exercise is good for us, and in a new school I found the enjoyment I had had many years ago with the martial arts. And I found too, as the Archangel said, my breathing becoming deeper, more rhythmic—and even, I thought, more powerful.

"Powerful!" he said, reading my thoughts. "That is the word you should relate to when you think of breath, proper breath. It is powerful. It is powerful for bringing in purity, for cleansing the body and taking out toxins. With each deep, deep breath, the toxins within your body are released, because your body begins to do what it should be doing all along, breathing as deeply as a baby, cleansing away anxiety and toxins, and bringing freshness and purity within.

"You can also meditate and get these results," he said. "But you rarely do it. You need only to sit quietly in prayer, or just in peace, and concentrate on your breathing. This is older than the sages. Put your hands on your stomach as you breathe. Allow the breath to move downwards, to your stomach, and feel it move up and down as it takes in, and releases, the air. All the muscles are working, the heart is pumping, and a new and fresh flow of air begins to penetrate more deeply into the tissues. It is a marvel of God. And it is available for you.

"Tell the others. This breathing not only helps the physical, but also, because of that, it helps the spiritual. When the body knows it is being cared for, it allows the doors of the spiritual to open, but when the body is ignored, it is like a petulant child, demanding more and more attention, demanding more and more material things. But once it is cared for, even if only for moments a day, it allows other parts of your life to be nourished also.

"And then the most powerful breath force enters, the breath force of the Holy Spirit. It is like a wind entering your body, sometimes forcefully, other times like a gentle wind that caresses you, but always it brings you knowledge from God, wisdom and peace. It helps you to see your path. This breath, the breath of the Holy Spirit, is the most powerful."

"And you receive this just by sitting?"

"Sitting quietly and allowing your body to return to its natural state of breathing calms the body and the mind. As we have told you before,

85

in a state of calmness you are more open to listen to God's whispers, to allow the Holy Spirit to enter you and give you wisdom.

In times of chaos, negativity, fear, you are not in a state to allow your mind and spirit time—you are caught up in the earthly. And the earthly, although important for your spiritual growth, is not the prime concern of your travels here. The spirit's growth toward God is what is most important."

"Tell me that again—the earthly body is the not the prime concern of our travels here. We're here on this earth, you said, to learn lessons. So aren't you contradicting yourself?"

"From dust to dust," he said somberly, "but the soul is eternal. The body is a means for you and others to learn what is essential for your spiritual journey. The body can speed this along, if it is open and at peace, because then it allows the spirit to be open and at peace. But if the body is consumed with thoughts of the earthly—survival, sickness, bills, and so on—it does not allow the spirit to take precedence. So although it is essential for these particular lessons, it is not the prime concern. Your spirit is most important and should be first priority, because your spirit is made in the image and likeness of God and is a partaker in the divine energy of Our Lord. All of this is magnificent and brings you toward your destination of complete peace of God, and a piece within God.

"Please pray the following, and ask others to pray it."

I bent my head in prayer.

"Lord, allow the breath of the Holy Spirit to enter my body, enter my mind, enter my soul. Allow it to fill me with cleansing, fill me with energy, fill me with kindness and compassion for myself and my neighbor.

Help me to breathe differently physically so that my body can be filled with life, filled with health, able to move to its maximum potential. And with these breaths allow my spirit to find the piece of God that resides within and around me. Amen."

Twenty-Three

I feel stuck today, as if my life is going nowhere, and I wonder if others go through periods like this. My self-esteem has hit new lows, and I wonder, am I alone in that too? I look around and everyone seems so confident, so self-assured, and I don't feel that way about myself.

I pray and pick a stone. Black. It fits my mood. In all the time I've been picking stones I don't think I've ever gotten a black one. I'm usually pretty happy, or at least I appear to be for the sake of others.

"Black is all colors combined," the Archangel tells me. We are at a new location, alone on a stretch of grassland overlooking the ocean, sitting on a small wooden bench. Rather than facing the stretch of beach before me, with the waves to my side, I am looking out on the vast ocean and the clear-cut division of water and sky. No boats are on the horizon, even though it is a glorious summer day. Usually days this glorious are in September, because even now, in August, I can feel the difference in the air. It is slightly crisp, not heavily humid as it has been through July.

"You need all the gifts today."

I nod. He hasn't told me anything I don't know.

"You are feeling this way for a variety of reasons. You are losing hope, and we have told you not to do that. These messages will spread and lives will change. We are telling you your time is approaching quickly. Do not be concerned with your work."

"But I am," I said. "I'm concerned that I have no work. I've given the talks on the first book and now I'm just writing down what you tell me. But I feel desolate and lonely."

"That is important," he said.

"What?" I asked, surprised.

"Do you not realize that the majority of people in the world feel desolate and lonely?"

"No," I said rather quickly. "I think quite the opposite. If I go downtown right now, people will be bustling, productive and busy. And I know people who have fulfilling jobs and children and families that are full of love."

"And you do not know," he said, staring directly into my eyes and speaking more slowly than he had ever spoken, "if they are desolate and lonely."

I shrugged, unconvinced. "They aren't," I argued.

"Many are," he said, "and we feel it's necessary for you to realize this, to experience these feelings so that you can help others with them. If you were right now overcome with happiness and had no insecurities, how could you learn the compassion that you chose to learn? You would not understand those in darkness. So you are taking on those emotions for the betterment of others."

"Taking them on?" I said. "I don't want to take them on. Make me feel self-confident, hopeful, happy."

"Did we not say that all things result in goodness with God?"

I didn't say so aloud, but today I wasn't really believing that.

"You, and the others, do not realize that you all have the same struggles. The most difficult one is the struggle of being connected with one another. When you turned from God you went as a one, but then you separated. Once in the darkness, away from God, you splintered and went on your own way, some with small groups, others alone. But during that time you learned the feeling of isolation because you were no longer one with God or with each other.

"And now the purpose of these journeys for each of you is to reunite with each other, and then return home to God as a one. But during these journeys you feel the isolation that occurred when you first turned from God and from each other. Sometimes you find comfort in this. It stops you from acting, from moving forward, from moving toward the light. You stay there because it is comfortable and known, and the alternative is to move toward the light, be vulnerable with each other, and reunite as a one. So in experiencing this feeling of isolation, you realize the importance of the community.

"We urge you to realize daily the importance of the community, because to return home you must return as a community. On this earth you struggle alone, and your society today encourages this to a large degree. Many people work more hours, leaving less time to interact with family, with children, loved ones and others. The feeling of isolation grows.

"When you find that others feel as you do, you often find comfort in each other, and then those feelings of isolation soon dissipate. That is because you have come together as a community, in your natural state of oneness, and therefore the fear leaves and you are one, and you can travel more quickly on the path to God."

"So I'm feeling this to realize what others feel?"

He nodded. "You can feel their isolation because you, personally, today feel isolated, and that isolation brings with it a darkness, a despair, a lack of hope. You need to face this and leave your worries and concerns with the Lord. He will care for you. But because you are suffering today in this isolation, you realize what others suffer.

"The key to all of this is to bring together the community, as it once was, and then face the light of the Lord."

"What about depression? I know people who are depressed and it is chemical. It has nothing to do with isolation."

"Yes, it does have to do with isolation. When they are together with others who care, the healing begins. This chemical imbalance may have been genetic, may have been from the ones before who felt isolated and abandoned and passed this on to their children. Or it may have come from simply a pattern in their own life of feeling isolated, hopeless and abandoned. If you, or your ancestors, have taken hold of this, it becomes a pattern in the brain. The brain embraces it and the chemicals think that is what is normal.

"It is as simple as that. The chemicals believe that this feeling is the feeling that is normal. Both drugs and other people can help the person see—and teach the chemicals—that the feeling of hopelessness is not the normal state. God wants everyone to be in the normal state of hope. That is the true gauge, the state of hope."

"It's all so easy for you," I said. "How can you tell me all this, as if you really understand it, when you don't have a physical body? You don't have chemicals that build and grow and accentuate feelings, whether euphoric or depressed, or chemicals that just allow us to worry."

"God does not want you to be in an unnatural state," he said, dismissing my tone of voice as if he had not heard it—or at least did not take offense at it. "And what you are talking about is an unnatural state."

"But what about Christ? In the garden before he died, he felt isolated and abandoned. His disciples slept when they should have been praying for him, and Peter denied him three times. If Christ felt like that how can you say that state is unnatural?"

"Christ took on the aspects of humanity; he took on the sacrificing of his life for his brothers and sisters. But even in that dark state that was both human and yet of evil, he constantly prayed. Prayer will protect you from this darkness. We have struggled to tell you this over and over. When Christ was in the desert and faced with Satan, he prayed. When he was in the garden, faced with his death, feeling the feelings of isolation, hopelessness and despair, he prayed.

"To guard yourself from these feelings, pray. Pray for God to allow your brain and your feeling of well-being to return to its natural state, a state of hopefulness. You should all be filled with hope, because you are returning home."

"I read at Mass yesterday something in the fifteenth chapter of Corinthians."

"Go read it. I will wait," the Archangel said.

"For as in Adam all die, even so in Christ shall all be made alive."

"Is that not what we are saying?" he asked. "When you turned from God, you all went toward the darkness, and in this darkness there is death, because not being with the Holy One is death, is hell. But when Christ came he showed the way to live your lives. He showed you the importance of kindness, compassion, community, and most important, prayer to the One Father who loves and cares for you infinitely and eternally.

"Once you as a whole realize Christ's message, you shall all be made alive again. You all will return home to Him who created you, to Him who is waiting with unending patience for your return. Christ knew this, suffered, and yet throughout this suffering understood the perils and concerns of mankind, but turned this suffering back to God, as all of you should. All of you can do as Christ did."

"Oh sure," I said. "Look at me. I have an angel dictating to me, and I'm still doubting that I can do what you say. I still doubt that the message will get out."

"Faith is believing in the unseen. You do not need faith to know these messages will go out because I have told you that they will. I have told you that you are to believe, and you are to understand. You also struggle every day with the responsibility you take on with these messages."

"Someone read the second book and was disturbed."

"Christ disturbed many people. The apostles and the disciples disturbed many people. Whenever you tell people the truth and point out the road to spiritual happiness, if it is not easy people will turn from it and be disturbed, angry, upset—a whole range of negative emotions. That is the human reaction when you are shown beauty and you turn from it—you will become disturbed. Many do not want to face the truth, so they discount it or become upset. Many do not want to take responsibility, or to change their lives. When there are forks in the road, many people stop by the roadside and camp indefinitely, afraid to make the wrong choice, and comfortable in their inertia. But in this inertia they do not grow, and their soul does not learn the lessons it needs to return to God. So this disturbance is like a storm on the sea— it is a storm of the soul. If the soul is not heard, the inertia grows stronger and deeper, and the fear and the shell around the soul grow thicker.

"That is not for you to fear, nor is it for you to take on. Give that to the Lord in prayer and it will be lifted from you. New challenges disturb people, and that is one way for the soul to get the personality's attention."

"But we don't always listen?"

"No, you don't, and you repeat and repeat the same lessons, the same fears, and live in states of hopelessness. Then you pass these states on both genetically and mentally to your heirs, as they may have been passed on to you by your ancestors."

"Well, tell me how to break the cycle."

He sighed. "Pray for the answers, and God will send them. If you are isolated and lonely, find the community and answers and doors will begin to open. Serious hopelessness may require medical procedures, which bring hope and are a gift from God. But it is important for everyone to realize that these feelings of hopelessness have been with you since you, like Adam, died in the spirit. You turned from God and entered a state of hopelessness. Now, through Christ's love and example, and his sacrifice, you can relearn the feelings of hope and see that the light of God shines within you.

"Take this message and share it with others, and realize that God is there for each of you, and that a community as one is the first step in returning to God. Being in isolation from the community will only breed darkness and more despair. You need one another. You had one another in paradise, where you were one with the One.

"And that is what will be achieved when you reunite. Amen."

Twenty-Four

Type this out, the Archangel tells me.

Breathe in the spirit to make me reunite with it, to waken my soul to its destiny, to allow me the confidence and self-worth that Christ has given to me, which is mine by being part of God, by partaking in the Divine Province that is ours. With this love for ourselves and each other, the rages and hates of the world will dissipate and each will realize that they are not only One, but need each other to be One, to be whole, to be reunited with the Maker. All of this comes from the love, wisdom and compassion of the Holy Spirit. Amen.

I'm surprised to find myself in the crystal arcade, which I had visited many times before with both the Archangel and other angels. It was a series of rooms off a corridor of thick creamy glass with an arched glass ceiling. Each room held different forms of wisdom, different books of learning. Some would be locked to me, and the angels would tell me it was not yet my time. Other rooms I would walk into easily.

The Archangel stands regally in the corridor, his arms folded beneath his flowing purple sleeves. An aura of white light surrounds him and the sunlight falls directly on him.

He barely smiles, only nods, and I walk toward him.

"Open this door," he said softly, standing in front of a large metal door. Next to the door was a store window, and I peeked in. It was dark inside, but I could make out shelves and shelves of ancients books.

I turned the knob of the door, and although it was of heavy steel, it opened easily and lightly.

"When it is your time for your destination, the doors open easily," he said. "Tell the others. When you struggle for something and do not achieve it, it is not your time."

"But struggling is important, isn't it? Because we need to struggle in order to persevere."

"No," he said. "Struggle is different than perseverance. Struggle has suffering with it, and it is a way to show you that the pathway may be wrong. Perseverance still has joy with it. Perseverance is your road, with changes, turns, detours, all of which are joyous learning lessons."

"Well, if I couldn't open this door, shouldn't I just have kept trying?"

"If you persevered, and it opened, it would have been God's will. But if you persevered, and suffered because of that, it was not for you to have."

"I think you're contradicting yourself," I said.

"No," he said. "Perseverance is a gift from God, and it is important to continue to move in that direction God gives you. In persevering you are always given signs by God; you can always hear His wisdom, and then you continue with joy and hope. But struggling does not have hope or joy, and it is often the indication that it is not the path for your spiritual development."

"I struggled with the publication of the first book," I said.

"No," he corrected me. "You persevered. Struggling would have meant that no doors were open and no indications given to you that the book should be published. Struggling is pushing against a brick wall with your hand, without strength and without results. Perseverance is slowly dismantling the wall, and seeing the signs of progress. Tell everyone that they are to look for signs, for openings, for God's light shining, and then they are to persevere. Your soul will recognize these signs. The more you are on your soul's original path and destination, the more you will realize and see these signs."

"These signs are around us all the time?"

"Yes, but you have blocked them out with the worldly. God and his messengers constantly send each of you signs and indications that you are on the correct soul path. The more you pray, the more the soul is in communication with the divine and understands these signs and allows you to view them clearly and without doubt, to view with faith."

"Are you talking 'coincidences'?"

He smiled. "You may see them as 'coincidences,' but what they are are doors opening and leading you toward your soul's path. Each of you at some time has experienced this, and most of you discount it. You discount it to such a degree that the shell begins to get thicker and thicker, and the soul cannot see the doors opening, the light of God, the pathway it wants to take. You block your own soul's pathway. But with prayer, and the aid and comfort of the community, and sitting in the silence of your being, you begin to meditate and understand the spiritual journey. You begin to realize that your pathway here was predetermined by you, and by the others (with your consent), in order that you and the one return to God.

"Yet many of you, once you are here, forget all of this. That is natural, but what is also natural is recovering those memories and journeying toward those destinations."

My hand was still on the steel doorknob.

"Enter," he ordered.

It was dark, and I fumbled on the wall for a light switch. There was none. The Archangel lit a small candle and suddenly the room was illuminated. Far more brightness came from this small white candle than would have come from a large overhead lamp. But I no longer questioned things that appeared illogical to me.

As I had seen through the window, the walls were covered with ancient books. The bindings were all leather, and some were stacked on their sides because they were so oversized. "May I?" I asked.

"Yes," he said. "Choose the book to which you are drawn."

Oh, I thought, now that sounds more responsible than just picking a book at random. I ran my hands over some of the books, resting them on an oversized tome lying on its side. Gently pulling it from the shelf, I saw the golden inscription on the burgundy leather. It read: *For Those Who Dare to Live Life Fully*.

I stepped back. That wasn't what I had expected.

"What did you expect?" the angel asked.

"I don't know. It looked so old, I pictured something in Latin, with Gregorian chants, and pretty medieval inscriptions."

"That is what your mind told you to pick, but your soul told you to pick the book which allows you to live fully."

I didn't open it. I didn't want to.

And then I wondered why.

"Do you need time alone?" he asked.

"No," I said. "I'm just curious why I'm not opening this quickly if it has insights into living life fully."

The angel said nothing, nor did he press me to open the book.

I held it, still astounded that I wasn't opening it. Didn't I want to live life fully? Of course, I thought. Didn't I want to have unending joy? Of course, I thought.

"Well," I said aloud to my friend, "what is holding me back?"

"Only yourself."

"Great." I said sarcastically. "Only myself. Well, right now that seems pretty big."

"We will wait until you are ready. "

He sat on a library stool, his hands still tucked within the large sleeves of his robe. He was all patience and understanding.

"Maybe it's not my time to read this," I said, already thinking up excuses.

"The door opened easily and swiftly," he replied calmly.

"Right," I nodded.

"Well," I said, "why am I holding myself back?"

"Fear," he said. "Again and again with humanity it is fear. That is why the majority of you do not talk to your soul, do not listen to God's whispers, do not hear the messages of the angels."

"Fear of what?"

"You tell me," he said softly.

I knew already; I didn't have to ask. Why had I even asked?

"Responsibility, change, and things we don't want."

He nodded. "Such as?"

"I'm sure that if I open this up, the book isn't going to say the key to happiness is having abundant wealth and security."

"You must open it to see."

"Nor will it say that thinking of your own needs will bring you a life of fullness and contentment."

He began to smile.

I slowly lifted the heavy leather cover.

The book was inscribed in gold again on the title page. The author was me.

"I wrote this?" I almost screamed. "How could I write this? I didn't even realize it existed! I didn't even want to open it!"

"Each person has written this book. Each has his own book, his own knowledge."

I turned the page and there was the first chapter: The Destiny of My Soul.

And I began reading.

Twenty-Five

Again I've received clarity, a clear stone that magnifies as I move it over letters on a page. I received it the other night when I gave a lecture in someone's home. I had asked that there be ten people there (because at that time I didn't charge) and there were probably fifteen, but the majority were teenagers who I had assumed were there under protest by their parents' orders. I had driven over an hour to get there and it was so far out in the country that some of the roads were not paved. My car had shimmied and automatically gone into four-wheel drive. To add to my discomfort, the weather was so hot and humid that at times I was afraid I was going to pass out.

I tried to change my lecture slightly so that the teenagers could relate to it, but I wondered if I had gotten anywhere. Some looked bored, others fidgety, and still others poked each other and laughed. And I thought, as I have so often thought, oh Lord, why am I here?

Afterwards one of the teenagers came up to me and I found out she had actually dragged her mother there. Another wanted to buy a book for her mother and told me how touched she was by the messages. And a young man who had sat in the farthest corner of the room, as if ready for a quick escape, thanked me quietly for telling my story. At the end of the lecture when we picked the gems, I picked another clear one, clear and magnifying. It made me think that my pathway was unobstructed and would be shown to me. I hope so.

I hold the magnifying stone in my hand, and the Archangel appears.

"The stones you continually pick are not only the gifts you need, but the gifts God wants you to have. Sometimes people think they need a certain gift from God, but in reality God is waiting patiently with the gift that will change and transform their lives. But they are too intent on wanting the other and thus never see the important and life-changing one."

"I'm ready," I said. I had thought I would say that hesitantly, but oddly it came out confidently.

"We know you are. And your time is very near. The messages are strong and will alter people's thinking." We had been sitting by the pool of water, but then we were back in the arcade and the book of my soul was in my hands.

"Read," he instructed me, and I did:

"This is for you to read now, in this period of time, for the goodness and journey of your soul. Your soul is not different than the others; you all must face the uncertainties of life, the challenges of living on this earth, the complexities of being with each other and dealing with their personalities. But your destinies are the same, to return home to God. Your individual paths may differ, and your soul will have to encourage you to make the soul choices. That is where many of you stumble and stop. The soul choices are those choices that seem uncomfortable, but are easily recognizable."

I wondered if it would explain those last two words. The text continued:

"Easily recognizable is through prayer. If you are faced with choices that seem overwhelming, and decisions that do not come easily, sit quietly in the body, breathe deeply, and ask to hear God's answers through your soul. Your soul will give you the answers."

I looked up at the Archangel. "It's not that easy," I protested.

"Continue to read," he demanded softly.

"When a decision is one of kindness and goodness, it will be from God. When a decision brings you joy in kindness, brings others joy, it is of God."

I spoke to the Archangel again. "But this doesn't work for every little decision in our lives. Like what do we do with a boss who hates us?"

He looked down at the book. I continued reading:

"Your soul's adventure began before the eons of time were understood. When God thought of your existence, you existed. You became one with Him and enjoyed the love and light of the heavens. But using the free will He created you with, you began to make choices of independence, choices that slowly moved you away from God and alienated you from Him. The darkness descended upon you. You had made the choice to leave the light, and now the soul's struggle is to return to the light.

"Many are still stuck in the darkness most of the time, and this is where the difficulty comes. All of you need to go back home together."

I stopped reading and turned to the Archangel. "A man asked me a question at a lecture, and I didn't know the answer. He asked, if there have been so many people on earth for so many centuries, and some of them have been horrible beings, how can we expect none to be saved until all are saved?

"I didn't have the answer," I continued. "Perhaps it was just mystical, I said. Then I added that reincarnation seemed to be the likely answer, but not one I was pleased with, since I didn't want to believe in that."

The Archangel shook his head. "First, there are many of you that make up the one. This was your time on the earth, but others have come and gone before and will come and go after you. Each soul has its own time to learn these lessons and return to God. Again, you as humanity, as a whole, begin judging your neighbors. And that stops your own progress. You do not know the choices the 'criminal' makes after his death. When he was brought toward the light, he may have fallen on his knees in remorse and pain, and turned toward the light and been with God. It is not for you to say."

"But isn't this our chance? On earth?"

"Do you truly believe that a God *Who is love* would give you only one chance at being with Him for eternity? He is waiting with unending patience for all of you to return home. Each of you, struggling or flying to your destinations, will be the recipient of that patience. When you die, there are different levels of light, different levels of alienation from the God Who loves you. And these levels are ones you have chosen in your life here on earth. You go to where you are at the end of your earthly time."

"Explain that to me more."

"If you are in darkness on this earth in a time of horrendous crime and you are part of that, or you have been selfish and hoarded the gifts God has given you, not sharing them, at your death you return to a level of darkness. That level, which some of you may term hell, is alienation from God. But it is not a hell to which God has condemned you; it is a hell you have chosen for yourself. Even in this hell God loves you. When Christ descended to hell after his death, he showed the souls there the light of God. Christ still regularly descends there and brings the light. At those moments the souls again have the opportunity to work their way back to the light, if they so choose."

"And the other levels?"

"They are different levels of learning and different levels of distance from the light and love of the embracing Lord. But, and we stress this to you, they are all levels which you have chosen on this earth for your afterlife."

"Is this like purgatory?"

"In a sense, yes, there are different levels of it. When you are in alienation from God, on the soul's levels, you are still struggling with

98

returning home. You are still struggling with making selfish decisions that do not help the whole return home. But you have chosen that level by your choices here on this earth."

"And then what?"

"You may work from that level to help others on the earth, or you may choose different lessons. Sometimes, even within those levels, there are souls who work furiously to help the other souls. It is heaven's soul work.

"But the soul is always trying to direct the personality toward the light, on this earth and on the other levels. Do not think a God Who created and loved you with His whole being, and allows you to partake in His divinity, would dismiss you or leave you. You must stress to everyone that it is you who leaves Him."

"Well, let's go back to the horrible person who dies, and then hits his knees and sees the light. Does he go to the level that he made on this earth?"

"Most times the level you make on this earth is the level you gravitate to, because you still have selfishness and alienation from God to work out. On each level the Christ visits. The light of God is shown at the intensity that the personality has asked for. But sometimes when people die, even after living a horrible life, the personality realizes its wrongdoing. They fall to their knees and ask forgiveness. These people have learned their lesson in the transition from earth to the Lord, and they are changed and move closer to the light of God."

"I'm Catholic," I said.

"We know," he smiled.

"And we believe that praying for someone in purgatory can help that person go to heaven faster. Is this what you're saying? I'm not sure. Are you saying there are different levels of purgatory?"

"I'm saying there are different levels of alienation from God. And yes, praying for a soul who has departed is immensely powerful, because those prayers, which are never wasted, allow the person to see more of the light. When you see more of the light, you want to be a part of it. But trying to just be a part of it, without desiring it selflessly, is the struggle. You must want, in the depths of your heart, for everyone to see the light, and to truly forgive those who have done transgressions to you. As Christ said on the cross, 'Father, forgive them for they know not what they do.' Christ not only saw the light and love of God, but he was selfless, both in giving up his life for his brothers and sisters and showing them such an example, and in being devoid of selfishness and revenge. That is true compassion; that is true love; that is being united with God completely.

"On these levels each of you must continue to learn, and truly encompass, these qualities and compassion for each other. When you have truly encompassed them and brought them into your being, you move toward God, because God is these selfless emotions, God is this love, God is this nonjudgmental and compassionate light, and to be reunited with Him, you must have all these qualities and have absorbed them at your soul level."

"Absorbed them at your soul level?" I asked.

"Continue to read."

The book went on: "Your soul knows all the answers because it is a part of God, and the soul is filled with the compassion, the light, the love of the Lord. Yet, as individuals and as a whole, you have turned from this light and thus have also turned from the compassion and light within you. That is your mission, that is your destiny, the destiny of each and every one of you: to unlock that compassion and unending love and live a life devoid of judgment, devoid of hatred, devoid of envy. Thus your soul becomes free. The more you live like Christ, the more the soul can direct your pathway home to the Lord. But until you have truly embraced all of this, and have absorbed it, and released the soul from your selfishness, you will not be in the total light.

"But the light will always beckon to your soul. Always. Even in the depths of the darkness of alienation from the Lord, your soul will recognize the glimmer of God."

"Does God's light shine less for those at lesser levels?"

"No," he said. "God's light is forever the same. It is just at a lesser level because your soul is still covered with the shell and so the light is dimmer. As you learn, and practice what you learn until it becomes one with your personality, and with your free will choose kindness and love, then the soul begins to crack the layers of the shell and shed them. With each shedding, with each lesson learned, you are able to absorb and see more of God's light and love.

"And eventually the soul will shed all of its armor, through your own choices, and at that level you will have freely chosen to be nonjudgmental, freely chosen to love your neighbor, freely chosen compassion, and compassion will be within you. Your soul will have no blockage in perceiving the light of God, and will be filled with the light and commingle with the light and be one with the light. Amen."

"Amen," I said.

Twenty-Six

I pray. I ask for serenity and the ability to accept it. As I pray I rest my hand over the bowl of the gifts of God and reach for a gem. I choose one that is entirely different from any I've ever seen before. It's somewhat clear, oval, with brown streaks going across what would seem to be a horizon.

I don't know what it means.

"Look closer," the Archangel says. I find myself by the small stream in the woods overlooking the mountains. The air is fresh and clean and I inhale deeply, as if needing it to clear my mind, to free my soul. The fresh pine scent invigorates me, and I look more closely at the stone.

"What does it remind you of?" he asked, keeping his eyes on a hawk that was circling across from us, on the other side of the shore.

"I'm not sure. It seems almost like copper sands, a desert, but inviting."

"Yes," he said. "The desert can be inviting. Christ went to the desert for forty days, and there he prayed to God to allow him to follow his pathway, his soul's destination."

"But was that the passage where Satan came, or am I confusing things?"

"Satan came to tempt the Lord," the Archangel said softly. "But Christ reached deep within himself, into the silent desert of his soul, and heard God speak to him, and he rebuked Satan and told him to leave. Then we came and we ministered to Our Lord.

"The desert is powerful in the physical sense and powerful in the spiritual sense. To go to a place of quiet is necessary for each of you. Find you own desert and then delve deeper into the desert of your soul, for there you will find the contentment, the happiness, the peace that eludes you when you are consumed with the physical, consumed with the material."

"But for Christ that silence also brought temptation, didn't it? So it's not all beautiful," I argued. The hawk was still circling along the shore, high above the trees, his wings outstretched and silent. He seemed not to be moving at all, as if he were just delicately allowing the air below him to keep him up, as if the faith in that alone would do it. And it did.

"Yes, in the silence you discover yourself. You discover your personality and you discover your connection with God. Because you began struggling with this issue eons ago, it still surfaces. The temptations of the Garden of Eden, the temptations of Earth, still call to all of you when you are getting closer and closer to the Creator. And that is both the beauty and the challenge. As you move closer to your soul's destination, evil will try to prevent you from following the path. The darkness inside you will try to cover the soul, and fear and greed will again seek to motivate you.

"But because of this desert and because of your *wanting* this connection with the divine, the power of the divine—if you access it—will overcome all evil, and you will be sent on your pathway. You will turn from the darkness, the temptations, and move closer to the light of the Lord."

"You make it sound easy, but Christ was still tempted. So if He was tempted, then how can I possibly think that I won't be, or that if I am, I can overcome it?"

He smiled, turning from the hawk, which had swept down and retrieved something. We saw it fly away with a small animal or fish hanging from its beak.

"Christ said to his disciples, 'I am with you always. You will be able to do even greater things than I.'"

"He did?"

"Yes, and what he meant was that when you learn your soul is divine, you connect with the most powerful source of all; you connect with the Creator. And when you partake in the divinity of this Creator, all things are possible. You are not doing it alone, you are doing it with the power of God Almighty behind you.

"So when you are in a desert, in the quietness of your being, and you find both the light and darkness within you, if you continue to pray—which is actually accessing the Creator to be one with you, and accessing His power and love to fulfill your purpose—you will turn away from the darkness and turn toward the light. That is why it is so important in the desert, in the silence, to continually connect with the Lord, because otherwise the desert periods of your life can become isolating, fearful and negative experiences. You will thirst and hunger, and not find fulfillment."

"The desert periods of my life?"

"The silent periods of your life, the times when you are alone with your thoughts and concerns. Those are the desert periods of your life. They can be glorious, such as the desert experience of Christ was. In that experience Christ grew in his humanity. Remember that he was both human and divine. He too grew as a person from this life."

"How could he? He was divine. He was the Son of God."

"Yes, but he embraced humanity when he arrived on earth. He knew his soul's destination and never deviated from it, but often was tempted and understood the darkness that pulls each of you toward it. In the desert he faced Satan. In the garden alone, he asked the Father to take away his cup. He, just like each of you, wanted to escape the harsh experiences that he was to face. But because of his constant connection with God, he turned from those temptations, and always returned to the words 'Your will be done.'

"And this too you all must do. When faced with darkness, when faced with temptation, you are to turn toward the Lord, and state, faith-filled, 'Your will be done.' And it shall, and your obstacles will fall aside, and you will be on your soul's path, following it to the destination for which you came here."

"To return home to God?"

He nodded. "To return home to God, and bring others with you. It is the only pathway that will bring you happiness and joy on this earth. Your journey on earth should be joy-filled, and it will become so when you realize your purpose. Kindness, compassion, love and light will emanate from you and you will find yourselves filled with the light of God."

"You make things sound so simple. But I gave a lecture to a bunch of teenagers the other day and I didn't know how to make it sound so simple for them. It's so difficult for kids these days. Violence and rage are everywhere. They're afraid to go to school because some one may come in and shoot people randomly."

He nodded and was silent for a moment. We watched a fish jump from the stream and fall back into the cool clear water. I wondered if I needed to repeat my question. Had he heard me?

I waited, not patiently, for what seemed a long time, although it was probably only a moment.

"Each person, as you have learned, is from God. You are all one."

"Yes," I said. "I think I've finally learned that."

"Others will learn that too. But learning that one principle is not enough to live it and fulfill it."

"What do you mean?" I asked, but I thought I knew where he was going with this.

"To understand you are all one is different than being all one, acting and living as a one."

This time it was I who was silent.

"When you talk to teenagers again, realize that they are going through difficult times emotionally and physically. Their bodies are changing faster than their minds are growing. Their bodies are maturing and yet they still have the minds of youngsters. On top of all this they are bombarded by materialistic and violent and sexual messages. Because their bodies are mature and their minds are not, they follow these messages."

"I can't tell them that," I said, raising my eyebrows in exasperation.

"In most cases they already know it. They are craving direction and guidance. They too, these youthful souls, are trying to understand their purpose here on earth. Sometimes at this age they try so hard to understand their purpose that they give up in frustration and never try again. As children you are born knowing your purpose, and then you begin to forget it, and the shell builds. Teenagers try to recapture it, and find it difficult, and it is at this period in many people's lives that they give up on their spiritual life.

"Each step is simple, as we have said before. If you don't know where you're going, you pray. Tell the youths to ask that the wisdom of the Holy Spirit descend upon them before they enter the classroom. With this wisdom they will choose acts of kindness and compassion rather than acts of selfishness and condescension. With this wisdom they will realize their own true worth in being a partaker in the divine with the Creator. When you fully realize that you are in partnership with God to return home, and are loved unconditionally by this Father, you will see yourselves in a light of kindness and acceptance. When you can see yourself in this light, you no longer need to cast shadows on others. Only light will shine from you."

"Explain this again," I said. I was beginning to wonder if I needed another cup of coffee, but then realized I drank it decaffeinated anyway so it wouldn't really help to clear my mind much.

"When you receive the wisdom of the Holy Spirit, embrace and accept it. Accepting it is the most important. The Dove descends all the time, but many do not open their hearts to Her. With this wisdom compassion for yourself and your neighbors comes into your heart, and your shells begin to break. When you have love for yourself, a healthy love that comes from knowing that God is with you and loves you, your self-esteem is healthy and whole. When this is so, you are a kind and wonderful person to others because the divinity of the Lord moves with you in all the directions you walk. The north, south, east and west become the setting for this love.

"When you are detached from God, and do not understand the beauty of your soul, or the destination of your path, or the worth of your being which is so wonderful, you are ashamed and fearful. Those emotions bring harshness and hate to the forefront. To make yourself feel more important, more loved, more likable, you ignore others, debase others, and find negativity with others. And that, in the mind of darkness, makes you feel more important—but only for a few moments. You will need to do it over and over. And finally the rage will come, the hatred will come, and the hate crimes towards others will come. All of this springs from your lack of connection with the Lord, because you are acting out of lack of love for yourselves. When you have the wisdom of the Holy Spirit, you understand the love and compassion that God has for you, regardless of your sins, your mistakes, and your shortcomings, and you realize that your opportunities to help others are limitless, your opportunities to move toward the light are limitless. With this optimistic and wonderful belief, miracles occur. Mountains are moved.

"But without it, rage and hate grow.

"And let the teenagers know that it is not just the 'different' ones that have this rage, the ones who are deemed violent. Each of you has had a part in this process. By not being connected with the Lord, by not treating each other as one, you are a part of the process of darkness.

"You are a circle of souls. None acts alone, because each is fed with the energy of the others. When you are enveloped in the love and kindness of a soul who has connected with the Holy Spirit, you too will spread that love and kindness and wisdom to others. You will believe in your own self-worth. You will have confidence and love for yourselves, a healthy and wonderful love, a love that is a reflection of God's love for you.

"You will want to share this and help others discover it. It is simply done through prayer, and then prayer results in actions, and the actions and attitudes will change others. The ripple effect will change the world.

"Do not think you are alone. Do not think the situations of the world are hopeless, because they are filled with hope through God's connection in each of you. You need only to access this divinity, to pray for the wisdom of the Dove, and then the peace and love that God has for you will be reflected within you. You will feel His love. Then you will embrace that love for yourself, and you will give it to others, and honor the love God has for others within themselves.

"And honoring the others will bring peace and light to the world."

I breathed the cool air again, overwhelmed with all he had told me today.

He placed his hand on my head, and I bowed down, expecting a blessing.

"Bow your head to the Lord the Creator Who loves you unconditionally and waits unendingly for all of you to return home. But each of you is a spark that must be ignited, and that spark must be passed from one soul to another, so that the light of God will shine throughout the world, throughout the universe, illuminating the pathway home to Him.

"God bless you and keep you," he said softly. "Believe and walk in faith. He waits for you, patiently. He waits to give you wisdom and guidance, and waits for you to discover the love that is within you.

"Amen."

"Amen," I said. Brushing away a tear, I looked up. The angel was gone, the hawk had left, and even the fish were no longer jumping. Quietly I sat in the green alcove, breathing slowly and deeply, praying for wisdom, praying to love myself and others with the same love that God has for us.

"It is possible," the Archangel's voice called from above. "Everything is possible with God."

Amen.

Twenty-Seven

Each of us interprets the gems we pick in our own way. To some, blue may mean serenity, the presence of the Blessed Mother, the beauty of the sea and the sky, or one of many other interpretations. At one of my workshops a woman picked a gem and started to cry. Within the gem were three small bubbles, two of them on the bottom of the stone and one floating away from the other two. She came up to me and told me what it meant to her. She and her husband had lost their ten-year-old daughter only a few months before, and she felt that the bubble was her daughter leaving, floating, moving toward heaven. The gem gave her incredible peace.

Today I've picked a white one. Some may see white as the absence of color, but my artist friend reminds me that on a light spectrum all colors combine to make white. Today I feel strongly that the gem means for me a new beginning, a clean slate, a washing away of my concerns. Yesterday, in the dark of the night, I asked God to take away my worries and concerns and give me the faith that His plans are marvelous for all of us.

Today the stone seems to reinforce that for me.

Some who read this will wonder if any of it makes sense. But I truly believe that when we pray, we must also be willing to accept and listen to the answers. That is where many of us stop. Often I have prayed and yet when the answer was shown to me I was blind to it.

The Archangel and I meet again at the top of the mountain. This time clouds surround us, so it seems as if a fog is on his robes of purple and gold. I find I am wearing a hooded down parka and heavy boots to keep me warm.

"Thank you," I said softly, admiring my clothes, which I had never seen before.

"Always thank God. He is the one who from all good things come."

I nodded.

"Why are we meeting in the fog?" I asked.

He pointed to the familiar spot where we had often sat, another rock much smaller than the large one we sat on at the beach.

"Many of you are in fogs," he said softly, "a mental and spiritual fog which envelops you. And one day, before you come to realize it, the fog is so thick that you cannot see in front of you; you cannot see your own hands or feet, or your own spirit."

"The other day," I said, "it was lovely at this spot. The river was clear, the fish were swimming, and I could smell the pine trees. Now," I said, blinking hard, "I'm struggling to see you."

He touched my hand lightly so I knew he was still there. Then he said, "The view is always beautiful from God's perspective. The view you saw the other day is God's view of this mountain. But each of you often fill your view of the world with clouds. You block the beauty with your concerns, with your materialism, with your greed."

"Greed is such a harsh word," I said, fidgeting on the hard rock.

"Greed is not only for money. Greed can be for love, for self-fulfillment, for any excess over your needs."

"But love is important."

"Of course," he said. "Love is why you are here. You are here to do God's will, and God is love. But when you want love only for your own gratification, and not to spread it, you turn the emotion into something that it is not. It becomes greed.

"Greed can never allow true love to grow. That is the lesson that many of you need to learn, that when you desire things and emotions and people for the wrong reasons, for reasons solely of self-gratification, you do not move closer to the Lord. Love is unconditional, love is unending. But it is also a feeling of contentment, wisdom, and peace that comes from God. All of this is a part of love. Compassion on the deepest level, compassion on the level Christ had for each of you, that God has for each of you, is the level that each of you is seeking."

"I have a problem with a passage from Matthew that was read in church on Sunday."

"Yes?" he asked.

"It was about the Canaanite woman who begged Christ to save her daughter, who was at home sick, from demons. The apostles tried to get rid of her, but she persisted. Then Jesus, who we have grown to believe is so compassionate, told her that he was there only to save the people of Israel."

"And what did she do?"

"She persisted, but then Christ told her, 'It is not right to take the children's bread and toss it to the dogs.' I read that as meaning the woman was no more important than a dog. How compassionate was that?"

"And how did the passage turn out?" he asked, although I knew very well that he knew the answer.

"Christ said her faith had saved her, and to go home and her daughter would be healed. She had begged, saying that 'even the dogs get the crumbs from the master's table.'"

"Christ was speaking to the people of Israel, people who for centuries considered the Canaanites enemies and inferior to them. Christ needed to show the Jews the importance of faith, that God embraces all people and all faiths, if they but persist in their faith.

"There were Jews there whose daughters were sick, and they did not ask Christ for healings. But it was their enemy whose daughter was healed, because of her faith and her persistence with Christ. Christ taught the lesson that all are the same in God's eyes."

"But he didn't say that in the beginning," I argued.

"No," he replied, "because he knew what the Jews were thinking, and he wanted them to understand and see the miracles of the Father. If he had just healed the woman without having the conversation, they would never have seen that the power of God is for everyone. They would never have seen Christ heal an enemy of his people. Christ's compassion showed in the healing, and his teaching was effective because he voiced what the Jews were already thinking. If he had agreed initially, they would have considered him a traitor to his own people. He wanted to show them that true compassion is for everyone, for your enemy as well as your loved ones."

"Couldn't he have said it more nicely?"

"The woman's soul and Christ's soul both knew their roles in this play. Consciously, neither did, but on a soul level they both knew what must occur. She had to approach him, even though a Canaanite woman would usually never be so bold as to approach a Jew. Nor would a male Jew answer her. So Christ had to reject her at first or else his listeners would have turned away from him, and his act would not have had the power to affect them as it did. Christ learned from the woman and went on to teach the message to his audience. People's attitudes toward others changed that day. Because of this conversation many people understood the love they must have for their enemies.

"So just as you do, Christ learned and grew from listening to his soul that day, and the woman learned and grew from listening to hers. Christ's role that afternoon was to teach others. To do so you must understand their viewpoint, their thoughts, and their fogs."

"Their fogs?"

He nodded. "Many are wrapped in fogs. They have seen beauty but they walk in a fog. It is for each of you to raise the fog from their eyes, as Christ did, to allow the clouds to rise above the mountains and reveal the beauty of the view. God's view."

"How do we do this?"

Again he answered, "You do it through prayer and meditation. And very often you do it in gratitude."

"Gratitude?"

"Yes, gratitude for the day, gratitude for the joy God gives you. Each day you must be grateful for this gift of life. The glory of this gift, this opportunity, is indescribable to you at this level. But you have all ached for this gift of your humanity for ages, and now that you have it many of you abuse it or disregard it, and some even end it.

"When you return to the level at which you have chosen, those who have not used their opportunities are filled with remorse and sadness at their lack of wisdom, because the wisdom was always available to them on this level but they did not access it. They did not pray, and they did not allow the community to help them progress spiritually. They returned with lost opportunities, and those lost times keep them from returning home to God."

"So make it easy for us. Tell us what to do."

The fog began to lift and the sun shone on the small creek next to us.

"It is all so simple," he said. "I have told you numerous times to pray for wisdom, but many of you ignore that, as if wisdom is too easy an answer. Yet wisdom from the Holy Spirit contains all the answers. It is the answer, and when you have it the fog with which you choose to surround yourself will lift.

"Because you choose this fog. This too is one of your free will choices."

"Why would we choose not to see? Why would we choose not to have wisdom?"

"Because you are comfortable where you are, and even in your darkness you find comfort. All change brings responsibility. When you can clearly see the picture, when you can clearly see your soul's purpose, you have no choice but to act. But taking action often fills you with fear, because you know that your life will change and you will have new responsibilities, and people may leave you. But Christ told his disciples to leave their families and go with him."

110

"I always wondered about that," I said. "That didn't seem too nice, to leave their wives and children. What happened to them?"

"Christ chose apostles with families that he knew would be taken care of, and he chose disciples who he knew would help their families on a spiritual path, the spiritual path that is the most important task you have here on this earth.

"Nothing else matters but to embrace the wisdom of the Spirit, learn love and compassion, and turn toward the light of God. Then happiness and joy will fill your being and you will be on the pathway home.

"Amen."

Twenty-Eight

I pray for the gift God wants me to have, and again I get a clear magnifying gem. It reassures me that God is showing me the clear way, and magnifying it for me. The Pope came out with a controversial statement last weekend that hell is a state of mind, a self-exile from God. I reread it three times, because he is saying exactly what the Archangel told me in *Songs of the Soul*—that it is not God, an all-loving God, Who sends us to hell, but it is we who choose hell by turning our back on God and embracing the darkness. Apparently many fundamentalist Christians are upset with this view, quoting Biblical passages about fire and brimstone and damnation.

I grew up with the notion of a white-bearded judgmental God sitting on a large throne declaring to people "You're saved" or "You're doomed for eternity." To the best of my recollection that's what I learned in Catholic schools, and here, thirty-five years later, the Pope explains the matter in a way I agree with.

I also think people are angry with the Pope's notion because they want justice. They want God to judge the Hitlers, the child-molesters, all the bad people, and banish them to an eternity in hell. I understand that completely, but now I also see that all of those criminals make their own choices, and even, I believe, when face-to-face with God they still have an opportunity to turn toward the light.

When I close my eyes in prayer the Archangel greets me at the beach. I tell him what I've just thought about.

"Is that not what we have said since we began our visits? You are all one. Christ told you that there can be heaven on earth, and yet most of you do not understand that statement either."

I frowned. "I understand the self-exile from God, but you're right. I might not understand the heaven on earth statement."

"If you are truly with God, truly find Him in the folds of your heart, and live your life according to kindness, love and unity, as Christ did, you will find heaven on earth. Seek out people who have given their lives to others. By doing so they have found heaven on earth."

"Like Mother Teresa?" I asked, remembering the nun who lived in poverty in India, tending to the lepers, the poor, and the sickest of the sick. I remember reading that she said working with the dying was a privilege because they were the closest to seeing God.

"Yes," he answered. "She had none of the material possessions that all of you crave, and none of the worries and burdens that come with that greed. She needed money only in order to tend her sick brethren, build hospitals, and try to comfort the dying. But she knew in her heart that even without those buildings and those medicines, her love and the love of her sisters for the poor and dying was what they needed more than anything else. They, the abandoned and shunned of the world, found in her and her sisters people who would hold them and care for them, and most important, see the Christ within them.

"That is what each of you must do. You must see the Christ within each other, the God within each other, and when you recognize that, the world will change. Peace will be on earth, and heaven will be on earth, because God will be seen and heard in everyone."

"How can that be possible?" I asked. "You have seen this earth from the beginning. There are always wars, wars for property, wars over money, wars over religion. Wars are even started over sex. And on a less grand scale there are the shootings we've recently seen in our high schools. Kids come into school and randomly—and sometimes not so randomly—just shoot people in the school corridors. Won't this hate and war be with us forever?"

"Everything is a chain of events. As we have told you before, each small pebble thrown into the sea affects the dynamics of the sea forever. It changes the sea forever. And as such a small ripple affects the sea, small ripples affect each of you."

"I know that," I said. "I say that all the time in my lectures. I use small examples of how people's lives can change. I talk about the express line of the grocery store, when the woman ahead of me has eighteen items in a twelve-item line and I can feel the anger growing within me, and how I can choose to let it go, and smile at the cashier, and then she in turn smiles at the woman behind me with a baby. Or I can choose to grunt at the cashier, and then she grunts at the next customer, and then the mother snaps at the baby, and the baby cries all the way home, and the husband comes home to a crying baby and a mother in a bad mood—all because I got angry about items in the express lane."

"Yes, that is the ripple effect. People do not understand the power of it, the magnitude of it. Today you picked the clear magnifying stone and in it you can see how things can get larger. You can put it on a small deed of selfishness, and it will grow. You can put it on a small deed of kindness, and it too will grow.

"The children who shoot other children are not the only villains in this story. They are in darkness, and their deed is evil and horrendous. But in many cases it is the ripple effect magnified. Others, whether their relatives or children in school, have criticized them, ostracized them, belittled them, and suddenly the pattern has expanded. A small remark by one person may then become the remark that pushes another off the brink of sanity, off the brink of thinking clearly, and the darkness rushes in."

"Well, explain this," I said. "Researchers are saying that in many of these cases, these children—or criminals in jail, or whoever commits a crime—may have a chemical imbalance, and therefore it is a biological function. It has nothing to do with the ripple effect of someone else's remarks."

He shook his head. The August day was gorgeous. It was cool, with a slight hint of autumn in the air. Around us people sat on the beach and children played in the ocean. The smell of the clear, salty air permeated my nostrils. I inhaled deeply.

"Yes, chemicals have much to do with this. But what you do not understand, and what you need to understand, is that these chemicals also have a ripple effect. If you begin a pattern and the chemicals kick in, and the pattern continues, the chemicals in your brain build up too. Each time the pattern or ripple moves, more chemicals come into being."

"I've had panic attacks. The doctor says that's chemical."

"Yes, but the chemicals build because each pattern reminds them to continue to build. The chemicals that are in your body, that God created you with, are there for a good purpose. Panic was originally meant for fleeing approaching danger. Stress in its original form was good because it helped move people from one land to another where more food was available. But when you live with constant stress, when you get accustomed to the panic, the brainwaves begin to build a path and the chemicals continue to build up."

"Can this be fixed?"

"Yes, in some cases by medication, and in other cases just by realizing the pattern and trying to break it.

"But," he continued, "I want to get back to the murders in high schools. The murderers, after years of abuse and neglect and struggling to find self-esteem, act out their pain. They cry out for attention. Those people in their pathways might have stopped both the murders and the hate with something as small as an act of kindness in school, perhaps a hug from a teacher, a word of encouragement from another, or some other student smiling and being kind."

"Smiling?"

"Yes. Everyone is one. When you are not kind to your neighbor, even in the smallest of acts, it returns to you. And this ripple effect compounds. It compounds in chemicals; it compounds in actions."

"It seems hopeless."

"Oh no," he said emphatically. "All of this can be broken. Throw a pebble into a pond and see the circles it makes. This is the pattern. But then throw another pebble into a different place in the pond, and the design will change. It is that simple with your lives. The chemicals, with the help of doctors—and most important with the help of changing your habits—change lives."

"What about people who have inherited this stuff? Chemical imbalances are inherited. Maybe those kids who murdered in school had no other choice. Maybe their chemicals were just out of whack from nothing that was their fault."

"You build your body, and your body carries those thought patterns. Those chemical pathways become ingrained to such a degree that they are passed on to your heirs. Each of you in the beginning was the same. But some took other pathways, and when those pathways become strong, they become impressed into your genes and then are passed on.

"But I am here to say that with medicine and changes in your lives and in your patterns, the ripple effect can make heaven on earth. Your mind is the most potent medicine you have."

"What do you mean?"

"It controls or creates your pain. It sends out the chemicals that cure you or make you susceptible to illness. In documented cases of people with multiple personalities, you will find that one personality may have a disease but in another personality in the same person the disease is nonexistent. Does that not tell you the power of the mind?"

"And you're saying that the mind can cure disease?"

"The mind is very powerful, but the mind is connected to the soul. That is what so many of you do not understand. The soul is the seat of knowledge. When your mind does not connect to the soul, it works on its own.

"Through prayer you can allow your soul, your connection to God, to be heard in your body and your mind. This will bring heaven to earth.

"Amen."

Twenty-Nine

White again. A clean slate? Purity? I have no idea what it means. I hold the gem and just pray. I hear the Voice say, "Each day is a new one. Each day is a clean slate for my loved ones. Disregard the mistakes you made yesterday and embrace the gift of life I give you today. Take this gift, cherish it, and work to help yourselves and others come home to our Lord. Come home to the paradise you once left. There in the place of unconditional love and peace a seat at the table awaits each of you. There are many rooms and many seats, but all are reserved for each one of God's creations, each one of your souls. Your souls long to return to this place. Allow them to return."

The Archangel greets me at the beach again.

"There is a seat for each of us in God's home?" I ask him.

"Yes. That is what we have been telling you. That is what Christ told his followers, that his Father's mansion has many rooms, each designated for one of His creations."

"Some people think that only certain people will be allowed into those rooms, allowed into paradise," I tell him.

The Archangel shook his head. "Paradise was conceived with each soul in mind. In the beginning of your creation God brought you to Him and allowed you to see and become one with Him, and you turned away. But always He is waiting for each of you."

"What about 'just the saved'?"

"As we have said before, God is willing to wait throughout eternity for each of you to return home to Him. God does not judge. Each of you alienates yourself from God. When you decide to return home, like the prodigal son, God is there, and so is your place in His mansion.

"But each of you must make this choice through learning and evolving and understanding the purpose of being here on earth. It is a privilege to be here, learning and understanding what holds you away from God and what brings you back to Him. Some of you learn quickly, and others, still struggling, still caught up in the worldly, find little time for the spiritual. Yet at the end of your days, you will be accountable for your time on earth."

"Accountable?" I asked. That sounded ominous.

"Yes, of course. Accountable. Not in a judgmental way, not in a harsh way, but you will see the gifts God gave you, and which ones you accepted and which ones you denied, or didn't even see, because you were consumed with the worldly. Then you will understand the opportunities and learning gained from this venture, or the opportunities and learning lost."

"Like a test?"

He smiled. "In your words, perhaps, but in reality it is not a test. You are the person who makes the judgment of whether you have done what you had planned on doing here on earth."

"We plan on doing things? Could you discuss that in more detail?"

"Your soul knows the destination it wants. Many of you are with other souls at a different level, and sometimes you decide together to learn the lessons, or perhaps one of you sacrifices his or her time on this earth so that the others will learn their lessons."

"I don't get it. What if we decide to do something on this other level, and then come down and mess it up and choose another pathway?"

"That is entirely possible. The others will still be guided by their souls and will have the opportunity to take a different path, one with the same destination. But the soul who changes its mind upon entering the earth has lost an opportunity for growth, and this lost opportunity slows down your process of reuniting with everyone and being totally one with God."

"Aren't we totally one with God now?" I ask. "If God resides within us, aren't we one with Him?"

"You were created as partakers in the divinity of God. God resides within you and around you and is always waiting for you. But to be an actual partaker in this divinity, you must actively partake. You must realize this divinity, and act accordingly. This action results in compassion, love and healing for others."

"Physical healing?"

He shook his head. "In some cases but not always. What I am talking about is spiritual healing. Think of it like this: Someone is standing by your side your whole life but you don't know it because you never turn your head in that direction. You must realize God's presence to grow. You must allow your soul to follow its destination."

"What stops us from doing that?"

He smiled. "What you think of as obstacles. For some it is poverty, for others it is wealth, for others sickness, lack of love, lack of trust in one another—the obstacles, as you call them, are many. But they are not always obstacles, because they can be learning vehicles that allow you, and your brethren, to move closer to God if you make the soul choices."

"Is that why you woke me up last night to tell me the name of this book?"

"Yes. It should be called 'Call of the Soul.'"

"When I woke up I couldn't remember it, until now."

"The soul calls you every day, every moment. It knows the way back home. But when you don't connect to your soul, you disconnect from God. You cannot hear His whispers, cannot hear your intuition, and cannot hear the direction of your life's path. That is when many of you change your course here on earth. Through prayer and meditation, and fasting for some, you can hear the call of the soul. When you listen to that call, everything falls into place and heaven is on earth for each of you. You find peace within your heart and you learn the lessons that you need to learn to move closer to home. Until you can embrace each other, have compassion and empathy and unconditional love for each other, you are not fully partaking in the divinity that God offers you, because God does all of these things. He waits patiently and with love for you, and you must wait patiently and with love for yourselves and each other. Become God-like in your forgiveness for your brethren, become Christ-like in your kindness for the sick and aging, and miracles will occur, not only for those for whom you pray, but within you too. Your soul will begin to crack open.

"As you listen to the call of your soul and follow its map to its destination, you will move quickly forward toward this peace and compassion which is divine and unconditional. It is there for each of you."

"When will we 'get it'?"

"I do not know. That is not for me to know. But the angels do know that we are here as God's messengers, to help you anytime on this course, this path of your soul toward the Divinity. That is one of our reasons for existence. We worship and adore the Lord, and He has asked us to help you do the same, to bring you back to him and to avert evil and darkness. But we can only help you with the work of your soul's destination, and only with your permission."

"My permission?"

"Not your conscious permission, but the permission of the soul. The soul knows where it needs to go and it knows how to get there. But if something is blocking the destination and we can help the soul, we can do so only with the soul's permission. Even then you as a personality can block our help. The soul always wants to get closer to the Divinity, but the personality may not, so you can use your free will to block our aid to your soul's cause."

"I am so tired today," I said. "I haven't even taken my poor dog for a walk, and he's desperate to go out. I barely had the energy to get tonight's dinner into the crockpot. I don't think I'm really understanding all of this today."

"This is enough. You may not understand it today, but you will understand it, and others will too. Because of this more people will be brought closer to the Lord, more people will listen to their soul's calls and see the map of their destination that they themselves designed."

"We designed?"

"Of course. Predestination is not what this is about. You each designed your destination. And then of course on earth you follow that, or you do not. That is your free will.

"Go now. Rest. We will be available to you and to all when you are more receptive and alert. God wants each of you to take care of your bodies, to rest when they are tired, to eat when they're hungry, to respect them as a temple for the soul, because when your physical being is not receptive, the soul cannot be heard. It is imperative that your mind, your soul and your body each listen to each other and help each other in the spiritual progress toward home.

"Therefore those who abuse drugs and alcohol do not honor their bodies as temples of God. They do a disservice to themselves, to God and to their neighbor, because many of you are dependent on each other for your spiritual growth here on earth. When you are not receptive to God's word, you can impede both your growth and someone else's.

"Go rest. Pray, and worship and adore the Lord Who loves you. Amen."

Thirty

I thought I picked another clear stone, but it has a slight tinge of yellow. I can't remember what the yellow gem means but I'll look it up. For me today yellow means hope. I know in *Songs of the Soul* the hope gem was pink, but hope is the word that came to me today.

I am beginning to understand that not only are God's gifts multitudinous, but each one has many meanings and attributes for each person, and that accepting His gifts is not enough. We need to realize that we must take them and bring them into our lives.

Hope is comforting for me today.

The Archangel and I meet on the mountaintop. In the far distance the crests are covered with snow, but the air is spring-like and filled with evergreen scents. I inhale greedily, sucking this clear air into my lungs, and I realize the altitude is much higher than my physical body could endure.

"It is your soul we are communicating with, and God takes care of your body when you are in these situations."

"Thank you," I said, patting my pants pockets for my inhaler. I've had asthma for years. I need the inhaler now only when I'm either sick with bronchitis or in an emergency situation, like running in cold weather. Although I've probably used it only twice in the last year, I always carry it just to be prepared. But today I don't feel it in any of my pockets.

"You have no need to worry. We will care for you here, and your lungs will be fine even at this altitude, because God has willed you to be here and will allow the cares of your body to lessen while you hear His word. Do not thank us, but thank the One who sent us."

I bowed my head and said quietly, "Thank you, God."

"You are here today to learn of the need to grow."

"To grow?" That sounded odd, I thought. Wasn't growth what this whole series of books was about?

"Yes," he said, obviously reading my thoughts before I voiced them. "But many of your read these messages, read about prayer and compassion, but don't truly understand that you are on this earth to *grow*."

"Grow into what?"

"Grow into the partaker in the Divine Energy at its most powerful level. When you are stuck in patterns that don't allow intellectual development or spiritual growth, you are not moving toward the enlightenment that you need to be truly one with the Lord."

"Didn't Christ save us to be one with the Lord?"

"Christ came to earth and saved you by offering his life for each of you. And I repeat that statement: *each* of you. Many Christians think that only a select few will be saved, but Christ came for each of you. He also showed you the way to God by his suffering, his actions, and his offering of his life for his brethren, and that is what you are here to do."

"Offer my life for my brethren?"

"Many of you are already doing that here on earth, and you do not realize it because you made those choices on another level. But as you follow through on those celestial choices, you grow. The shell that keeps your soul in darkness cracks open more and more. Growth is very important."

"You mentioned intellectual growth. What do you mean? I thought all of this was spiritual."

"The end route is spiritual. But many of you will not find the end route without understanding and learning the vastness of God. The more knowledge you acquire, the more compassion and understanding you have".

"I don't think that's right. Take someone like Hitler. He probably had knowledge, but that doesn't mean he knew anything of compassion. He knew only evil."

"But with his knowledge he also had the option to choose. He had free will."

"What about people who are retarded or just slow? They can't learn any more than they're capable of."

"They may be your teachers," he said softly.

"What?"

"They may have already, easily, achieved knowledge—both spiritual and intellectual—that far outdistances some of their peers on earth. They may have chosen their earthly condition to help others realize their pathways and grow."

I shook my head.

"I don't think I believe this thing about choosing our pathways."

"Why?" he asked.

"Because people are suffering. They're sick, they're hungry, they're addicts, or suicidal, and I don't think anyone chooses those things."

He rearranged his glistening bronze robe around him, and tucked both hands into the flowing sleeves. I knew I was in for a long lecture.

"People have chosen what they need to know in order to grow, in order to learn and to embrace compassion for each other, and to finally return home to God. What you do not see, nor do you understand, is both the brevity of this time on earth and also its immense power. It is a short but extremely important time for the souls here on earth. It should not be wasted.

"Those who you say 'would not choose this path' may not have. Here is how it works. Your soul on another level, before your birth, plans its lessons. It knows what it needs to learn to return home and be one with God. On your soul level you, with others in your circle and other advisors to you, map out your pathway."

"In heaven?"

"On another level," he said, as if dismissing the word I had used.

"And then, with that pathway in hand, you are brought to earth accompanied by angels to encourage your work. You know at the time of your decision that this suffering or pathway which you chose is so brief, so small, in the realm of eternity, that you are willing to undergo it in order to grow. You choose others to accompany you on this level and help you achieve this. Some souls come to earth solely to help another. Christ did that. He came solely to help his brothers and sisters. He was one with God. He was united with God and understood the plan.

"When he arrived, like you, he followed the plan and remembered it. Still, he had times of darkness and temptation, because he was human and understood the power of suffering, the pain of the body, and the ache of leaving those he loved. But he chose, through his free will here on earth, to follow the plan he had designed and accepted with the Holy Spirit.

"All of you too come with a plan and a map for your souls' growth. With this plan you will grow or will help another to grow. But the trouble lies in that you may suddenly, in your human body, forget the brevity of this life and the gift and power of it for growing toward God, and get stuck in your humanness, choosing not to remember, not to follow the spiritual plan. This may happen if you do not keep in touch with your soul. If you ask small children about us"—he pointed toward himself—"many will talk of us as you talk about your friends. They see us; they remember the plan and understand their purpose here on earth. But as the earth and its material concerns bombard them, they close the spiritual doors.

"That is the obstacle. That is when free will comes into play."

"But if we pray?"

"If you pray, you still have your free will but you will be open to your soul. You will be open to the connection with God and the Holy Spirit, and you will live your life the way you had planned, either for your own enlightenment or for the enlightenment and growth of another. Christ chose to follow his plan, and through prayer he always knew what it was. Christ chose his parents, as do you."

"We choose our parents?"

"You choose groups to come to this earth with to grow and move closer to God. You often sacrifice for each other, or they for you, all with the purpose of moving closer to God."

"But what happens when someone doesn't follow the plan?"

He turned to me, his deep blue eyes filled with sadness. "It happens often. It obstructs the soul's development."

"But what about the others who are depending on that person for help?"

"If they pray, and continue to know their soul's destination on the soul level, and listen to their soul's call, their pathway will change from their original plan but go in the same direction."

"Like a backup plan?"

"Yes," he smiled, "like a backup plan. What many of you don't realize is that if you follow your worldly side, ignoring your soul and God's calling, you may not only deter your own development, but by a ripple effect you may hinder the development of another. If you came to earth to teach another compassion, and then do not fulfill that, the other soul must look elsewhere to learn the lesson of compassion."

"That's a lot of responsibility."

"You are one. Of course it is a responsibility. This task of returning home to God, although simple, is not easy for you. There is evil lurking to tempt you away from your destination. Greed, materialism, and egotism lure you from unconditional love, from giving and compassion. But if you continue to pray, and allow Christ's message and life to enter you, you will stay the course, and help others to do so.

"Go now. This is a lot for you to understand. But you will, at one point."

I was embarrassed but I needed to ask a question. "Could you hold on a minute?" I asked. "I've been awfully worried lately, anxious about everything, stupid things and serious things. I wonder if I'm losing the joy I used to have."

He looked at me, his face kind, not stern as it often was when he was delivering messages to me. "Joy rests in doing God's work. Joy rests in realizing that you are one with God. Joy rests in the self-esteem that springs from knowing you partake in the divine energy. Although you have come along well, you still do not understand this in the depths of your being. You do not think yourself worthy of many things. God wants all of you to think you're worthy of wonders. Wonderment and heaven on earth are here for your taking."

"What's the difference between healthy self-esteem and pride?"

"It is good to be proud of yourself, in your religion, in your work, in your accomplishments. But like everything in life, there is a yin and a yang. When the dark side of pride overtakes the healthy side, pride becomes evil and destructive. Be proud of your accomplishments, because they are done in co-partnership with God. But when the ego takes over and you begin to think of them as solely your own, then it is a destructive pride and no longer healthy.

"We picked you for a variety of reasons, but one, as we've said before, is that you are ordinary. What you battle, many people battle. In order to find this joy that you are currently lacking, you need to know that you must delve inside yourself and believe that you are united with God. Once you believe that, then all your decisions made with Him, all your actions in conjunction with the Holy Spirit, will bring you only goodness and light, and lead you back home to God."

I wasn't sure if he had really answered my question, but I nodded. He had hit something on the head. Why do so many of us question our worth? We measure it by accomplishments, money, houses, social connections—by all kinds of things instead of by what is truly important.

"When you give lectures at the convalescent homes to the people locked in body braces, confined to wheelchairs, paralyzed and unable to move, you say the truth. Listen to it."

He didn't need to tell me what I said to them. I knew. At the end of each lecture to the elderly, the ones who could barely move from one room to another without a walker or a wheelchair, I say, "As long as you have had a day in which you've prayed, you've had a magnificent day."

"Those are God's words, which He gives to you to remind those souls of their purposes. Often they are depressed and think their lives no longer hold meaning. Yet when you deliver those words, they understand the beauty of their lives. You," he said to me, his voice firm but compassionate, "need to realize and live those words too."

He disappeared.

And I knew he was right.

Thirty-One

I picked a clear stone with a large section of orange in the middle. It took me just milliseconds to figure out what it meant.

The Archangel appeared on the rock overlooking the mountains. I wondered briefly why we weren't meeting at the beach more, but I didn't ask. The mountain air was wonderful, and the panoramic view was one I would never otherwise see because the altitude was too high for me with my asthma.

"You know what the gift was today, don't you?"

"Energy?" I half asked, half stated.

"Yes, and did you see that it is only one-third filled?"

"Yes. Shouldn't God have given me a whole one?" I asked, and then thought how rude that question was. God should know what He's doing, and I'm getting greedy.

The Archangel disregarded my question. "The gift today was a message that you are living with only a third of your energy. This message is for many people. Most are barely using the energy God has given them. By using this energy you can move mountains. Energy translates into faith, love, action, prayer. As you grow in energy you are able to do more of God's work. But without energy in your lives, you cannot."

"Explain this in more detail, because I don't know if I agree. I see people in nursing homes and they are able to do God's work, because they pray. Right?" I asked.

"Energy comes in different forms, but all energy begins in the mind. That is why people who are depressed, even though their bodies are capable of energy, do not perform athletic endeavors, because their minds are not informing their bodies of their energy capacities. Elderly people are still capable of tremendous mental energy, and in many cases this energy can transfer to their aging bodies, but also in many cases their energy is solely for their minds.

"But the point of this lesson is to allow people to realize that this energy—which is a gift of God—is available in each person. The energy you need to focus on comes with breathing correctly and eating correctly. Correct breathing brings energy to different parts of your body; it moves and energizes the cells that can become stagnant. When you sit and breathe deeply, and meditate, bring the breath into the center of your being. This will revitalize your energy, calming you in different areas of the physical and mental, and it will begin to heal you."

"Give me an example."

"Breathe slowly and deeply, and close your eyes. Concentrate on your breath and bring that breath all the way into the center of your stomach. Feel your stomach move up and down. Place your hands on your stomach and continue to breathe. Remember always to let out the breath slowly and precisely. Concentrate as you do this. See the breath moving through your body."

On the mountaintop, in the clear air, I could feel my breath enter, cleanse my body, and leave.

"Do this many times a day, and you will begin to access the chemicals from your mind, chemicals that are stagnant because you are not breathing deeply. The ancients knew the connections between the body and the mind, and you have forgotten this. As energy moves through your body, you will begin to accomplish actions you did not know you were capable of. You will begin to pray with more fervor, you will begin to see things more clearly, and you will begin to understand the necessity of action and prayer. Together they move mountains."

"I thought faith did."

"How can you have faith without communication with the Creator?" he asked. "And that is done through prayer. When you communicate with the Creator, when you face the light, you will be able to access the energy of God. That is what makes prayer so powerful. But when you are listless in your bodies and listless in your minds, it does not work. You will find yourselves hungry for the energy of life, which is from the soul. The soul has the most profound and moving energy available to it. But again, when you do not access the energy of your mind and body, the soul becomes trapped. You are on this earth for a reason, in these bodies for a reason. The soul cannot act alone on this level without the mind and the body. Therefore, to access the most profound energy you must access the energy of the mind and the body. Each of you can do this easily.

"Even the elderly can practice this. Sit quietly, breathe deeply, and think of a place of calmness and quiet. Bring that breath into your being, bring it down, and then allow it to cleanse your cells, reinvigorate your cells, and move away those that are stagnant and unproductive, allowing new, energized cells to grow. There is beauty in God's map of the body and the mind and the soul. Within you, though you do not realize it, is the capacity to perform great acts, acts you would consider miracles, all because you have accessed this energy and thus, eventually, the energy of the soul.

"You can also access this when you walk. Walk, breathe, and understand the necessity of moving the stagnant emotions and bringing in thoughts of creativity. Your breath does all this for you, but in your fears and your darkness you have made your breathing shallower, and this shallow breathing results in more fear and anxiety.

"Breathe deeply. Breathe in the air of the world, and then breathe in the spirit of the Holy Spirit.

"You do not realize, nor do you access, the energy that God has given you, that He has made available to you. When you realize this, your accomplishments will be magnificent.

"Amen."

Later that day the Archangel spoke to me again.

"Energy comes from purpose, from hope, from having a goal. All of you came to the earth with a goal. But many have buried that goal, and buried energy and hope along with it. Therefore it is essential to release your energy, and prayer is the vehicle to do this. Listen to God's plans for your life, listen to your soul's destination, and remember it. Those words are the key: Remember it. Then the energy that you have buried because of pathos, laziness, darkness, and in some cases turning toward evil, will be refreshed and renewed through prayer.

"And through prayer you will begin to remember your purpose. Energy will move through your body and refresh your cells and your mind. This energy will release the soul and you will remember your plans and your purpose. With this remembrance hope will return because you will know your final destination is one of unending love and compassion. It is to abide with the Creator for eternity.

"Breathe in the Holy Spirit, remembering that the energy God gave you is there for your taking."

"When I was sick," I argued, "I was really really sick. The doctors didn't know what was wrong with my liver. I was scared and my body had no energy. None. I couldn't even leave my bed. I could have breathed all I wanted to, and done all the visualization you wanted me to do, and it wouldn't have helped at all because my body had no energy—I had a real problem physically. So what about that?"

"When your body is physically without energy due to an illness or accident, your mind and spirit can still access energy for themselves, and that hope and knowledge of your destination of which I spoke are still possible."

"I couldn't do it. I couldn't even pray. I asked others to pray for me because I was so sick."

"That was a step in your development, but if you practice what we are teaching you now, you will be able to do it later, when it is truly necessary for your well-being."

Thirty-Two

We meet on a hillside overlooking a large bustling metropolis. Many months ago, in *Circle of the Soul*, we were often at this site, but not since this third book began. It was early evening, when dusk was just beginning to settle over the city, and lights from the buildings and streets were appearing.

"Hello," I said to the Archangel, unsure of why we were here or what today's lesson would be.

"We have told you before that you are a community, and still many do not believe it. You do not understand that each of you resides within each other, that a part of you is always with your brothers and sisters, and that therefore when you hurt or maim or get angry with another, you are also doing that to yourself."

"You mean it ricochets?"

"It ricochets back to you, but you are also a part of everyone. As Christ resides within each of you, as God and the Holy Spirit reside within each of you, a small part of you and your brethren resides within each other. That is why it is so important to realize that deeds done to another will come back to you, because you are in effect doing it to yourselves."

"I don't get it," I stated. "Are we talking karma?"

He paused. "Not really. What we're talking about is more profound and deep. Karma means that if you do not learn your lesson now, you will need to repeat it and repeat it until it is learned."

"You've said something like that."

"Yes. You are here to learn the way back to God. When God first created you He gave you free will, which you used to turn away from Him. You made that decision as a whole, and that is where part of you and part of others all reside within each other. Now you must learn to use that same free will to return home to God. In the darkness that you chose you ached for the love of God, for the light of the Creator, for the love of Christ and the Holy Spirit. Because you realized this, as a whole, you used your free will to decide to repent and return to God."

"That sounds easy enough."

He smiled. "But it was your souls that needed to guide you in doing so. Just as your personality guides you on earth and you make decisions without consulting your soul, so you did that then. The soul is the map-keeper of your destinies. And now, just as then, your personalities, your egos can turn you away from the destiny of the soul. But the soul is the life-force of the body. It is the navigator of this map. When you consult with the soul, using your free will as God gave it to you, your soul encourages you to make the decision that leads you home to God.

"But when you do not understand your neighbor, nor pray for him, you are clouding your own destination, because God aches for all of you. And because you are a partaker in this divinity, you will ache for those not following the path."

"I don't even know if I'm following my soul's path," I said. "Sometimes I think what you're saying is very odd. My soul picked my destination, my parents, my career? I don't know. Maybe I would have joined a computer company in Silicon Valley fifteen years ago, been a salesman right out of college and retired a multimillionaire with stock. Looking back, I don't think that would have been a bad career choice."

"But that is not the choice you made on the other level." He shook his head. "Let's assume you did that. Then you would not have chosen all the pathways that brought you here, to these messages, to the messages that are being spread around the world."

"Oh, let's not get carried away," I said. "I self-published *Songs* and I did well for selling them out of my basement, but it's hardly a runaway bestseller like, say, the diet books of some actresses."

"The messages we impart to you from God change people's lives. They have circled much farther than you know, and they will continue to do so. Lives will be changed on their soul level. People will allow their souls to listen to the call of God, and all of this is because your soul guided you in this pathway. Sometimes you have stopped and gone in different directions, and the soul has had to gently, and sometimes not so gently, bring you back to the original road you chose.

"This message is not just for you. It is for everyone. You chose your life for a reason, to learn what you so desperately needed to in order to understand and return home to unconditional love. Until you understand compassion and unconditional love, by experiencing them yourself, you cannot really be one with God in paradise. You still need to learn. Once you embrace these emotions, bringing them into your personality and your being, your souls will reunite with God and each other in paradise. You are a partaker in the Divine Energy, and God is always there, waiting for you to come home. Even though you as indi-viduals are still tempted by evil and by darkness, your prayers for each other and for all of you to reunite and return home to God will bring this to fruition.

"When you see the enemy, or those you perceive as the enemy, realize they are only other souls longing to return home to God. If they are not walking toward the light you must pray for them, because you are a part of them, as they are of you."

"I don't think I really understand that part. I understand that we're all alike, but I don't understand the other part. We're all individuals, right?"

"Yes, you are all individuals, with your own personalities, likes and dislikes. But you are a family connected by the same elements. Just as a family has many of the same genes running through it, a part of your soul runs through everyone else. You are a family."

"Maybe I'll understand it better later on."

"Yes, reread this tomorrow and ask me questions later. You may not understand this initially, but eventually you and the world will, and that will be a huge stride in realizing that the pathway to God is unity and love.

"Amen."

"Amen," I echoed softly, barely hearing it myself. The Archangel rose into the sky and floated over the city. I could see his majestic blue robes flowing in the wind. He blessed the city with the sign of the cross, and I followed, making the same sign.

Then he disappeared, and I brushed a tear from my cheek.

Thirty-Three

In prayer, again the gem I take is yellow, a very light yellow, almost clear. To me the color symbolizes hope, and the clarity and magnification of the stone remind me that with God's help all things are clearly seen, and His aid magnifies everything.

I ask the Holy Spirit to protect me and give me wisdom today. Sometimes each day seems like such a struggle. Small things—lost dry cleaning, car trouble, errands and chores that must be accomplished—get in the way of prayer.

The Archangel meets me on a different beach, a small section of sand that overlooks a bay. To our left and right are beautiful dunes and marshes. I inhale the still-humid September air that somehow hints of fall. The setting is beautiful.

"This is new," I said.

"Yes, God's beauty is everywhere, tucked near marshes, overlooking the creations of His ocean—I stress, it is everywhere."

"Right," I said.

"Everywhere," he repeated.

I looked at him, cocking my head to one side. Obviously I was missing something because his tone of voice was emphatic.

"Yes?" I said.

"His beauty is everywhere. You need not come here, to nature, although it is often soothing to your souls. And the fresh air is good for your bodies, and thus your spirits. But His beauty lies in every creation He has made. When you went to lecture at the maximum security prison for women, how did you feel?"

"I felt the presence of God in that room more than at any other lecture I had ever given."

"The beauty of God is everywhere. That is today's message, one that many of you do not understand. Nor do you want to listen to it. When you go into a hospital, a nursing home or an inner-city school, God's beauty is there. Each of these people has a Living God within them, nourishing them. They have an immortal soul guiding them, helping them to follow the map of their destination."

"But there's evil. You've said so."

"Yes, there is evil in the midst of beauty, but God's love and light will overcome darkness. Each of you must remember the beauty in each other, or else darkness will encompass you and blind you. You will go into the convalescent home and see only sickness, despair and death. But that is not what resides there."

"Of course it does," I said. "I've lectured there. Some people are so sick they are in wheelchairs that are flattened out because their bodies can't bend. It's terribly sad."

"But you have not looked into their souls. I said that you will see only sickness, despair and death. I did not say they don't exist. What I said was, 'That is not what resides there.'"

"Oh," I said humbly. I was always jumping to conclusions.

"What resides there are souls, souls who have all the knowledge but need others to help their personality guide them to their pathways. Each of you guides and helps the others to their souls' destination, which is always a destination of love and compassion and returning to God.

"When you see only the earthly—the sickness, the death, the aging and despair—you have been lured by evil and then you are not open to see the beauty of the souls."

"I try to do that," I said.

"We know, and you are progressing. But these messages are not only for you; they are for everyone who reads and listens to this. People see pictures of fights and terrorism and are caught up in only the evil. That evil then makes people afraid, and their fear takes them away from God. Whenever you see a situation that appears difficult, remember that within each person is God's guidance. Each person, even those who have not been following their souls' pathway, is a partaker in the Divine Energy. And if someone has not been following God's pathway, and the soul is still keeping the body alive, it is for each of you to redirect that person so that the soul can fulfill its destiny here on earth.

"You are your brother's keeper. You are the one who can guide and help him, as he can help you. You are all one. But you must not be caught up in the earthly picture, because that picture, as you know by now, is not really what you see—it is what you do not see. Your life here is a spiritual one, in a physical body. Because of that, the reality of your life can only be spiritual. If at the end of your life you have not fulfilled your spiritual destiny, yet have accomplished many earthly feats, it is of no avail. You are here solely to help yourselves, and others, return to

God. By doing this on earth, you find happiness and heaven on earth. It is possible."

I sat down on the soft sand. It was damp and I felt my body sinking a little into it and making an indentation. "It's always so beautiful when you say it, and I always agree with it. But then I'm distracted by worries and concerns, about health or material things or whatever. I get caught up in them. These bodies God gave us can also give us a lot of trouble in maintaining them."

"Remember," he said, "they were given to you for a divine purpose. The purpose is to find God here on this earth, to find God within you and around you, to realize that you are loved unconditionally. The bodies teach you many lessons, and all of these lessons—if you learn them— bring you to God. Lessons unlearned will be given to you again and again until you realize your soul's purpose for this adventure.

"Go, pray, and share this with the community.

"And love yourselves and each other. Amen."

Thirty-Four

It's been a while since I've been able to sit quietly and pray. Work, charity stuff, and day-to-day living have made these last couple of weeks hectic—and then I feel so guilty. I pray in the car and at other odd moments, but I have not been just sitting and contemplating God.

The gem I take from the bowl next to my computer is sky-blue. It's large and round and has a slight metallic color to it. In some ways it reminds me of the sky outside this morning. A cool strong wind, left over from a hurricane that downgraded to a tropical storm, came through last night, but today is breezy and gorgeous. Except for the broken branches on the ground, no one would ever know that something so horrendous pounded us for almost twenty-four hours.

The Archangel appears and I sit next to him. We're on the mountaintop again, with a small pool of water nearby, and for the first time I realize that this pool streams downward to the bottom of the mountain.

"I'm so sorry I haven't prayed for a while. Things have been hectic, and I've been trying to go around talking about *Songs of the Soul*, but it's been somewhat discouraging this week. A radio station, instead of interviewing me on the phone, insisted I drive a two-hour round trip for an eight-minute interview. A library began a program and told me that twenty to fifty people would be there, but just a handful came. Between driving there and driving back, and the time there, I lost a day."

"We know," he said.

"Well, I'm getting a little impatient," I said. I was in no mood for a simple response. I was tired, my throat was scratchy and I felt overloaded. "If these messages need to get out, can't you help me?"

"We help you every day. We keep you from getting discouraged by surrounding you with a community that believes in this. The community is important. You do not realize that you touched people this week with the messages. You will never realize the true impact of the messages until you have gone on to another level. If they touch one person that day, those messages and the actions they inspire spread and move on to more. It becomes monumental."

"It would be nice to see," I said. Even to me my voice sounded curt.

"You will never see the entire picture here on this earth, but you will see the movement of the messages to a larger group."

I didn't even feel like pressing it any more.

"What you need to tell people, again and again, is not to get discouraged, to take the gifts of hope and perseverance and use them in their spiritual journeys. Did you see the gem you took today and did you fully understand that it was a gift from God?"

I looked down and didn't answer.

"You understood the meaning without even realizing it."

"I did?" I asked, bewildered.

"In the darkness of the storm, when the trees are falling and the floods are rushing and the rains are pelting at your roof, and danger is imminent, you feel fear and apprehension."

"Sure," I said.

"And today?"

"Today is beautiful."

"Yes. That is the lesson. The times of darkness are short, and always, if you persevere and hope, the times of beauty, of clear and blue sky, will return. But those of you who do not wake from the darkness do not understand this. You shutter your houses in a storm, and you shutter your souls in the dark times of your lives. Until you open those shutters, you do not even realize that the light of day has returned."

"Just one more time, tell me about why we need this darkness."

He smiled. I know I had asked him a zillion times, but still, on some days I understood and on others I just felt it was so unfair.

"We were with you at the bookstore Wednesday night. You already know the answer to that."

"You were there?" I asked.

"We are always with you."

I had begun coordinating an inspirational book club at a major book chain near my house. A famous television talk show host had started a book club three years before, but though she often spoke of spiritual books, most of her choices were fiction. I thought it was important to have people come together to talk about spiritual books.

For the month of September we had read a book by the Dalai Lama called *The Art of Happiness*. In it he says that suffering is a normal part of life. In his belief system suffering comes from past lives, from karma, but still it is normal. According to him, as I understand it, if you think suffering is abnormal, then you will never find happiness.

"Is that what you're talking about?" I asked.

"Yes," he said. "Suffering is a part of life. But it is how you view suffering that is the real tool for your soul's journey. Each of you views suffering as negative and bad. Yet suffering can be a journey to growth of your soul. Remember the passage you read to the group?"

"Yes," I laughed. I don't usually read from the book at the club meeting; we just discuss it. But I read that paragraph because it hit me so strongly. It says that in his book *The Third Man* Graham Greene observes that in Italy thirty years of Borgia rule produced horrible terror and bloodshed, and also Michelangelo, Leonardo da Vinci, and the Renaissance, while Switzerland's five hundred years of brotherly love and peace gave the world the cuckoo clock.

"What do you understand from that?"

"Well, there's a dichotomy here, isn't there? With suffering comes growth, but look at the Swiss. They didn't suffer, nor did they grow a lot, but they did practice brotherly love and had peace. Isn't that what you want us to do?"

He laughed heartily. "Oh, the more we know you the more we truly love you."

I swallowed hard. I knew he said he was always with me, but I didn't remember his ever saying he loved me.

Well, I wasn't going to let that get me off the track. I still wanted the answer.

"Yes, of course we want people to be peaceful and love their neighbor. That was Christ's message, the message that God wants us to pass on to each of you. But what you also don't understand is the difference between peace and apathy and boredom. Apathy is not brotherly love. When you see your fellow man in trouble you must help. With stagnation you may have a kind of peace, but you do not take the opportunities that God gives you daily to move closer to Him, and to use your creativity to better the world, to beautify the world. Peace doesn't necessarily mean that there is brotherly love. You must realize that. Peace may just mean that there is complacency and stagnation.

"People in Switzerland during that time still had suffering in their lives, but many of them were stagnant because they did not move on. They did not take chances to help others who may not have been in safe situations. I have told you before, not all fear is negative. The fear that runs through your body when you see a barking dog approaching allows you to move, to get out of the way and run to safety. If you carry that feeling of fear with you after the dog is gone, then it becomes toxic. But when people are in the storms of their souls, they have the opportunity to move closer to God. When people are stagnant because of comfort and safety, just as a pond gets murky and does not flow clearly, so do your souls become stuck. And that is the worst destiny for your soul, because your soul wants to move.

"Therefore the key to moving closer to God is to constantly move. And when you do not move, whether from complacency or fear, your soul does not grow."

"You know how you said 'your soul wants to move'?"

"Yes."

"Well, my friend, a minister, said that my soul is moving faster than my personality."

He smiled again. "And do you disagree?"

"No." This time I smiled. "I see exactly what he's saying. With all these messages and lectures and so on, I know that what you have told me is true and profound. But still I'm scared about sharing them sometimes. What if I've transcribed them wrong? I'm scared about the final outcome."

"Your soul is not," he said with empathy. He turned, rose, and walked over to the pool of water. I noticed he was barefoot, and although he walked on pinecones and other brush he never stumbled or stopped. I was sure he did not feel any discomfort.

I jumped up and followed him.

"See this pool of water? "

"Yes."

"Think of it as God, the Source, and from this Pool all knowledge, love and kindness emanate, moving downward through the skies as this water moves downward on the mountain. All who wish can stop, admire the rushing streams, and quench their thirst from the cool clean water. God's love is always near you, wanting to nourish you, wanting to nurture you. But many walk past the stream. They think they are not thirsty, or they say they've seen streams before, or they bring their own bottled water in case the stream is contaminated. Always excuses."

"You mean we just walk past the beauty of God?"

"Many do, yes, because they either do not see it or they think what they have discovered on this earth is ample and sufficient. They never realize the strength and power of the lake above them.

"If you partake in the Divinity of God, drink from His water, you will be filled with His love. And the suffering you face will bring you closer to Him, bring your soul closer to the destination it wants and wrote before your birth. The suffering will be only a thirst, a dry parched time of your life—but a necessary one, for you to need to drink the cool water of the stream."

I almost asked a question, but then knew the answer. If life were easy, and we were never thirsty, we'd never drink from the stream.

He turned back to me and smiled, obviously reading my thoughts.

"Yes," he said, "you now understand that. So the suffering, the thirst, is necessary and it is the way you must approach it, because the darkness of the storm will bring you the clear, brilliant blue sky. The thirst from climbing the mountain will bring you the quenching water of the Source.

"Amen."

"Amen," I said softly. He rose into the sky, and as I walked closer to the shore, I realized that the small pond was in fact not small at all. Much of it had been hidden by a line of trees. It was a magnificent, large, still-glistening lake. A heron swooped down, perched at the edge and drank.

"Watch and observe," I heard the Archangel say. "Watch and observe the innocent because they know from whence God comes."

I sat down on the edge of the grass, watching the heron finish his drink. Then, with barely a movement, he glided upward. His majestic wingspan scarcely moved as he opened yards and yards of distance between us. He too disappeared into the sky, the same color sky as my gem.

"Amen," I whispered, feeling as if I had just *seen* a prayer.

Thirty-Five

I haven't sat down and prayed in a while, and I'm ashamed about it. I've prayed during the day the way many of us pray, in the car or in the shower, but I haven't just sat down and tried to listen to God's message for me, nor to hear the angel. I quiet my mind, pick a gem, and laugh. I've picked this gem before, a clear one with a large block of blue within it. The blue always makes me think of calmness, and how I need it so much. The clarity of the clear stone doesn't work when I have anxiety. And today I feel that piece of blue represents the anxiety that blocks me, not the calmness that I need.

"Good morning," the Archangel says to me. I look up and we're in a new place. It's still a rock, or a cliff, but it's very low and we're looking out over fields, acres and acres of ranchland. It's country I've never seen before, and it's beautiful. I inhale and smell fresh air, warm and clear, not the crisp clear air I'm used to in New England. I inhale again.

"I have a friend who wants me to ask you personal questions."

"She already knows the answers."

"No, she doesn't," I say, "because she asked me to ask you to pray for them."

"We pray for everyone. Each has an assigned angel, and other angels around them for a variety of reasons."

"But this woman is a good woman, always doing charity work, always helping others, and she needs help right now. I don't know exactly what the request is, but she asked me to help her through you."

He looked at me, his blond hair shining in the sunlight; today it took on the hue of the hay I could see in the distance. His robes were a shade of deep plum, almost black. His clothes have an iridescent shine that is beyond description.

"We are here to deliver messages for all mankind. She can pray to God and receive the message she needs in her own heart. But these visitations are for everyone. We are not here for the individual on these visits; we are here for the whole."

"Can't you help a little?"

"Tell her that her soul is following the path that is allowing her to return to God, and that any other circumstance right now is not the circumstance for furthering the development of her soul. And that is also a message for many of you. Your soul is always working to follow the agenda it picked before your birth. This friend picked her destination, her soul's goal and work, before she was born, and her soul is allowing her to follow it. Often there are difficult times in life because your soul's destination and your human personality conflict and you want only what your personality deems right for you. But tell her that everything is for a purpose, and that in order for her to change her destination yet keep with her soul's progression, she must pray for the guidance to combine the two. Up until this point she could not have combined them without losing sight of her soul's destination. And that is the most important part of it. But if she wants to pursue her personal quest, she must ask her soul for permission, and thus she is asking the divine. When she does so, she may be able to combine the two. But tell her that her soul's destination is the most important and she has chosen this, for this exact time in her life, for now."

"Will her soul choose something else down the road?"

"It may, but only if it will work with the soul's destination. Remember that it was she who chose this pathway before her birth because she knew and understood it was the pathway to God."

"I don't know if that makes sense."

"It will to her," he said somberly. "And I am answering this particular question because it will help others too."

"You mean that if you are sick and struggling, and your personality obviously doesn't want that, your soul may have chosen it because it moves you toward God?"

"Yes, and you cannot see it, because you block out your soul's work and concentrate on your personality's work. But your personality's work has little to do with this. If you listen only to your humanity, you will lose sight of your soul. You will block your soul, and thus block what you have chosen. Your friend has not blocked her soul, but if she prays to God and allows herself to combine her humanity's choices—as long as they will work along with the soul—with her soul's choices, she may be able to have both. But often people's personality choices do not mesh with their soul's choices. Sometimes your soul's choices seem the hardest and most difficult, but they are not. And they are your choices."

"I'll tell her. But if it doesn't make sense, then what?"

"She must pray that she understands that she chose this, when she understood better what she needed to advance toward God. And she is on that pathway."

"I told my friend Henry, a minister, that these messages seem overwhelming to me and that sometimes I worry about them. What if they're wrong?"

For the first time in a long time the Archangel laughed. "You constantly amaze us. You see people's lives change toward God, make great progress forward, and still you question the messages."

I looked away from him. I felt so ungrateful.

"This is a big responsibility," I said softly. "It is soul work, telling people things that could change their soul's destination."

"I am here to tell you these things, and to reassure you. You pray each day before my visits, and you ask God to protect you. These visits are only for the good of mankind. As the Bible has stated, 'Test the winds of the Spirit.' You have done so with each book, and you have found people praying, returning to God, meditating and praying for their enemies. That is a testimonial to their Source, the God Source. It is no longer in your hands. Do not worry about it. It is God's will, we are His messengers, and you are to continue to write these down until we are told to stop visiting."

"Will that happen?"

"I do not know."

Oh, I thought. Gee, usually they knew a lot.

"God's will is my will.

"That should also be a mantra for all of you. If you say it daily, you will find peace and contentment in it, and you will find peace within yourself. 'God's will is my will.' By stating it, it will become so.

"Realize that what you state, what you think, becomes who you are. If you think fear, you become fear. If you think love, you become love. And from these thoughts, actions result. Therefore continue to act as if you believe it."

"But you know I struggle so much with worry and anxiety."

"We know. But each day just say, 'God's will is my will. Care for me, lead me, and allow the peace which resides within God to reside within me.' It does now, but you are not accessing it."

"You make it sound so easy, but it could be chemical."

"It obviously results in chemical changes in your body. You feel the anxiety in your chest. But what we are saying, contrary to some physicians, is that you can alter those chemicals by your mind alone. Do you understand this?"

"I don't know. Because then if I don't, it means I'm not doing something right, and I'll feel worse."

"You always are so impatient. Did I say you would change them overnight? No. It will take practice. It may take years. It has taken you years to become anxious—patterns develop and they become the norm for you. New patterns will not be made overnight.

"But it is possible. Each day, remember, 'God's will be my will. Protect and lead me, and allow my soul to fulfill its work today.' Then, because you relinquish your control to God, chemicals do change in your body; the chemicals that result in anxiety no longer pop into the forefront. This change brings amazing and everlasting peace."

"Thank you," I said. "I must go. Yesterday was my birthday and my family's coming down today."

"Yes, we celebrated your birthday yesterday."

"You did?"

"Of course. We celebrate the birthday of each soul who comes to earth and chooses to move closer to the Lord, our God. The day of birth is a beautiful day. We pray especially fervently for them that day, that they will continue to listen to their souls, and if they are not listening to their souls, that they will.

"Tell the others that. You are not alone on your birthday. We are surrounding you and celebrating your existence."

I thanked him, and he disappeared into the cloudless sky. I inhaled the smells of the ranch and was transported home.

Thirty-Six

I pick a gem, and it speaks to me.

The angel appears on the mountaintop again, and the clear air is crisp like a fall day in New Hampshire. The mountains glisten, and again, although we are high in altitude, I have no trouble breathing.

"You have questions?" he asked, without bothering to say hello. Today he was dressed in white. I looked at his glistening robes and marveled. Threads of gold and silver ran through them at the bottom hem and the hems of the sleeves. Today for the first time, at least that I noticed, he had a golden cloth rope wrapped loosely around his waist.

He smiled at me.

"Yes, I have questions. Can we get back to the soul's choice, this question of the soul's destination?"

"Yes."

"What is it? Doesn't free will get in the way?"

"Do you think that you have free will only on this earth?"

I didn't answer.

"You have been created with free will. Before your birth on earth you had free will, and using this free will and your soul's knowledge, you picked your pathways."

"But it seems so wrong. We all have so many troubles. Many people have childhoods of hell, with alcoholic parents, abuse, sickness. And you're saying to me that these people chose this hell? I don't believe it."

He looked upward toward the heavens, as if he were praying or, I thought, perhaps calling to more angels to come and help with this difficult human.

"Here is how it works. As Christ chose his parents, you chose yours, and you all decided this prior to your coming onto this earth. Most of you knew the obstacles that would appear in your lives, but you understood those obstacles were opportunities to learn and grow toward God, the only way you could learn and grow toward God.

"But once you have arrived on earth and then do not listen to your soul's destination, but only to your humanity, often the soul is taken from its path. Constantly, and I stress that word, *constantly* the soul is moving in the direction that you chose before birth. But oftentimes,

144

because others listen to their personalities and not their souls, they infringe on your pathways."

"Huh?"

"Let us say that before your birth you and another soul decided that you needed to learn compassion. So that friend through some method would teach you the need for compassion. But when the friend was blinded by her humanity, and used her free will not to follow her soul's path but for immediate earthly gratification, she is no longer available for your soul's pathway."

"So then what?"

"Your soul, always aware of this, must reroute. Before it comes to earth the soul knows many different pathways to return to God. Because the soul is a partaker in the divinity of God, it knows how to use free will to change while staying on the path you chose before your birth."

"What about the woman who didn't keep her end of the bargain? What happens to her soul?"

"Her soul continues to strive for her pathway toward God. If the personality moves in, and blocks out the soul to such an extent that it can no longer move toward God, the soul leaves the body, and thus the body dies."

"So you die when you've either accomplished your soul's work, or you're so far off the path that the soul can't get back on track?"

"Yes," he said. "And this is all with your knowledge and permission. But I also want to stress to you that you are all one. When you decide to come here to help another, and then do not, it is of the darkness. It is a waste of your lifetime."

I caught my breath. It sounded so harsh, and he never sounded harsh or judgmental.

"Isn't that kind of hard on us?"

He looked toward me, his eyes a deeper blue than the sky. "No. It is a fact. You have chosen the pathway your soul needs, and the lessons your soul craves, for your advancement to the Light. When you do not follow your path, and especially when your earthly free will neglects the soul's work with another soul, you have lost an opportunity to return to God, and to help your neighbor return to God.

"None of you realize the shortness of this life or the huge importance of it. You have waited for eons for this opportunity and some, upon seeing the materialism of the earth, forget their purposes, just as all of you did in the beginning of time. Thus it is so important for each soul to help the others realize their divinity, because the story of the Garden of Eden happens daily on the earth. You must help your neighbor souls not to turn toward the darkness, but to turn toward the light."

I rubbed my eyes. I was tired and, truthfully, somewhat lost in his profound talk this morning.

"Can we talk of other things?"

"Yes," he said.

"I need practical application for the things you are speaking about. I need practical methods to get rid of stress and worry. It's great to say it, but I need to do it."

"We have told you many times to pray, to meditate, and often you do not."

I looked down, ashamed. He was right. By the time I sat down to meditate my mind was cluttered with thoughts and worries. I wish I had the discipline of people who followed Buddhism. I wondered what their nervous systems were like. In every picture of the Dalai Lama, he looks happy and content.

"For the physical, you must breathe. Breathe like the child you were upon your birth. When you were born you were still carrying your knowledge from before. Watch a sleeping infant breathe. His chest does not move up and down, but his stomach does. This allows oxygen to get into your systems and circulate, refreshing you and revitalizing you. Studies will be done showing that the lack of this circulation brings on harmful chemicals and adverse effects. God gave you all you need, but you have forgotten this.

"Breathe with a word, or a thought, and consciously move your stomach up and down, to bring in the air your body needs. If you take small shallow breaths, your body and your mind will begin to become nervous, shallow and small. If you take in large breaths, deeply within you, you will begin to feel the life that pulsates through you."

"Thank you," I said, trying it.

"Continue to do this," he said, "because doing it just occasionally is not enough. It is similar to food for your body. God made these bodies with the capacity to heal, but you often do not allow them to. You do not eat correctly, sleep long enough, or breathe correctly. All of these things would help build a healthy body and a healthy mind.

"Work on the breath today. Each time you are anxious or nervous, look down and make sure your stomach is moving in and out like a small child's. Be like the children, Christ said, not only in kindness and innocence but even in their physical activity. Breathe as you were told to breathe before birth, move your limbs as you were told to move before birth, and thank God for all of it each day."

I was so horrible—I thought of people in wheelchairs who couldn't move their limbs.

"They still are breathing, and people should always help them move their legs and arms and bodies to circulate the oxygen and keep the muscles strong, because with this ability to breathe you will move anxiety away."

"I'll try it," I said hesitantly.

He smiled again. I was always amazed that he didn't just leave me, complaining, You are always arguing with me—just do it.

He knew what I was thinking. "No, that is not my place. My role is to allow you to see your pathway, so that you in turn can allow others to see theirs. It is a monumental and joyous role."

He left before I could question the word "monumental." Was he referring to me, or to all the others?

I breathed deeply, consciously watching my stomach move up and down, trying not to be worried about the word "monumental."

I called into the empty sky. "I'm sorry I'm so difficult. It's just that . . ."

His voice called back from the clouds. "It is how it was planned. It is why the messages will have importance to the world. Eventually you will accept this gift as part of your life and you will not question as much, because you will see the fruit from the seeds. But for now, it is as it has been planned."

Oh, I thought, that sounded somewhat better. Then I breathed again, very very deeply.

Thirty-Seven

I wonder why I don't sit down and meditate every day. I know that most people would be delighted to receive life-altering messages daily. I feel guilty for not doing it.

"You are who you are," the Archangel said. I looked up and found myself, once again, on the top of the mountain with the large lake next to us. I was dressed in a warm sweater and the weather was cool and pleasant—early September in New England. But we were high up, where it should have been much colder.

"I am who I'm supposed to be?" I asked, not believing that. Didn't we all grow and aspire to be better, changed people?

He shook his head in answer to my unspoken question. "You grow and aspire to move closer to God, to be 'better' if that means more compassionate and loving. But the core of you, the soul of you that you were born with, is also unique. It is who you are. In the Bible God says, 'I am who I am.' So too each of you 'is who you are.'

"That does not mean that you don't improve on your path. But do not discount the uniqueness of your souls. You are all one, but yet, like a puzzle with a thousand pieces, none of the pieces are the same. Otherwise the puzzle would never become whole, never become one. Think of each of you as a piece in a puzzle. Each of you is different, unique, and each uniqueness is essential for the whole to become one."

"Oh," I said. "But how can you say that 'we are who we are'? There are people out there robbing, murdering, abusing children. You can't say they are who they are. That doesn't make any sense."

He sighed. "They were born as they are. They were born an integral piece of the puzzle of the whole. They may have chosen difficult lessons, difficult childhoods, difficult places to be, all in order to grow and be compassionate. Some of them chose such things before their birth, but did not follow through on their choices. But the soul *always* continues to circumvent the detours to follow its original pathway. Therefore, if you chose to learn lessons and you haven't and have turned toward darkness, the soul continues to move you in the direction where you learn compassion and wisdom."

"But what about the people who were molested? Did they choose that?"

He smiled at me. I knew he was thinking of my impudence, my difficult questions, my refusal to just nod blindly at his answers. "Some choose to confront evil in order to destroy it. But those choices are from the other level, and on this level they may not be able to destroy it. They may choose to succumb to it. Or, in many cases, it was not a choice. The people with whom they decided to travel chose the wrong path, and the child was in the way. But the soul will take care of the child, and move the child always to learn its lessons. That is why 'everything is possible through God.' Even those who have been victimized can turn that into goodness by following their souls' pathways.

"The soul always learns in the storm. It is the storm of the soul that continues your evolution. If all circumstances in your life were without turbulence, you will not learn your lessons. The soul seeks out the storms."

"Great," I said sarcastically.

He laughed, a rarity. "But," he added, "the soul also knows when you need to rest, when you need to reflect on the turbulent seas. In the midst of a hurricane no one can imagine a clear sea. But after the hurricane, the sea can be calm and peaceful. It is respite before another storm approaches. It is during these respites that the soul allows the personality to recover."

"Oh."

"Do you understand?"

I shook my head. "Not fully."

He didn't seem concerned. He looked away from me and kept his eyes on the large lake. Today he wore blue, royal blue with a tinge of purple.

"It is such with suffering," he began again. "Suffering to those who are in the midst of it is hellish and dark. But suffering can teach you much. It can teach you compassion, love, understanding of others going through it. Then you can understand the sacrifice Christ made for his brothers and sisters. If you pray profoundly, you can take your neighbors' suffering upon yourselves instead. Suffering can be a blessing, if you accept it for yourself."

"A blessing?"

"Yes. Christ suffered, but he suffered in place of his brothers and sisters. Such can it be for you. When you are suffering, remember that it may have been a choice you made on purpose to allow another soul not to suffer, and that somehow this suffering helps another to learn earthly and celestial lessons."

"Can I go now?" I asked. "I'm so tired. I think that's why I don't sit here all the time. It's such heavy stuff and lots of it I don't even understand."

"You all understand it. You all understand it in your souls. You need to get in touch with your soul and remember your pathway. Once you do, you will be joyous in all that you encounter."

He rose slowly, his wingspan huge, and then he just disappeared.

From the heavens I heard. "Pray. Pray for yourselves. Pray for your neighbors. Pray to God, the One who wants you home, the One who beckons you home. He is waiting, patiently, for all eternity. Amen."

Amen, I said, finding myself back at home sitting at my computer.

Thirty-Eight

I pick a stone today that is unusual, one I've never picked before, a metallic bright green. It reminds me of the woods, of health, of nature, and just seeing it makes me happy.

The Archangel returns, and we are in the woods sitting on the rock, overlooking a rambling brook.

I'm holding my stone in my hand, rubbing it and turning it over.

"Nature is God's gift to humanity," he says. "We have told you that before."

"Yes, I remember. I remember how you said that we often ruin it with pollution. I thought you were an environmentalist."

He tries not to smile, and I smile broadly at that, watching his expression out of the corner of my eye. He often seems so intent on his messages that rarely does he smile or laugh. But I know he appreciates my humor because he's told me so.

"Yes, that is essential, to take care of God's gift to you. But also nature can bring you back to God. It can help center you and allow the breath of the Spirit to enter you. The beauty of His creation will allow you to connect with other living things, and thus realize that God takes care of the smallest of the creatures and He will take care of you."

I looked down at my stone, so smooth, so bright—so inviting.

"You don't believe this?" the Archangel asked.

"I don't want to be difficult," I answered, knowing that I was, "but sometimes realizing that seems hard to me. Sometimes it seems that God takes care of the swallows, the deer, the crows, more than He does us. They know their jobs, do them, and survive. But there are people all over the world, especially in third world countries, but even here in the richest nation, who don't have food to eat or heat to warm them in the winter. It seems to me," I said, not meeting his eyes, "that maybe some of the chipmunks are taken care of more than we are."

I looked up.

"The chipmunks and the squirrels are God's gifts to you to provide a beautiful environment. They serve a purpose in helping the earth grow to its potential. Although many animals are predators they are all in the cycle of life, and this cycle allows nature to grow and prosper.

But each of you, as I have stated before, has chosen the lessons you are to learn. God has given you this freedom of choice, and you—and you alone—chose what you needed to learn in order to return to God and to allow the wisdom of the Holy Spirit to enter your minds and souls and bodies."

"But there are still people starving."

"Yes," he said sadly. "And do you not realize, although we have told you, that you are all one? That Christ said, whenever you feed my brother you are feeding me? Whenever you clothe my sister you are clothing me? When you take in a person you are taking in Christ? Do you think that he meant only Him?"

"What do you mean?"

"Say the words aloud."

I said, "Christ said: When you feed my brother, you are feeding me."

"Now just say Christ's statement," he ordered.

"When you feed my brother you are feeding me."

"Repeat it and say it aloud."

"When you feed my brother you are feeding me. When you clothe my brother you are clothing me."

"Yes," he stated simply.

"Yes, what?" I asked softly, but thought I understood.

"Christ was not only talking about himself. You all are extensions of God's love. You all are partakers in the Divinity of God. Therefore when you say 'God' has abandoned the poor, the sick, He has not. He has sent you to do His work. You are a part of Him.

"And each person who is needy, sick, poor and destitute, mentally ill, or hungry—each such person, you must realize, is you. You are all one. Therefore it is your duty and it is God's wish—which is your soul's wish—to care for the others. The others may be here to teach you that lesson, and you do not learn it because you say, 'God is not taking care of them. God takes care of the chipmunks, but not the people starving.' But I say to you today that God resides within each of you. You are connected to the Creator and the Spirit, and are part of that. So if some are hungry, you are to help. As Christ said, 'When you feed my neighbor, you feed me.' So you too must say the same thing, because when you help another, you are helping yourself. You are helping yourself grow, you are feeding yourself, and you are clothing yourself in the glorious robes of the Spirit. When you feed your neighbor, you feed both Christ and yourselves, because you are all children of God and connected to the Creator, the Great Spirit.

"So do not say, 'God does not care for certain people,' because you are a part of God. Take responsibility for this statement and act on it. Pray and action will result."

I breathed in deeply, still holding my stone. I had expected a conversation about trees, clear air, maybe meditating by the ocean—and I got a profound and powerful message, one that was meant to get me off my chair and stop blaming God.

"Not only you, but all of you must realize this.

"And all of you must realize that some souls have chosen to be without earthly possessions in order to help other souls. They are waiting to teach the others compassion, giving and being one."

I felt so humbled, so regretful. "I'm sorry," I said.

"It is all right," the Archangel said softly. "You are learning, as are the others. You are progressing at rates much higher than you think. As we often say, do not be hard on yourself. But realize that with wisdom comes action. Once you understand, you can no longer turn away. Once you realize that you are one, that you are your brother and he is you, and each act of compassion leads you closer to home and to God, you will be filled with the Spirit and understand more deeply the Word of God. Remember Christ's words: 'Forgive them, Lord, for they know not what they do.'

"Ignorance can keep you from God, keep you in the darkness. But now you and the others are learning, and this wisdom will change your lives and the lives of others. Amen." he said.

"Amen," I replied. He disappeared before my eyes. He did not fly into the sky, or move into the clouds, but just was gone.

"Thank you," I said softly, knowing that he would hear me. "Thank you."

"You are welcome," I heard in my mind. "It is a blessing and an honor to deliver the Creator's messages to each of you."

Thirty-Nine

I pick a yellow stone. It has a heart within it, or at least what I think looks like a heart.

The Archangel and I meet again beside the running stream, and I inhale the cool fresh air. In the distance the snowcapped mountains are majestic. Beauty surrounds me, but I feel lonely and sad.

"Each day that you can greet the Lord, you should be filled with joy. That is how He intended it to be."

I nod, and wipe away a tear.

"I don't know what's going on with me," I said softly. "I used to feel better about myself. I used to feel more confident. Ever since I've been sick I've been more anxious, more worried, about silly things and about important things. I second-guess myself and worry obsessively. I worry about the future, and as I do, I realize I lose the preciousness of the day."

"Yes," he said somberly. "Today is the only gift you have."

"I know," I said. "But that doesn't stop my brain from worrying. I worry about thirty years from now. Does that even make sense? I worry about security in the future."

He turned to me. I had never seen him wearing this particular robe before. It was such a dark brown that it appeared almost black. There was no shimmer of gold, but silver threads ran through the hem. His wings, clear yet silver, seemed to match the robe's hem.

"And what is it you need to ask me? You know I am here to deliver God's messages to the world, but I am also here to help you do that."

"Well," I said, "there's medication that may help with this worry. Can you advise me about that?"

He looked away. "Do you remember the passage in the Scriptures that says the sins of the father are passed on to the child?"

"Yes," I said vaguely. "I always thought that was awful. Why would innocent children be punished at birth for the sins of their ancestors?"

"No." He shook his head. "It is not as you interpret. It is the sins of the body, the alienation of the body from its true healthfulness. That is why humanity inherits certain genes. You have different genes than your neighbor. You inherit the looks of your family, the mannerisms of your family. You may not even know that some of your traits are traits of ancestors who died decades before you. It is because their traits become ingrained in their DNA, and thus, as they procreate, those genes are passed on to new generations."

"So what are you saying?"

"'The sins of the father' are oftentimes the worry, the alienation, the concerns, the disease of the body. They become ingrained in a person, and if they aren't stopped, move onward to their children."

"Therefore you're saying some of this worry and anxiety is inherited?"

"Oh, yes. The patterns are there. They are patterns an ancestor made decades or centuries ago. If an ancestor was greedy, at some point that 'sin' will be passed on to heirs. If an ancestor was kind, so too that trait is passed on. You are not 'punished' for the sins of the fathers, but they become a part of you. Realize that your ancestors were you and you are your ancestors. You are all one. Therefore, if an ancestor was selfish, you are capable of that too. You cannot blame your ancestor, because you have the same capabilities. But all of these alienations can be broken."

"By free will?"

"That is the key."

"It seems you're contradicting yourself."

"No. Just because the traits, the DNA for some of these alienations from God, are within your body, it does not mean that they cannot be changed and altered. If your ancestors created them, you can dismantle them."

"I don't think the doctors would agree with you."

"At some point in the future the doctors will not only agree, they will propose this."

"So where does this leave me with the medication?"

"You must stop the process. We cannot make those choices for you, because those choices are of free will. But we do say to you, that if you cannot stop them on your own, for whatever reasons, then God has supplied medicines to the world to help. That does not mean those medicines need be in your body for the rest of your life. Your free will can alter your body. Remember these words. The medicine only works if you allow it to, and during that process, you will return to the natural healthy state you need to be in to function well."

"So you're saying I have two choices. One, I can try on my own to change my predisposition to this, using free will."

"You do not realize the body's capacity to heal, to change, to move closer to its natural state of health, if you allow it. People often do not allow their body to work the way it should. They get in the way. The body is a finely-tuned machine, and with the right diet, exercise, and most important, the right choices, it can often heal itself."

"But in cases when it can't?"

"You need to use medicine to realign it. God created the world knowing that everything that each of you needs in on this planet. Much of it is not discovered yet, but much is. If you feel you need to realign yourself, do not get caught in the web of thinking it is permanent, because realigning yourself, ridding yourself of the pattern from your DNA, is possible through choices."

"No one would believe that. DNA is DNA. I don't know for sure, but that's what I'm guessing."

"Attributes from your ancestors can be brought to the forefront or left behind. That is evolution. That is choice."

"So let me get this right. Taking medicine to free me from worry may in effect help me to change my patterns, but I don't have to be on it for life?"

"Yes. Remember, when a pattern has been imprinted on your genes, and each of you reprint a different pattern to pass on to your heirs, it can be changed by your thoughts and by your body."

"But if someone has a horrible disease which is hereditary, and they're born with it, what you say doesn't make any sense."

"What I say is, the sins of the father have been passed on. But in the future the attitude you all have can change those patterns. The sins of the fathers need not be passed on. You can alter them at *any time* with free will, free choice. Many of you resign yourselves to no choice.

"You have chosen this lifetime for compassion. Without a body compassion is difficult to understand, and you begged and begged for this opportunity. When the opportunity arose, a bevy of us had to bring you to the earth's threshold, because you suddenly weren't so sure."

"That sounds like me."

"You realized that it would not be easy, yet your soul knew that compassion was the essential key."

"So how does this teach me compassion?"

"It teaches it very simply. You realize you are vulnerable, human, and capable of errors. You realize that you can fall into alienation from

God. Yours is not alienation by evil, but by worry and the need for security. There is no security on earth. There is only security with God. Please understand this and learn it."

I stopped and whispered the words. "'There is no security on earth. There is only security with God.' That sounds rather terrifying."

"No," he replied, "it is just the way the earth works, and it is essential for the lessons of life. You must understand all this before moving forward. Last visit we talked about God taking care of the animals. He takes care of you too, if you allow it. That is where many of you falter. You do not allow it. You control and control, repeating the choice that banished you from the Garden. You wanted control of your destinies.

"And now you have it, but often you continue to make the wrong choices. Your soul knows the right choice, and always moves you back to the Lord. But here on earth the soul exists in conjunction with the body and the mind. The struggle many of you have is in aligning all three.

"Because you turned from God with a body, now with a body you have an opportunity to *return* to God. The same choices confront you daily: control, security, ego and turning from God. To turn to God, give your lives—body, mind and soul—to God. Then you will understand your purpose and live it peacefully.

"You are still in the Garden, still fighting for control. But when you relinquish that, you will be given more freedom than you ever imagined.

"Go now. Pray and rest.

"We will be with you through all of this. Remember that during the storms of your soul you are growing and progressing and moving closer to God. Without the turbulent seas you would not understand the smoothness of life with God. Those seas allow you to delve deeply into who you are. They allow you to see life head on, to take all that is good within you and use it to survive the seas. That is why the storms of the soul are so important, because they allow you to find within you qualities, needs, strengths and love that you did not know you had. These storms put life in perspective.

"Appreciate this time. It is a storm for you, but you are growing because of it. You are delving deeper. You see your faults and you see your strengths. Without this storm you would see neither.

"When you see your own faults, you are less likely to see the faults of others. Pray for those around you, for your neighbors and for your enemies.

"God bless you and keep you," he said, disappearing into the clouds over the mountain peaks. The only motion I could see in the distance was from his wings, shining silver in the sky.

I felt so small, so tiny.

"And yet you are gigantic," the Voice said, "gigantic in the scheme of things, gigantic to God. Each of you is not small or insignificant but essential to God and to each other. Remember that and take joy in the day.

"Amen."

"Amen," I said.

Forty

I pick a black stone, and now I understand why picking that color frightens some people. I always tell them that if you combine all the colors of a palette, you will end up with the black. Today I tell myself the same thing.

The Archangel sits beside me on the rock, next to the crashing waves of the ocean.

"Do not be afraid of the darkness," he said, "and tell the others the darkness, like the light, is a gift from God. Without darkness you would not realize the importance of light, When a single candle is lit in the darkness, light beckons throughout the cavern, throughout the room, with a warmth that was there but unseen."

"I thought darkness was always what we avoid."

"You avoid the darkness of your soul, the lurking evil. But in avoiding it you learn to understand the wonders of your soul. So when darkness appears, it offers a lesson to be learned, a lesson to show you that you have the capacity to turn to the light. Learn that no one needs to be swept into the darkness. The choice lies with you, your soul and the divine connection. It is a learning opportunity. When the darkness engulfs you, and you do not use the powers of your soul to find the light, then you are sucked into evil, and that is fear. But facing darkness, facing evil, facing fear is essential for the growth of your soul."

"But what if you don't face it?"

"Then you begin to be sucked into the evil the fear encompasses, and you find comfort in the darkness. The darkness is not comforting, but it is not to be feared, because if you fear it you will become it."

"What does that mean?"

"Darkness is fear. When you align yourself with fear, you align yourself with ignorance and sorrow. But when you see the fear and face it, you align yourself with love.

"It is essential that you realize that your soul has a tremendous power, that your free will is tremendously powerful when you align it with the divine will. Everything can be accomplished. Heaven can be on earth. It is so simple. But the first step, as always, is your choice."

"Choice?"

"Yes. Oftentimes humans choose to stay in the darkness because they are afraid of what they may see when they light the candle. Many of you are stagnant in your lives because you are afraid of taking another step, afraid of rocking the boat. As Peter began to walk on water, fear engulfed him, and then he did not follow his soul's direction and he fell into the sea. But had he aligned himself with Christ, he would have walked on the water. A common ordinary man would have done the miraculous simply by agreeing to do it—and agreeing to allow God to create this miracle with him."

"Allow God to create a miracle *with* him?"

"Yes, with him. God can create miracles without you—that is understood. But on this earth, because of your gift of free will, He will not intervene unless you agree to create the miracle along with Him."

"Through prayer?"

"Yes, prayer and aligning yourself with your divine inner self, aligning yourself with your soul's destination. The power of prayer is accessing the power of God, but many of your have forgotten this. You have wandered away from the power that was yours at the beginning, the incredible power you had when aligned with God. Now, like an art or exercise no longer practiced, you can barely remember how to do it."

"How do we do it?"

"You pray to God, you listen to your soul, and when you face the darkness and your fear you realize the darkness is there for you not to run to, but to stand up to. Then, when your fear is gone, it cannot mesh with the fear of the darkness. You worry often about security. But security is in standing firm with God and your soul's plan for your life. That is the only security any of you need. When you follow your path, and create miracles with God, heaven will be on earth. All of this is possible."

I must have looked dumbfounded, because I felt dumbfounded. "Let's go over it again. Darkness is not to be feared?"

"Correct. It is to be faced."

"But if you don't face it?"

"You will follow your old patterns, because darkness is fear and your own fear will mesh with it. You will be stagnant and deaf to your soul."

"And darkness is an opportunity?"

"Yes, it is. "

"I don't know if everyone would agree with you on that one, that evil is an opportunity."

"Fear is an opportunity. How can you grow without the storm of your soul? And how can there be a storm for your growth if everything is stagnant and calm? It is not possible. When you turned from God, you broke your connection to Him. He is always there, but you, by free will, became enmeshed in the darkness.

"Now your struggle is seeing that, and turning from the fear, from the apprehension, and creating miracles daily."

"Creating miracles daily?"

"Yes. When you create with God, when you align yourself with God, miracles become everyday occurrences. You may not see them as miracles, but we assure you that they are. They are events that wouldn't have happened without your own permission and your own partnership with the Lord."

"Christ performed miracles daily, always accessing the power of his Father. He said, 'Do as I do.' If you do, miracles will happen.

"Remember these words and tell the others.

"Amen," he said.

"Amen," I echoed, watching the waves crash near my feet and feeling the ocean spray on my legs. He was gone, but I knew he would be back.

Forty-One

I haven't sat down and prayed in over two weeks. I'm ashamed. I kept "doing things."

The Archangel greets me on the rock by the sea. "We have asked you to pray every day, and you do pray every day. Do not be so hard on yourself."

"But I haven't prayed the way you've asked me to, sitting down quietly, meditating, listening to God's plan for me."

"No," he agreed, "but you have constantly communicated with God, and when people do that the Creator is pleased. The quiet sitting and listening to God is important because it gives you a sense of God within you. It allows you to understand the peace of God with each breath."

"It's difficult for many of us to do that—and for others it seems so easy."

The Archangel nodded. "Everyone has different paths to travel, different struggles, different choices they have made in order to return to God. Each must face them, and overcome what blocks them, and move closer to God."

"Can we talk about the concept of time again? I was reading what you said and I got so confused. You said time as we understand it does not exist. But you gave me patience as a gift from God."

"Because you are still at the learning point where time is essential. Also, patience was one of His first gifts to you so that you would begin to understand that when time is eternal and now, your need to hurry, to rush, serves no purpose. Once you understand that all time is now, all time is infinite, all past and present is one, you will no longer need the gift of patience, because you will see that impatience and patience have no meaning.

"But while you still do not truly understand the concept, you need to embrace patience, because it is a steppingstone to understanding that time is infinite."

I looked down at the sands. The glistening grains gave off rainbows of colors, prisms of pink and gold as the sun reflected off them. Quietly I said, "It's hard for me to understand." I was both ashamed and humbled.

He moved his hand and placed it under my chin, tilting it up so I was looking into his eyes. He rarely touched me. His fingers felt like a light breeze beneath my skin.

"This is the school you have chosen. Do not be ashamed for not understanding the lessons that are not of this school. I am only telling you this in order to help you understand God's infinite patience with you, and your infinite ability to return to Him. What the Creator wants you to understand is that all mistakes can be rectified, and all guilt can be abandoned, when you continue to move forward to God. And there is no time limit on this."

"No time limit?"

"No, no time limit. God in His absolute love and understanding does not watch the clock and give you only one chance. Time is forever, and you are His child forever, and He wants you home. Although you may think this is beyond your understanding, you have understood this at another level, and you—personally—constantly fight this."

"I personally?"

"Yes, you have been 'impatient' since the beginning of time—even when you realized there was no time. So this lesson on earth for you, and for many others like you, just allows you to grasp this more fully. This earthly lesson allows you to see things in slow detail, allowing you to understand the infiniteness of time, because each minute means something to you here."

"But doesn't that defeat the lesson? If time is important here, then doesn't that make time important?"

"Do you think that all your earthly lessons are learned here?"

"Sure."

"Well, upon your death, your soul looks back and what you have not fully comprehended on earth, but have completed, suddenly is learned."

I must have looked puzzled.

He sighed. "When you buy ingredients for a cake, none of it looks like a cake. When you stir together the milk, the cream, the sugar, and so on, it becomes one mixture, but still not a cake. Yet with the heat of the oven, a cake appears. At your death, if you have used all your ingredients, mixing them according to the pathway that your soul has chosen, you still may not see the cake. But when you have passed on you do see it, and understand what you have done."

"And we have to wait until we die?"

"No," he said, "some foresee the cake and understand it completely.

Others do not fully comprehend their lessons as they go through these processes. But they do on the other side, and it is beautiful to see, because the wisdom from these lessons is powerful and strong and brings you closer to the Lord. This expansion of wisdom and love that you have come to the earth for is what you return home with. As we have said before, you take only two things with you upon passing, wisdom and love. Nothing more."

"Thank you," I said. "I wish I could implement all that you tell me. I wish I could live it. At my lecture the other night a priest asked me how the messages have changed my life. Of course I answered that they did. But I also said that it's easy to write them down but hard to live them. I wonder if I'll ever be able to fully understand them or fully live them."

"Do not concern yourself with that. You are moving on your own pathway, learning compassion and understanding. Remember that these messages are not solely for you but for everyone. Some of these messages will be easy for you to grasp and learn, and others are difficult. Yet for another reader or listener it may be the exact opposite. These messages, although given to you, do not revolve directly around you."

"Yes, I understand," I said softly.

"Go now, and take joy in the day. Do not be anxious or worried. God has you in the palm of His hand and will care for you, as He will care for the others."

He blessed me with the sign of the cross and disappeared before my eyes. I sat quietly, breathing in the salt air, savoring it.

"Relish your senses," the Archangel said from above. "We are glad to see you do this. This is a gift of the body. Breathe in the salt air. It is healing."

Healing. I wondered what he meant. Healing spiritually? Emotionally? Or actually physically?

I breathed deeper, not taking a chance on missing out on any opportunity for healing.

Forty-Two

A couple of weeks later, I was praying to be free of the anxiety that plagues me. The doctor had put me on some anti-anxiety medicine and even that didn't seem to be relieving it. I picked a blue gem, a color that for me always symbolizes calmness, serenity, the ocean, the Blessed Mother.

The Archangel appears before me in the middle of a large meadow. We have never met here. The day is sunny and bright, and wild grass and wildflowers are all around me, some up to my knees. He beckons for me to come closer, but I hesitate. I'm allergic to bees and poison ivy, and I even worry about Lyme disease ticks in high grass.

He smiles, as if reading my mind. "Come," he says. "You are protected here." Immediately I know that I am.

I walk toward him. His robes are bright yellow, not garish but the hue of a sunlit living room, or of a baby's new hair, comforting and warm. Next to him is a small stone bench. He sits down and nods toward the empty part of the bench. I sit next to him. "Inhale the air," he says.

I do, and it is clean and refreshing. A light breeze blows around us. The flowers bend and move slowly, as if they too are breathing.

"Christ asked the people why they worry," the angel said, "because the Father takes care of the animals and dresses the flowers and lilies in the most glorious robes. Why do you worry?"

"Because we're not flowers. Actually I'm glad you brought that up, because most people in the world aren't dressed beautifully. Many of them don't have clothes and they're homeless. Slavery still exists, and in many parts of the world, including this country, children are hungry and cold in the winter. Yet you tell me about the beauty of the flowers. Please, explain this."

"You look only at their outside beauty. God cares for everyone."

I shook my head. "I don't think so. There are children who are hungry. Didn't you hear me?"

"And then there are people who are not," he said.

"What do you mean by that?"

"What do you think I meant by that?"

"I don't know. That some are more favored?"

He answered calmly, but shortly. "No, of course not. God's love is equal for all His children."

"Well, then, what did you mean?"

"Those who are clothed need to clothe the others. Those who are well-fed need to feed the others. The others, those you think God is not taking care of, are here for a multitude of reasons, maybe their own growth or maybe the growth of someone else. The poorest and least-educated among you may be the closest to God on a different level. As Christ offered up his life for others, so may have they offered up their lives for others."

"I don't get it."

"If some are poor, seemingly slow or retarded, handicapped, homeless, or any other label you give to the unfortunate, do not pity them. In many cases they are here freely to help others learn compassion."

"You mean in some cases they already have the compassion?"

"Most certainly. Did not Christ say that the first will be last and the last first? Do you not understand that?"

"I thought that had something to do with a meal or something."

"It has to do with the level of compassion each of you has for one another. When the downtrodden are shown to you, each of you has options. Some people use the poor, abuse them, set up sweatshops or put them into slavery, and thus they miss their opportunity for leaning compassion. Others may ridicule them, not understanding that each of you is a child loved equally by God. Yet others may embrace them, give them care, give them nourishment, give them compassion, and in doing this they have seized the opportunity."

"Is this true all the time?"

"Not all of the time, because sometimes people have chosen the route of what you call poverty to learn the abundance of God's riches, and to understand that true wealth is not in the material. But in other cases it is for the others. The Bible says to be kind to strangers because they may be angels unaware."

"Yes, I remember that passage."

"What it means is that the poorest of you may really be the closest to God. The homeless person may really be far along on the path toward love and compassion, and has offered his life up for others to advance as well. As Christ said, whatsoever you do to my neighbor, you do unto me.

"Each of you is one with all the others. Each of you, when you truly understand God's love, and your purpose in the universe, will willingly give up your lives for each other's growth, for each other's spiritual enlightenment. Thus all of you will return home to God.

"Do not worry. Do not be anxious. Breathe in the air of the meadow and thank God and your neighbors for the opportunity to grow and return home to God.

"Amen."

He left me. I remained sitting on the warm stone bench, wondering, and watching the flowers bend, but not break, in the wind.

"God made all of you, even the flowers, with an inner strength which is His. Rely on that strength each day, and thank Him for it," the Archangel's voice said from above.

"Thank you," I said to myself. "Thank you."

Forty-Three

I picked a beautiful stone, one I'd never had before. It is clear, with blue lines through it like the horizon or the sea. Yet as I hold it up I see there's a crack in the side, upward through the sea, and now I think I don't like it as much as before.

The Archangel greets me by the ocean but in a different place, which I recognize as a spot fisherman use. The flat rocks are everywhere, and the sea is crashing against them. Today the ocean is not calm and we sit closer to the beach roses, away from the ocean's spray. I know this place from my childhood, and I also know that when the sea is turbulent it has come across the rocks and snatched away fishermen, who were never seen again.

"You are always safe with me," the Archangel says.

I look up at him, but still I am glad we're away from the shore, near the rose bushes. It's winter and the pink flowers of the beach roses have long gone, but I can still smell their unusual scent and am thankful for such a small gift.

"A lecture I gave last week drew a large audience. I was grateful that so many people came, and bought the book and enjoyed it," I said. "I keep wondering where all these messages you give me will eventually go."

"Do not worry. It is not even your concern. It is for God to take care of. You are to do as He asks, and then the rest is in His hands and the prayers of the others."

"The others?"

"Yes, many people and angels pray for these messages to enter the world. It is not your responsibility alone. Do not shoulder it all.

"As always, but especially now, the world is in need of messages that bring them comfort and understanding. Many of you have lost the memories of your journey and can no longer rely on the faith that is essential. You need to understand the purpose of your journeys, that the love that you give out will come back."

"Oh, that 'what goes around comes around' stuff?" I said. I shook my head and pulled my knees to my chest as we sat on the rocks. "I don't always see that. I see people who live dishonest lives, or aren't nice to others, and their lives are happy. They're healthy, they're well off, and they are content. Don't tell me they're not."

"The energy you send out comes back to you. It is that simple."

"No, it isn't."

"Yes," he smiled, "it is. When you do unto others, you do unto yourselves. This is a fact. You are not here to judge others, as I have said many times. You do not know their inner journeys, their inner fears, their inner feelings. Even if you did, you do not know their pathway or journey to God. Each of you is here to save each other. Do you not yet truly understand this?"

I looked down at my knees, not sure what my answer would be.

"I guess I really don't," I said.

"You are here to save yourselves and your neighbors, and to leave with love and wisdom and move closer to the realm of God. With each act of jealousy, each inconsiderate thought, each sin of greed, you move yourself away from the path. There is evil in the world. No one wants to hear of it because they don't want to believe it. They talk of the absence of love, but the absence of love is fear. And fear breeds evil. Evil is lurking, waiting, but it will be overcome. Messages such as these will do it. Each blocking of these messages is only evil trying to stop them.

"That's scary," I said. "I don't really want to think about stuff like that."

"Nor do any of you. Many of you believe in the angels but do not believe in Satan."

"No," I said. "People don't want to talk about that."

"Well, Satan exists. Evil exists and it lures each of you with its comfort."

"Wouldn't God and kindness and love be more comfortable?" I asked naively.

"Yes, of course it would. But God does not live in the realm of materialism or greed or covetousness, and these things bring instant comfort to many of you and you find yourselves swallowed up in it. Then it becomes a circle you cannot escape."

"How do we then?"

"You step out of yourselves. You pray to be able to step out of yourselves. You pray to see yourselves as God sees you, with unconditional love. When you see yourself as He sees you, your attitude toward others changes and the gifts of God are bestowed upon you one after another. It is a beautiful and miraculous thing. You must be open to the gifts of God, and when you are, they will in turn allow you to give to others."

"So we need to love ourselves in order to love others? How do we do that?"

"You forgive yourselves your transgressions, as God has forgiven you. You let the past go, to the best of your ability, and realize that each day has a new dawning, a dawning that is a new gift from God. You need not bring along to that day all the indiscretions and omissions from before. Give each day to God and start anew. Once you feel that, and actually do it, you will begin to believe, really believe within your soul, that God has immense love for you. Then you will be able to spread that love to others. Many of you understand God's love for others but cannot understand it for yourselves. You must. If all of you in this world truly grasped the love that God has for each one of you, crime and hate would disappear from the earth. Heaven would be on earth. It is as uncomplicated as that."

"As that? I don't know," I said. "If Christ couldn't get that through to people, how will anyone else?"

"Through prayer. Christ came with the message and was the example and the symbol. He loved himself because he knew God's love for him, and because he knew God's love for him he was able, and willing, to give up his life to show God's love to his brothers and sisters. That is how it works for all of you. Once you understand God's love, understand God's plan, you will perform miracles. You will step out into the world and do deeds you never imagined you could do. You will want everyone to understand this love. None will be saved until all are saved, and you will understand this and want everyone to participate in God's love."

"Oh," I said, nearly speechless. It seemed so daunting.

"But it isn't," he answered, as if reading my thoughts.

"But so many people have had such horrible, horrible lives. They've been molested as children, have alcoholic parents, were abused or neglected, and as adults they do the same to their children, and turn to crime or drugs. How does all this work?"

"As you say, those crimes, those sins, are against each other and God, but can you not see that they are all acts of people who have no regard for themselves, who do not understand God's love for them? There is so much love, and this love is an energy, a healing energy, a curing energy, a powerful prayer energy that goes out and goes in. It goes within your soul."

"I've told you before, and I'm sure you remember, that I worry all the time about stupid things. I'm even on medicine for that. Now this makes me feel even worse, that I'm not letting this energy come in, or go out, or whatever."

He took my hand and patted it. "God created each of you to help one another. If someone discovers a medicine to help you, then why are you ashamed? It will just take you away from the anxiety and allow you to see the truth of what I say. No one should be ashamed of taking God's medicine, but of course, just like anything good, it must not be abused. But if anxiety and worry block you from prayer, then medicine is a gift from God. Let the issue go, and find the peace of God. The peace of the body is different from the peace of God. But God's peace can heal the body.

"Go now," he said. "You look tired. You will understand these messages much more as the days and years go by. They will spread and God's work will be accomplished. Amen."

"Amen," I said, standing up on the rocks and holding tightly to the bushes next to me. The waves crashed and a spray of ocean air hit my cheek. I heard from above, "You are always safe with me. Go. Tell the others of God's love for them. Tell the most destitute, tell the most sinful, that God loves them. Tell them to turn away from the evil and see the goodness and divinity within them.

"Amen."

Forty-Four

I picked a green gem and knew immediately what it meant for me. The gems can easily mean different things to different people, but to me green always means healing. I associate it with grass, with life force, with nature, and with balance. That's what I'm always searching for: a balance, health in both body and mind.

I'm taken to the notch in the mountains where a stream flows. Usually it is green and warm but today the scenery is wintry. The mountains in the distance are shining with new snow, and the stream next to us, although flowing slightly, has a thin layer of ice in the middle, a sheet of it floating downward as if it had broken off.

I look down and notice I'm dressed warmly in heavy boots and a warm winter coat touching my ankles. The Archangel sits next to me on the rock, attired in a simple navy robe without all the winter accoutrements I'm wearing. The robe glistens, as do most of his clothes, and the cuffs of the flowing sleeves and the hem shine with silver. Even his large wings seem to have silver flickering on their edges.

"Thanks for the coat," I said.

"You don't need it," he answered, "because you are protected here, but we knew you would want it."

I laughed. He knew me so well.

"You are so concerned with the earthly that it gets in the way of the heavenly."

I bit my lower lip.

"Even here, during these visits, when you are sitting on the cold rock but not able to feel the cold, your mind would be distracted from the messages because you would keep thinking that you should be cold. So we wrapped you in a coat."

"I'm sorry." I said, really meaning it, and knowing that his analysis of me was correct.

"You do not have to be sorry for who you are," he said softly. "But you, and the others too, have to realize that who you are today is not who you will be tomorrow, and that with each step of growth you can walk with God and grow into the person that you have asked to become."

"Asked to become?"

"Yes. The journey is of your own request, and you know your goals. Someday you will be able to sit with me here, with the cold and the ice, and not be concerned about the temperature but only about listening to God's messages for you."

"I'm interested in the message now," I said. "Aren't I?"

"Yes, but the earthly concerns still get in the way."

"I talked about this with some friends in a prayer group and they said they understood my concerns. We live here where it is cold, where we need shelter, where we need money and food. We're human. We're not like you, just floating around with no illness or . . ." I let my voice trail off. Did he need sleep? I wondered.

He laughed. "No," he said, reading my mind. "We do not need sleep to replenish ourselves. We sing and give praise to God and that is our replenishment. That is our joy."

"Oh," I said. "That sounds beautiful."

"Everyone has that opportunity. We have noticed you giving thanks daily, and God is pleased."

"He is?"

I had been giving thanks daily. Last year when I was so sick for so long, I didn't think I'd ever feel good again. From November to March I didn't leave the house. I couldn't cook for Thanksgiving, Christmas or Easter. Now, with my health back, I was so grateful to be in the long lines at the supermarket for Thanksgiving. While other women were complaining, I was thanking God that I could be there, that I had the health and stamina to stand in the lines. I was so grateful.

Usually I'm the type of person who, once I'm well again, kind of forgets all my pledges and deals and negotiations with God. But after last year's illness I was different. I hope I'll never take my health for granted again, and I don't think I will.

"It has been an enormous lesson for you. It has been a lesson of thankfulness and compassion."

"Compassion?"

"Yes. People who are ill need the compassion of others, and now you realize this. You realize what it is like not to have the energy to clean your home, do grocery shopping, put up Christmas decorations. You realize that for the ill or the elderly even the smallest of tasks is overwhelming. That has made you realize, on another level, that you are truly one."

"It's too bad I had to go through all that in order to realize it."

"How else could you have?"

"If you, or God, had just told me how important it was to understand it, then maybe I would have grasped it. Or maybe if I had just been sick for a few days, I would have grasped it."

He looked at me intently, his blue eyes boring into me. "Do you agree with your own statement?"

I looked away from his gaze, because I knew I didn't. I just wanted it to be that way.

"People have chosen paths, and those who have chosen challenges have the opportunity to grow from them and learn the lessons that they need to know. You can grow from these challenges, or in some cases you can regress. It is always your choice. It is always your free will. Your soul will try to lead you in the direction of learning and growing, but your personality, your humanity may lead you away from it. I tell you, and I tell the others: Listen to the songs within your soul. Listen to God's plans for you. Listen to your soul's plans for you."

"My friend says she prays all the time and yet she doesn't know her soul's plan for her. Maybe mine might be getting out these messages, but even then, how do I know that is my soul's plan? And how does my friend know her soul's plan? She wants it in neon lights."

"She must sit quietly in prayer. Sometimes your soul's plan will be given to you, but in most cases it too is a lesson to learn. You must follow the goodness, the kindness, the warmth of the soul, and you will be led to your plan, knowingly or unknowingly. If you follow Christ's example of love for each other—and that includes love for yourselves, not a selfish love but a love that honors that divinity within you—you will be led slowly and carefully in the direction of your soul's plan. It is when selfishness, greed and evil come into your lives that you can be led astray."

Looking down I saw that the heavy coat and the boots were gone. I was wearing just a regular blazer with my jeans and turtleneck, although snow and ice were still all around me.

He smiled.

"While you were listening, truly listening, to God's words for you and your neighbor, you no longer worried about the flesh. You no longer worried about the cold. When you were listening to this you no longer needed your coat, because you are safe in His Word."

I felt like Peter walking across the water, and then realizing that he was walking on water and falling into the sea. I expected any moment to feel frozen.

"No. Today the Word has engulfed you. Your doubts and fears will not block you from the Word of God.

"Go now," he said, making the sign of the cross over my head. "Listen to these words and heed them."

He disappeared. I sat in the frozen glen without warm winter clothes and didn't feel cold at all. In fact, I was as warm as on a day in July.

"Thank you, God," I whispered. "Thank you."

Forty-Five

Again I pick a green gem, this time an iridescent one, and I think of health, well-being, and nature.

The Archangel arrives. We're sitting by the beach, and his first words to me are, "Your health is many-fold. The most important task is to keep your soul and spiritual life healthy."

"I understand," I said, "but we've been through this before. Life gets in the way."

"Of course. That is the plan."

"What do you mean, that is the plan?"

"How can you relinquish what you all coveted at the beginning of time without being shown it again?"

"What?"

"You relinquished the kingdom of God for your own earthly pleasures and possessions. The story is of an apple, but it is a metaphor for the earthly possessions you all craved. Now the only way back to God is to realize the futility of them, that they hold no purpose in the scheme of your eternal lives, and to turn from them. But unless the 'earthly' was in your realm, you would never have had this opportunity.

"God has given you each the opportunity to return home to Him. In order to do this you must turn your objectives and goals away from what you once coveted and return to what truly feeds and nourishes you: the God Who created you, the God Who loves you, the God Who waits with unending patience for each of you.

"But it is free will that allows you these decisions.

"The earthly encompasses much: greed for property, for security, for love of another, for physical health. There is much that is earthly."

"Love of another is good," I said.

"It is good and a blessing to love each other, but not to covet each other.

"You are here for your spiritual healing, your spiritual growth, and without the temptations which you originally turned to, you will not be able to turn away from them. You will not understand their pull."

"So we're here fighting this battle for a reason?"

"Of course. You are often anxious, as are many in this world. All of you have forgotten the source of true peace, the source of true comfort."

"You always make it so easy, but it's not. Sometimes I wake up for no apparent reason, and the panicky feeling in my chest engulfs me."

"We know. It is an obstacle that you must overcome in order to help you find the peace of God. Some can be helped by medicine, some by breathing techniques, some by stepping out of their own lives and sacrificing for others. Anxiety is oftentimes a self-absorption."

"That's not a nice thing to say. It's also a chemical condition."

"Yes, but it feeds on itself. The more you give it energy, the more it grows. You must understand this lesson with many things. It is a universal lesson. The more energy directed toward something, the more that something will be nourished and grow. If it is negative energy, it will grow negatively."

"Explain this."

"If it is positive energy, it will grow positively."

"That's not necessarily true. I know people who have positive attitudes about their cancer, and the cancer still grows."

"Ah, but it is the positive energy that allows the person's soul to grow through the experience. If the person gave it negative energy, not only would the cancer most likely increase at an alarming rate, but the soul would not move closer to God.

"Negative energy begets negative energy. And the picture that you look at is not always God's picture."

"Then how do I change?"

"Each day when you pray, simply give the day to the Lord and ask for the view of the world that is His view, the view that each of you is loved unconditionally, that there is a magnificent plan for each of you, and that if you do this each day, the plan will be revealed to you."

"Just like that?"

"Perhaps, or perhaps in steps so slow you do not even realize it. But the plan will be revealed, and your soul will grow in astounding leaps because you will be accessing God's positive energy. That is what you can do. This energy from the Source is the most powerful energy imaginable. It can change hearts, lives, and worlds.

"Ask for His energy, which is always positive, and implement it in your lives. You will be blessed beyond your understanding.

"Amen."

"Amen," I said as he disappeared. I was wondering about the energy.

I would try. I would try to say each day, "Lord, this day is Yours. Allow me to follow Your plan and the plan of my soul, and allow me to open up to and access the energy You want to bestow upon me."

It was simple enough to say. Perhaps it was so simple that it might actually work.

Forty-Six

The Christmas holiday is over and I'm so grateful (initially I spelled it greatful, which I am, too) that I had my health. After being so sick last Christmas, I took joy in the small things of life. Standing in line in the supermarket became an opportunity for gratitude. Others were complaining, but I remembered that last year I couldn't be there. This week we had ordered a cord of wood. A cord is a lot of wood, basically a truckful. The loggers just dumped it on the front lawn. I took a wheelbarrow, filled it with wood, wheeled it to the edge of the backyard stairs, dropped each log onto the patio, and then started the process all over again. My dog took at least one log for every ten I threw down and made his own pile in another section of the yard. It took me two entire mornings to move and stack the wood by myself. But as I did it, again I was so grateful for my health. Filling the wheelbarrow, dropping the logs, stacking them, became almost prayerful, like a mantra. A mantra of thanksgiving.

When a situation feels like an abyss, dark and terrifying, and the light seems non-existent, we often do not know the reason for our pain. During the abysses of last winter, I didn't know. But today I look back with gratitude for my health, and with an amazing compassion for those who don't have theirs. And this compassion has grown. I pray much more now for those who are sick and unable to do the smallest of tasks.

Perhaps the lessons are not easy, but when we learn them, we do become more developed, more whole. I find with myself that my biggest problem is living through a lesson but not learning it. I don't understand the point of it, and therefore I am shown the lesson again somehow, in a stronger way.

The gem I pick today doesn't seem to have any particular impact on me, but I know that God has a gift for us each time we ask, so I'll just wait, and pray to be able to accept it.

I close my eyes in prayer and the Archangel meets me on the mountain. Snow is everywhere, and I am clothed in a heavy coat. He is wearing a bluish purple robe with silver threads running through it. The silver reflects the snow and ice from the mountaintop.

"You do not need that coat," he says, "but God has clothed you in it

179

because otherwise your mind would not be on our conversation."

I nodded. I knew exactly what he was saying—wasn't I always concerned with the earthly? I took off the gloves I was wearing, and I noticed that although everything was frozen around us, my hands were not cold.

"I can take off the coat," I said firmly. "I believe."

The Archangel just stood looking at me.

I took off the coat, and doubt started to attack me. It was frozen around here. Shouldn't I keep the coat on?

I felt the cold for a moment.

"Faith is walking into the unknown, realizing that God is walking with you each step of the way," the Archangel said.

I dropped the coat.

I was as warm as on an eighty-five-degree day in July. I stood there in my jeans and turtleneck, almost too warm.

The Archangel smiled. "That is a step for you, a big step, to realize that God provides for you all the time. He provides for your spiritual path. That is what you are learning, and that is what each of you needs to learn. You all need to realize that the spiritual path is open to each and every one of you."

I cast my eyes down, feeling ashamed.

"Yes?" he asked, seeing my hesitation.

"I saw a show on television last night. There were kids no older than seventeen who had been in jail and were now back on the street in a gang. They all had a razor blade in their mouth. They could move it around, like a stick of gum, without cutting themselves but hiding it from others. One of them said that's what they all learned in jail. A young girl, flipping the blade in and out of her mouth, said that she could easily conceal it and then take it out and carve her initials on someone's face."

The Archangel stayed still, almost motionless.

"There's such evil in the world," I said. "I know what you'll say, to pray for them. Amazingly I did. But I also thought, these kids will come up to an innocent person someday, perhaps me, and do something violent. How would I react? With the love of Christ or with hatred of evil?"

"That is your choice," he said sadly, "and it is theirs. Their souls' paths are not going in the direction God wants them to. But each of you can change that through prayer." He sat down next to me on the rock, which was warm from the sunlight and not covered in ice at all.

"You have grown mightily in the last few years," he said softly, "and so have many others who have read these messages. Now you understand the ignorance and the power of evil that pervade the world. When you are confronted with people who are not following the pathway home, you understand now that they are filled with anger and sadness. Many years ago you did not realize that. It is a human condition to get angry. Christ got angry. But the anger must be directed only to soul work, not to revenge or hate but to growth."

"What do you mean?"

"If you are attacked, it is a natural, animalistic response to try to save your body. That is what is human. So anger surges through you, energy surges through you. But to keep that anger, harbor it, and savor it—that is the sin."

"The sin?" He didn't talk much about "sin" and I stopped him at that word.

"All sin is omission," he said.

"Omission? I don't think so. Some sin is active. Someone murders someone and it's an active sin, not an omission."

"It's an omission of love. It's an omission of connection with God, with peace, with the Holy Spirit. Therefore sin is turning from the light, turning into the abyss, turning into the void. It is going where there is nothing. Coming home to God is returning to the land of the bountiful, the land of beauty, the land of our Lord."

"There are hostages who have been held on a plane for five days now, during the Christmas season. People are holding them in the name of God."

The Archangel looked away. "Again," he said, "it is the void, the omission, the ignorance of not knowing that God is a loving and compassionate God Who made each of you, even the terrorists on that plane, and He wants each of you to return to the love that is waiting for you.

"We are there, but evil is there also. Pray. Pray for those people, and pray for the peace that Christ brings into each person's heart."

"I will," I said softly. "I haven't been, but I will."

"Remember what we have told you before, that no power on earth, not nuclear power or any other power in the universe, is as powerful as the God Who created you, the God Who is Love.

"Amen," he said.

He left, and suddenly I was scared and I put the coat back on. I felt like Peter walking on the water and then realizing what he was doing. I need to work more on my faith, because with it I felt no cold but without it I was chilled.

"Amen," I heard a chorus of angels call from above.

"Amen," I sang back. "Amen."

Forty-Seven

I keep picking a yellow stone, although each one is different. This one is bubbly, and I wonder what it means in my life. Yellow seems so happy. Perhaps that's what I should take from it, to be happy and accept the bubbles that are always there, regardless, like the trials and tribulations in life.

"Is that not what we have told you?" the Archangel asks me, interrupting my thoughts and bringing me to the deserted beach on this cold January day. The wind whips though me and I shiver. Immediately I am clothed in a warm coat, but he, of course, is wearing only his robes.

"When you truly have faith, when you walk and live in faith, you do not need those cloaks. Your faith in God keeps you warm."

I knew this because it had happened to me before, but still, like Peter falling into the sea, when I doubted I was cold.

I stuck my hands into my pockets. "Told me what?" I said, going back to his first comment.

"That God wants you all to have a joyous life, a life fulfilled and heading home with love and understanding. The bubbles that you see and interpret so accurately are the happenings of life. They are the ups and downs, the lessons you have asked for, the paths you have chosen before your birth. But through all of this you—and you alone—have the ability to find joy in this life. Each occasion is an occasion of joy."

I shook my head, still keeping my hands tucked warmly into the pockets of the fluffy lining. "No, I can't always do that. Yesterday we went to the eye and ear hospital in Boston because my husband Tom is still having trouble with his retina. I had prayed and prayed, and each time before his condition had been stable, and this time I assumed it would be again, but it isn't. How can I find joy in that?"

"And did you continue to pray?"

"No," I said, "because really, don't you think God knows what my prayers are? If I've asked Him a zillion times, do I need to keep asking Him? Many people say that God knows from the first request and so we don't have to keep asking."

"Have I said that?"

I thought about his question. "No."

"What is our message?" he asked, rather formidably.

"To continue to pray all the time."

"Yes," he said. "It is not because God doesn't understand the request the first time. Of course He does. But the communication that you have with Him when you pray is of the utmost importance for your soul. When you make requests of Him you are speaking with Him, and each time you speak with Him He bestows blessings, understanding, and compassion upon you."

"Oh," I said. "So you're saying that if I had prayed this particular time, and not taken it for granted, Tom's eyes would have been stabilized?"

"No," he said. "I'm not saying that God answers all the prayers in the manner you want. But I am saying that if you had prayed this time, and the news was not the news you wanted, you would be fortified, you would be grateful for what news you did receive. The blessings of understanding would have been set in your heart."

"How could I be grateful?"

"Because the news could have been much worse. Because he might have been operated on that day. But you did not see that. You saw only the bad part of it."

I felt ungrateful, but still. . . . "I have a friend whose husband is going through a horrible cancer treatment. We laugh sometimes because we say she's so lucky to have found a wonderful hospital, and a chance for a cure. We laugh only because we really feel that to be lucky would be *not getting cancer* in the first place."

"But the lessons of sickness are great. We have told you that. As the yellow stone suggests, everything is a blessing when you understand that God wants you to live in joy and accept both the good and the bad with love."

"But even Christ, when he was on the cross, said, 'Father, Father, why have you forsaken me?'"

"Yes, it is human reaction. But still, even in his darkest moments, when Satan tried to tempt him in the desert, when he felt alone in the garden, when his friends betrayed him, when the people chose crucifixion for him instead of for the criminal, and on the cross—even during those times, he allowed them to be only brief. That is human growth. True human growth is seeing the need for the growth, seeing the need to return home to God, and learning compassion. Christ learned compassion in his lifetime on earth. He was a human child, and in the temple when his parents lost him, even he did not understand their worry at the time. He continued to grow as a human. When the woman who was not Jewish begged for a healing, he said to her, I am here for the Jews. She replied that even the dogs get scraps from the table. All of this was a growing experience for Christ. At that moment, in his humanity he realized that this simple woman of faith had taught him. Had taught him."

"People taught Christ?"

"Of course. You are a circle, and each of you has a magnificent task of teaching and learning from each other. Even Christ. All the great prophets do, too. They needed people.

"We urge everyone to find a community, whether it is a small community, such as a friend at your kitchen table, or a large one. This age of technology will bring the blessing of many advances and medical cures, and will also be a blessing in allowing people all over the world to understand how basically alike all human beings are. But technology also brings the concern that the one-on-one, face-to-face community may suffer. So please urge everyone to share their feeling and actual physical presence with each other. Just communicating online will not be enough. Human beings need the physical presence of others. They need to touch, feel, smell each other. Just as babies need to bond with their mothers, humans continually need to bond with each other. Such is the circle of the soul."

He turned to me. "We have not spoken since the millennium," I said, looking up at him with my coat wide open. My faith strong, I was oblivious to the cold and the wind. I wondered what he would say.

"May it be filled with blessings and wonder, and love for the world," he said softly. "And that is possible if each of you pray for each other. Pray especially for those in darkness. The passing of the millennium last weekend without incident was due to the prayers of the world. Never doubt the power of prayer. Never doubt the circle of the souls. Last weekend you saw it on a worldwide scale. It can be an everyday happening. Heaven can be on earth.

"Continue to pray."

"Thank you," I said.

"Thank the One who sent me," he said quietly. "It is an honor to do the work of the Creator."

I sat alone on the rock, watching the cold waves roll in and recede, the sun beating down on my chest. I felt hot, almost as if it were July and not January.

And that morning I knew the power of faith.

Forty-Eight

I pick an oddly colored gem this morning, a metallic raspberry-coral hue. It's large, much larger than the rest. I hold it tightly in my hand and pray for some insight.

I pray these words: Dear Lord, take me where you need me. Help me to do Your work. Allow me to listen to You, for that is one of my biggest obstacles—not listening to You.

The Archangel appears and we sit on a different rock, overlooking the deserted beach. The beach is familiar to me. The past weekend, in the midst of the January cold, I had taken my German shepherd for a walk there. He was delighted that the long, expansive stretch was ours alone because I took off his leash and he romped, ran and played along the sands. I threw a tennis ball for him until I felt like a baseball player on the injured list.

"The sea has always been a place of learning and peace for you," the Archangel said. "It is a place where you replenish your soul life. It allows you to understand the comings and goings of life, even at a subconscious level, a level you are not even aware of. All of you are filled with the sea, and returning to it allows you to mesh and connect with nature. The ocean draws many of you to it, and one of the ocean's purposes is to allow your soul to find the peace God has planted in it."

"Oh," I said. His words were beautiful but not surprising to me. I had always found solace and happiness at the beach.

"You need to tell the others of the need to understand the tides of life."

"The tides of what?" I asked.

"The tides of life. People are caught up in them, and they do not understand that the tides of life are not only in the ocean but also within each of you. There will be turbulence and storms, and what goes out comes back in. So many of you do not understand this."

"What do you mean, what goes out comes back in?"

"What goes out comes back in, and what comes in, goes back out. If you simply sit by the beach and watch the waves and the tides, you will understand the importance of what you give out into the world, because what you give out does come back to you, and what comes back to you goes out again."

"Are you talking about karma? That's an ancient belief that everything returns to you, that if you give out good karma, good karma comes back."

The Archangel looked at me. "Why would you discount such a theory? You see it in nature, and you see it in the ocean tides. Why would it not also be fitting for each of you? You too are composed of water."

"But it's not like that," I said. "Recently I heard of a man who continues to be one of the most successful men in the world, and he doesn't believe in God. He thinks religion is a weakness."

"Yes?" he prompted me.

"Well, doesn't that ruin your premise? The man criticizes God and people who believe in God, and he ridicules certain religions, yet his life is comfortable and healthy. Then you take the person who is volunteering in the soup kitchen and can barely pay her own medical bills, but still helps others. If karma really worked, it wouldn't be this way. The man who is cynical would be unable to pay his medical bills. The woman who gives her last dime to help others would have the billions of dollars to do more."

"Again you are judging. You have come to this earth to learn compassion and not to judge. And you continually fight it."

"I'm not judging," I countered. "I'm just stating a fact. I'm just saying what others who read this will say. So answer me." My tone was almost defiant.

He looked sad as he turned toward me. The sea in the distance roared, and a large wave broke onto the shore and then rolled back, taking with it some sand from the beach. I bit my lower lip, half ashamed of my defiance, and yet still intent on an answer.

"You judge when you know not the facts."

"I know the facts."

"No," he said. "You do not know the facts. You do not understand the theory or the way it works. You must learn this, because it is what you have asked to learn in this life. I am one your teachers in this lesson."

Never before, that I remembered, had he told me, "You must learn this." I looked intently at him.

"You are judging another person. You are thinking that what has gone out has not come back to him. But this you do not know. You see

186

a material life of ease—"

"And health," I added, because that was always important to me.

He continued, "and you think that is his reward. You never for a moment think that it may be the bane of his existence. Does he have love? Does he have compassion for others? Does kindness permeate him and does he live a Christ-like life, walking with compassion and understanding for all? Most important, does he realize that at the end of his life, he cannot take his homes, his bank accounts, or his success with him? He can take only the love and wisdom he has acquired.

"That is the true test of the tides. What goes out comes back in. If he does not give kindness, compassion, and the wisdom that comes of knowing his pathway on earth, what returns to him is empty. At the end of his life what he takes with him will be no more than what he brought into the world as an infant.

"The soul struggles to teach him, sends him teachers along his pathway, but he is caught up with other, tangible, things.

"So the 'karma,' as you call it, is still in force, and though you may think he is being rewarded, I assure you he is not. What you, and many others, do not see is the inner lives of people, the inner souls of people, the inner torment of many people. And it is not for you to see. It is their pathway. But if you asked them on their deathbeds what is truly important, you would see that many of them realize it too late, because it is only then that they understand that you arrive on the earth with nothing, and you leave with no material possessions. Before you are born you know that you are coming to the earth to grow in wisdom and love, and when you are facing your death, you realize that those are the only possessions you can take with you. But during your time here you forget that. We are here to remind each of you of the importance of life, the importance of the tides of your lives, the importance of taking stock, of not judging, of not being envious. Because many of you, if the choice were given to you, would not choose to have the inner life of another.

"At death, you who have followed the tides will return smoothly to the Creator.

"Live life with this understanding, and do not judge anyone else. Understand that they are on their own path. Teachers have been sent to them, people have been put in their pathway, as they have in yours. It is for each of you to choose, with your free will, what your soul needs. Some of you choose it, and others disregard it, because they have forgotten."

"But your only job is to pray for each of them, and pray for yourself. Pray that all of you understand your pathway on earth. Pray that you understand your souls' tasks, and that you remember your purpose here on earth.

"And I reiterate: God is love. You are here to learn to love, unconditionally, and to return to God with love and wisdom. Because with wisdom come understanding, compassion and a greater sense of others and of yourself, and a greater connection to the Spirit who created you. That is your only task.

"Your only task.

"Amen."

Forty-Nine

I seem to continuously pick stones of the same colors. Today, as it was a few days ago, it's yellow, muted but lovely.

Usually the colors or the shape of the stone means something to me immediately, but this one doesn't. I just sit and hold it, appreciating its smoothness against my palms.

"It is the ray of hope, it is the sun warming you, it is the strength of happiness," the Archangel says, standing in front of me. We are in a valley surrounded by mountains. Everything is green. Although I've never been to Wyoming or Colorado, I feel as if that's where we are, out west somewhere.

"Strength of happiness?"

"Yes," he said, "strength of happiness. The gifts God makes available to each of you are gifts for strength and perseverance. Hope, serenity, and other gifts all bring you strength, spiritual strength. Many of you often get depleted of spiritual strength, and you wither and stray from your path. By accepting the gifts, not only do you breathe in and become a part of the gift, but also the gift brings you strength to continue on your path.

"Prayer brings you strength to continue on your path.

"We look at you and see that many are desolate, depressed, overcome with the burdens of this earthly life. When you made the choice to come here, to learn the lessons, you knew it would be difficult. But now that you are here, many of you cling to the humanity of your being and not to the soul of your being, which is when you need the strength."

"Of God?" I asked.

"All power, all love, and all strength come from above, come from the Source, come from the Lord. Alone you cannot return to the pathway, but when you communicate with God, His strength moves within you. The energy comes into you. You accept it and become a partner with Him. When you partner with God, all things are possible. All your spiritual dreams and aspirations become realities. Because you have partnered with God you have accessed His strength, His love, His compassion and His wisdom, and you move toward the Light of the World."

"You always make this sound so simple."

He smiled. "We have told you before, it *is* simple. Simple means uncomplicated. God wants you to find joy in each day, in each moment, in each opportunity and each situation."

"I know," I said softly. "You've told me that before."

"Yes, but you keep forgetting, and challenging it, and judging the situations."

"Judging the situations?"

"Yes. You see a situation—take illness for example—and immediately you judge it to be 'bad.' You see it as a setback, a reversal in your life or in someone else's. Yet it may be just what is necessary for your growth or for another person's spiritual growth. So you should accept each situation with joy. Once you do, the situation will become joyful for you."

I shook my head. "My friend's husband with cancer? Joyful? Please, give me a break."

"Do not judge the situation, but judge the growth and the learning, and the spiritual journey of the situation. The opportunity to move on the pathway to God is given to you in *every* situation. When Christ was tempted by Satan in the desert, he moved closer to God by rebuking Satan. It was a situation he could have viewed negatively, but he grew as a human being by resisting the temptations of the earth.

"That is the choice all of you have. You have free choice but you often limit it to certain situations and feel you have no control over others. You have control over every situation, because each situation in your path is one for your spirit, and it is your free will that determines how your spirit accepts the situation. Do you understand?"

"I think so," I said. "I read an article about a woman of great faith whose daughter has been in a coma for thirty years. The woman is filled with joy as she takes care of the daughter around the clock. The quote in the paper said something like, I asked God for two daughters and I have them. She went on to say that she didn't put conditions on the request. And she was joyful."

"She has found the strength of the Lord and accessed it. She has found the joy of the Lord and accessed it. Nothing is possible without the Lord, but when you co-partner with Him, all things are possible for you. All things. You will find joy and growth in all situations because in your heart you know you are here to grow spiritually. Only that is important.

"Go in peace," he said, rising from the log we were sitting on. He rose above me, his yellow robes floating against the blue sky. The mountains in the distance seemed greener and more alive than I had ever seen them. They pulsated with life.

"Find joy in each situation. Realize that the opportunities are given to you each day for your spiritual growth. Do not ignore them. Embrace them, relish them, and access God's strength. Amen."

"Amen," I said, shielding my eyes from the bright sun. The sunlight seemed the exact color of the gem I had picked today.

"Go find joy. It is there and it is abundant," his voice called from above.

"Amen," I said again, hoping to be able to do such a "simple" task.

Fifty

I pick a deep blue stone. If I hold it in the palm of my hand it's almost black, but if I hold it up to the light, it's a translucent sky-blue.

The Archangel appears. "And what do you make of that?" he asked.

I was surprised at his question because usually I had already thought about what the stone meant to me before he appeared.

I smiled. "I know what you're going to say it means."

"It is not for me to say what gift of God is appropriate for you today. You have asked God yourself, and you have received an answer. It is between the two of you and your spirits to co-create the miracles of the day."

"Well," I said, "what I think it means is that looks are deceiving, sort of what we talked about yesterday. When I first picked up the stone it seemed so dark, so forbidding. It reminded me of the sky before a storm. Quite frankly I got a little scared. Then I had to remind myself what I tell people in the lectures, that all of the gifts of God, all of the gems He gives us, are positive. There are no negative gifts from God."

"And?" the Archangel prodded.

"So I looked at it more closely. I held it, and still I thought it reminded me of a storm. It wasn't as smooth as the other stones, and it had imperfections in it. Then, so I could see it even more clearly, I held it to the light."

"And you saw the color of the sky on a beautiful day."

"Yes," I said, surprised. "That's just what I saw. It was entirely different."

"And you realize?"

I smiled again. I felt as if I were with a psychiatrist who already knew my answer but wanted me to state it out loud, to hear my own voice say the words and give them impact. Perhaps that's important in life. Saying something out loud, giving it impact, giving it to the universe.

"I realized that what we see as negative may in fact be a beautiful gift, something wonderful. But fear usually keeps me back. Usually I would hold the dark stone and then toss it into the bowl again and try to ignore it. But today, perhaps because of yesterday's conversation, I held it, turned it over, examined it, and then, wanting to see it even more closely, held it to the light, where it was transformed."

I stopped. I repeated out loud the words I had just said. "I held it to the light, where it was transformed."

The Archangel smiled. He did not do that often, but today it was a large and knowing smile. "The Light transforms everything. God transforms everything for the good. Today you have realized this, and we pray that you continue to hold to that realization. Many of you do not understand this, and so are stopped on your spiritual path. Listen to your soul, for it will always try to lead you in the direction of the light. It will always try to disregard the fear and take the pathway to joy, because the soul knows the transformation of each event in life. It knows that what you see as darkness is truly a gift from God, if you take the opportunity to reach for the light and see it in the light. If you stay in the darkness, fear will engulf you and you will never see the beauty of the situation. You will lose a learning opportunity, and that is tragic."

"Tragic?"

"To lose a learning opportunity is always tragic. It is a waste of your time, and because the soul knows that, it is saddened. The soul wants to lead you back to the light. When you let fear shut out the light, you lose opportunities that you need to progress. Change the fear, allow it to dissipate and leave, and look at the situation, the gift, the gem, and hold it to the light. Hold it up to the Lord, and the answers will come. This is a form of prayer. Giving what frightens you, what you do not understand, to God, will bring the light of wisdom shining into your being. Then you will understand, on the deepest level, the meaning of the situation, the need for the situation, and the opportunity it offers for growth.

"But, as we emphasized yesterday, each of you has human free will. Your soul can show you the way, but your humanity can disregard its advice, and when it does that, you are headed away from the pathway, away from returning to the light. Then the soul must find new opportunities for you to learn."

"Is that why some people keep repeating their mistakes?"

"Yes," he answered. "They repeat and repeat their mistakes, because if they could overcome their fear and learn from their mistakes, their soul would progress onwards. But the soul knows that the wisdom it needs to acquire on this earth can be learned only through lessons that are different for different people. If you do not pay attention to the lesson and understand it and gain wisdom from it, the soul will continually search out the same situations, until you have turned toward the light, turned toward the right path."

"Wow," I said. "But how does this fit in with free will?"

"Prior to your birth, through your spirit's free will you gave your soul permission to lead you back to God. You do not remember this, and it is not necessary that you do. You realized, even at that time, that your humanity might change the path. But your soul is constantly trying to return you to God. Unfortunately, many on this earth listen only to their humanity's free will, and disregard what they have already decided on another level for their spirits."

"Oh," I said. "Some days everything made so much sense." And today it did.

"Go. Spread the messages we have given you. Shout them from the mountaintops. Never hesitate to share them with anyone. Lives are being changed with these messages, lives that you will never know about on this earth. But rest assured, they are moving closer to God because of these messages. Continue to spread the word and continue to believe."

He disappeared, and not until then did I realize I was sitting on a log in the midst of a dense forest. Normally I would have been afraid of being alone in a place I didn't know. But I looked above me, saw the sun shining through the tall pine trees, and thanked God for the opportunity to breathe in the clean air and to sit in His natural world.

The fear gave way to beauty.

Was I finally learning?

Fifty-One

The first snow of the season is falling and everything looks so clean and white. I woke up today still searching for God's peace, still anxious about the day, and I wonder why. I inhale slowly, trying to breathe in the Holy Spirit and the wisdom that is Hers, and the peace that comes from God. I choose an unusual stone, one that is clear with a strip of translucent blue through it. It looks as if the sky or the ocean is suspended in air.

I close my eyes to pray, as usual not knowing if the Archangel will arrive or not.

"Did you understand the gift God gives to you today?" he asked.

We are on a mountaintop overlooking a village that seems to be Austrian or Swiss. A light snow covers the charming scene. Smoke from fireplaces rises into the sky, which is clear with the clearness that comes after a storm.

"I don't think so," I said, looking at the stone. "It's clear with a blue middle. What does it mean?"

"It's what each of you knows in your heart it means. It is not for me to tell you, unless you are completely at a loss, and then I can lead you."

"For me blue always means tranquility, or the Blessed Mother, and clearness always represents clarity. If you put a clear stone up again a sentence, the sentence gets larger and the words are easier to read."

"Yes?" he said.

"But the part I'm still not sure of is why the blue band is completely in the middle."

I stopped, and a thought came to me.

"Am I completely in the middle? "

"Yes," he said softly. "You are in the tranquility but do not even know it. All of you can find heaven on earth and you do not even realize it. On each side of you is complete clarity, clarity to see it, to understand it. The wisdom of the Holy Spirit is around you all the time. The gift God gives each of you, that each of you do not always accept, is the gift of tranquility. To receive it you must also access what surrounds that tranquility: the clarity of wisdom. Heaven is on earth when you understand and accept the wisdom of the Holy Spirit. Because as we have told you before, with wisdom comes understanding for your neighbor and yourself, with wisdom come compassion, love, and unity. Everything is made clear, and that clarity brings heaven to earth, because you understand your path, you understand the reason for each event. You understand that it is *your acceptance* that allows you to grow."

"But," I said, "there's a glitch in that. Acceptance. If something bad happens, we don't just say, 'Oh, okay, I'll accept it and grow from it.' You need to pursue it. If someone robs you, you don't just say, 'Oh, I'll accept it,' and let the guy go."

He shook his head. "That is not what I am saying. I am saying you accept each situation as a growing movement toward God, toward the path your soul wants. When you do this you will be able to deal with the situation with clarity. That is not to say that you accept loss or hatred or injustice and do not try to resolve it. But it is how you accept it that brings about reconciliation with God and reconciliation with each other."

"Explain that."

"Say someone robs you. Obviously it would be foolish to say, 'Oh, I accept it; too bad,' and let him go on his way. But it is *how* you accept it that makes a difference in your life, makes a difference in how you deal with it. If you take in the situation and get angry and filled with revenge, then that is the energy you will send out. You may find the perpetrator, but that energy will continue to grow until you get justice, or worse, revenge.

"If you accept that situation as a negative one, but still one that gives you the opportunity for growth, then you have changed your attitude. You see more clearly. You still seek justice, but more because the person who committed the crime needs to understand that he or she has taken the wrong path. And you continue to try to find justice to keep the robber from robbing another innocent person. But you do it for the sake of others, and when you do it for the sake of others, including the perpetrator, you become healed. Your physical body is not filled with revenge and anger, you accept what you need to do with *love*, and then you grow, and that energy moves out from you. And others may be helped."

"May be?"

"Sometimes others are not helped in one single instance. It may take many people with the same caring and love to help another."

"So you believe in justice?"

"I believe that others should not be harmed, and I believe that you need to understand where you have gone wrong on your soul's pathway. Punishment isn't necessarily the answer, but education and understanding are. And of course we stress that those who turn from the light need to find the light. Otherwise the evil deeds will continue to spread throughout the earth. Justice in your terms is different than justice in mine. Justice to me means lighting the path, correcting it by bringing the person back to the one the person's soul fixed on, and doing it with love."

Fifty-Two

I don't often pick a black stone. When I did today I had the same reaction that many people in my audiences do when they receive one. Suddenly you think of darkness and death. I always assure them that black is all colors combined and that it is a magnificent stone, and that none of the gifts from God are negative. They are all bountiful and blessed.

So I breathe in deeply, trying to take my own advice. It seems to work.

The Archangel appears. We are sitting on a picnic bench overlooking a lake. In the distance children are swimming and playing in the placid water. Although it is January, here at the lake the air feels to me like July, hot and a little humid but delightful. Breathing in the smell of the pine trees around me, I say hello to him.

"You have received a black stone today," he said. "What does that mean to you?"

I told him my initial fear, and what I always tell people in the seminars. "Yes," he said, "you are right. Every gift from God is a blessing. People are afraid of the darkness."

"Shouldn't we be?" I asked. "We always associate the darkness with evil, with the devil, with bad things."

He paused. "The darkness is evil if you enter it and succumb to it. But being faced with it can be a growing opportunity for you."

"I don't understand. "

"How else can you grow unless you are able to compare good versus bad, kindness versus selfishness? When you see the yin and the yang of life, you realize that you have choices. But if you never had these choices to face, you would never grow. Entering the darkness is entering evil because evil is in the depth of the darkness, and once you enter that, it is difficult to leave. Your prayers and prayers of your neighbors allow you to escape it. You do not learn in the midst of the evil. You learn at the brink of the abyss."

"I don't truly understand."

"If you enter evil you are swallowed up in it. If you enter the darkness, and move too far from the light, you cannot find the light again on your own. That is where the circle of the souls is so important, because others, through prayer, can lead you out. But once in the bowels of evil, you are consumed with it and you cannot progress, you cannot learn, and you need others to help you escape."

"So evil serves a purpose?"

"The existence of evil, the existence of the darkness, serves a purpose, because it is what you chose in the beginning when you turned from God. God in His goodness allowed you to see the light, and allowed others to pray for one another. Its existence now reminds you of your past choices, and allows you the opportunity to turn from it, and thus to run toward the light and grow. But if you enter the darkness, and move so far into it that you no longer see the light, without prayer you become lost, and evil consumes you."

"Wow," I said, thinking to myself that I wished today's conversation was light and airy.

"It is not to be frightened of. You must realize that the stone you received today, the black stone, is God's combined gifts, the colors of all stones combined—serenity, peace, courage, and all the others. It is how you face the darkness, how you use your free will, that allows you to move and grow."

"People often say 'I'm in a dark place' when they talk about their lives and their emotions," I chimed in, as if I really understood what he was talking about today."

"Yes," he said, "that is when things are troubling, because being in a dark place can consume you, can move you closer to the darkness and away from the light. That is why all of you need the prayers of others, as well as your own prayers. Facing the darkness and understanding are the keys. Christ was tempted by Satan in the desert and also many other times. Each time he faced the darkness, and grew from facing it, but he did not surrender to it, did not enter it. Even as he was dying he was facing a 'dark place' and cried out, 'Father, Father, why have you abandoned me?' He faced the darkness and spoke to his Creator in prayer, and through that prayer he overcame the darkness. Upon his death he entered hell, and through his resurrection he showed the light to those in the deepest darkness. His prayers, his giving up his life for his brethren, allowed them to see the light and choose the light. Up until that time they were consumed by darkness and had no understanding that there was a light to lead them back to God."

"I need to reread this to understand it."

"Yes," he said, "we realize that. But tell the others that facing the darkness, facing difficult times, facing evil, are all opportunities for growth. The key word is facing, not being engulfed in it, because if that happens, the darkness consumes you. By facing darkness you grow, and choose light, and with that choice all the gifts and strengths of the Creator become yours. *All the gifts and strengths of the Creator become yours when you chose the Light.* Remember these words and heed them. Amen."

"Amen," I said. He disappeared, and I sat quietly on the picnic bench, hearing the laughter of the children in the lake. I don't know how long I stayed there before being transported home, but it was peaceful, light-filled and calming.

Fifty-Three

I should be at my tae kwon do school this morning, but the round trip is an hour through the country and it's snowing out. I'm such a wimp driving in the snow that I've decided to cut class. Guilt still nags at me, but perhaps I'll go this evening when my husband goes, and then he can drive.

Because my mind is elsewhere I find it difficult to sit and pray. I think of all the monks and people who meditate and can easily block out daily concerns to concentrate on their prayer lives, and I become a bit jealous. I want to be able to do that, to let go of earthly worries, at least while I pray, and concentrate only on the spiritual. But I'm not there yet, and I wonder if I ever will be.

The Archangel meets me in the glass arcade. We haven't been there in months, and only twice since this third book started. It's a corridor with a ceiling of pure glass, arched and shiny. Along the corridor are doors of wood and of glass, each leading to a different room. One was full of books; another had led me to different countries with an Asian angel. Looking around I see that we are farther down the corridor than I have ever been before. I hadn't realized the corridor extended this distance.

"Your sight is always limited," he said in greeting. "You see only what you are capable of seeing and understanding at the moment. To give you the entire view of the world would overwhelm your body. Therefore, as each of you progresses, you move to a new spiritual territory and see and delight in new opportunities."

"Oh," I said. That made sense, I guess. "But I hadn't even realized that the corridor was this long."

"You cannot realize what you cannot envision," he explained, "and you cannot envision growth until you are ready to grow."

I must have looked perplexed.

We walked down the corridor. Each of the room had glass storefront windows but they were tinted so I couldn't really see into them. And each of them had massive, heavy-looking wooden doors.

"I'll repeat the statement," he said. "You cannot realize what you cannot envision."

"What do you mean by that?" I asked. "That I can envision things and they will happen? I was talking with friends last night and we were discussing visualization."

"Yes," he said, continuing to walk slowly past the doors. Today he wore a muted dark red robe. Asian-like characters were embroidered in gold along the flowing sleeves, which billowed as he walked, his arms crossed and hands tucked into the opposite sleeve.

"Visualization is an aspect of faith. When people say they visualized something and then it occurred, it is true faith. In sending out the prayers and the energy, they have made it happen. When Christ said, 'Faith can move mountains,' he was in reality saying that if you believe it will occur. Although many people think they believe, they falter as Peter did in the sea, and fall into the water."

"What about what you said, though—you cannot realize what you cannot envision?"

"Think of it. You did not realize that this glass arcade continued, that the hall filled with knowledge and opportunity extended this far. When you limit your imagination you limit your growth and you limit your faith. When you cannot imagine, or envision, you cannot realize.

"The greatest thinkers of the world allowed their imaginations to go to places that were unexplored, and then, once there, they found a way in their world to reach that place."

"So you're saying to envision beyond your imagination?"

"I'm saying, when your intuition speaks to you, when the Holy Spirit wants to pour knowledge and wisdom upon you, allow this to happen. Be open to it, and your vision will broaden. Your ideas will become larger and more expansive, and although they may seem unbelievable, those are the ideas that are necessary for humanity's true growth."

"Do you mean things like technology, or do you mean envisioning world peace?"

"Which seems more difficult for you to imagine?"

I shrugged, still walking next to him at an incredibly slow pace. "I don't know much about technology's future, so it would be hard to imagine something."

"Precisely," he said firmly.

"If I imagined something, it would probably sound like science fiction."

He stopped walking and motioned toward a closed wooden door. I opened the heavy door easily and entered a small shop, which was filled with knickknacks, things I would hardly think were important—little ceramic angels on a table, candles, books stacked on a shelf. It looked more or less like a small gift shop, one with not much inventory. I wondered what the point of this was.

"What people called science fiction fifty years ago is reality today, because some people had a vision, and that vision led them to discoveries. If everyone in the world envisioned world peace, prayed for world peace, and had *faith* that it could occur, it would. That is visualization at its most powerful. That is faith becoming action, faith moving mountains as Christ said."

"Is it possible?" I asked, sitting down on a little pink chair and mentally criticizing the decor of the room.

"Everything," he said strongly, "for the good of mankind is possible through faith. If you believe you can move the mountain, the mountain will move. If you can believe in world peace, the world will find peace. If you can envision a future with 'science fiction' technology, it will become reality.

"But most of humanity closes its mind to envisioning the impossible. They may visualize something for themselves—a job, a spouse, healthy children, a home—but even then, once they have it, the seeds of doubt and darkness enter their thoughts, and the vision often goes away, even though many of these visions are realistic and limited. So to step into the outer boundaries and envision what you do not understand, you need the wisdom of the Holy Spirit and the guidance of the Lord. And you need the faith that so many of you are lacking.

"If you create with God all visions can become realities. You will envision what you cannot describe or image, because God has allowed you to see with His eyes. And then you must employ your faith."

"That's the difficult part," I said.

"Yes, for many of you it is. Your faith wavers. Some days it's strong, but when the impossible is shown to you, it falters. Faced with the impossible, you must grab hold of your faith even more. Pray that your faith will stay with you and guide you and guard you from doubt, because fear and doubt can break the vision. Fear and doubt can close you off from God's words and eradicate the faith. Pray continuously for the courage to hold onto faith, to be able to see with God the creations He wants for the world, and to implement them. Your vision is limited but God's is expansive and infinite. Tap into His vision and you will be given answers that you never even knew existed, because the questions did not exist for you.

"The possibilities are endless, but none of you realize it yet. The possibilities for faith and growth are within you, when you connect to the Divine Maker and tap into His power."

He left me as quickly as he had arrived. I sat on the soft little pink chair for a while, inhaling the aromas of the room. I smelled roses, although I didn't see any. I stood up, stretched, and picked up a small white ceramic cherub. I had a similar one at home. I still did not understand why this room was so important for my growth, but as I put down the little statue, I prayed silently.

The Archangel's voice came from above. "Envision what you have never dreamed of, and know that with God's power, all things are possible for goodness. Amen."

"Amen," I said, leaving the store and quietly shutting the wooden door behind me.

Fifty-Four

I sit, feeling sad and exhausted and not much like praying. Closing my eyes I pick a stone; it is a light yellow one. I always associate the yellow with happiness, hope, the energy of the sun. But today I don't feel that way.

Last weekend I visited a friend who is going through a difficult time. We went to an elegant party, and because I hadn't planned on drinking that night, it had already been decided that I would drive home. She had a lot to drink, and outside the party insisted on taking the keys away from me. I refused. The scene got out of hand, and I returned to the party with the keys still in my hand. Eventually someone there convinced her to let me drive home, but she was so angry with me she barely spoke. And the next day she was no different.

I would do the same thing again because losing a friendship is less important than losing someone's life. But at forty-three years old, I had never before had to experience fighting for car keys. I had always assumed it was a "teenage" thing, and now I so admire teenagers who can take away keys from angry friends and risk losing their friendship and their cliques.

I have no anger, but I am profoundly sad. We had been good friends for over twenty years but now she will no longer speak to me. She said I embarrassed her in front of her friends and working associates. But in my view she embarrassed herself.

Yet I can't shake my sadness. I close my eyes in prayer and ask the purpose of all these trials.

The Archangel appears. We are back in the crystal arcade, sitting in a library. There are books from ceiling to floor, and the warm chestnut wood of the shelves comforts me.

"Pick another stone," he says to me, handing me the gem bowl. I pick a green one, like the color of June grass. Bright, yet comforting.

"Many of you forget that the gifts of God are abundant and everlasting—and readily available. You hold one gift, the yellow stone of hope and happiness for you, and yet you still need God's strength and gifts to continue your journey. Always be open to all the gifts He is willing to bestow upon you."

I hold the June grass stone in my hand and think of health. Green always reminds me of health, even though I've forgotten what the color originally meant in *Songs of the Soul*.

"The colors of the gem change, the need for certain gifts changes, as you progress on your path. But they are always available to you."

"Health?"

"Growth and health. You do not understand yet, nor do you see, the destination of your path. But your soul does. You look at this weekend as a sad weekend, and of course the situation is sad. We know that you wonder why you even went to the party."

"Did you know," I asked, "there's a saying 'No good deed goes unpunished'?"

He smiled. "It is a saying made by humans who do not see the final destination of each good deed. Good deeds are just that, deeds which reflect the love of God and the love humanity has for each other on its soul level. Nothing can ever destroy that."

"Well," I said, shrugging, "I'm not so sure."

"We cannot see the future or the time of an individual's death, because that is between the soul and the Lord. But we can tell you that what you think was a horrible evening was for the greater good."

"How can you say that?"

"Because what you did you did from love. You gave your word to her husband that you would drive home, and you honored your commitment. That in itself is honorable. But even if you hadn't given your word, what you did was the right thing. You may have saved her life, you may have saved an innocent driver's life, or spared her children or someone else's children from having to grow up without a mother."

"I know," I said. "Her child's face kept flashing in front of me."

"Yes," he said. "We did that."

"You did?" I asked, but I wasn't surprised. That evening, as I fought for the keys and the scene escalated, my fingers clutched the key ring and I saw her baby's face. Oddly enough, people who have had too much to drink can often be convincing, but it's the tone of their voice—angry, raging—that gives them away.

"Yes, she was trying to convince you that she was fine, and for a brief second you doubted your own judgment. That is when we intervened."

"You do that for people?"

"Of course," he said. "We are God's messengers. We are here to help you return home to God. If you are open to returning, and are doing His work—as you were that evening—you are open to seeing our messages. We know that many times people tell you, 'I wish I saw an angel as you do.' You always respond correctly, 'It's not important to see the angel. It's important to listen to the messages and realize the angels are with you.'"

"Thank you," I said. He usually didn't give me compliments.

"But most people don't realize when we are working. Even you, that evening, did not realize we were helping you have no doubts about your judgment."

"I doubted myself for only a brief moment."

"But that was enough. We were there to help you to do your job, to continue your work of love."

"Love is hard sometimes, isn't it?"

"Giving it is never hard, but for many accepting it is. It comes down to self-worth, and people who do not realize God's love for them do not value their own being. Thus they find it hard to accept love, because they find it hard to accept that they are worthy of love."

"I always want to be perfect. I always want to be loved by everyone."

"That will not happen," he said firmly. "Your soul is perfect; it is an extension of God's love. It is your humanity that sins, and because of this, until the end when all are returned to the circle of souls, not everyone will love you. At the deepest level each soul loves the other, but the personality of the human blocks that love from reaching out. The free will of the person often stifles that unconditional love.

"When your friend raged at you and swore at you and threatened you when she wanted the keys, how did you react?"

I closed my eyes before replying. The question had so many answers. "Well, we were in a city I wasn't familiar with, and I had no idea if that section of it was safe or not, so of course I kept my eyes on the people passing by, for fear of being mugged or worse. So I was much more alert. But what surprised me the most was that as she raged at me, I felt no rage at all. None. The only time I got angry was on the drive home when she reached over, still berating me, and put the car into neutral. That upset me because she could have gotten us killed if she had done that on the highway—or even worse, shifted it into reverse. But otherwise I just felt a tremendous, deep, profound sadness. And love."

"And that is why when you do things in love, and you react in love, you are protected. Although you may have lost a friend, you did God's work. Christ and the disciples had many enemies, but they continued to work in love and do God's work. When you work in love, you react with love."

"I was telling a friend recently that before these messages, I would not have reacted in love. I would have been angry, embarrassed for what she screamed at me and upset at her cutting words to me. But somehow, even when I delve deep inside, I can't find those feelings. Are you sure that is healthy?"

"Yes," he said quietly. "But it is an important question. You may block out emotions and say you 'love' when in reality that love does not bring you peace. Each of you needs to delve deeply into your soul to make sure that you do not harbor feelings of jealousy or anger. When you are sure of that, you have love."

"And how can you be sure?"

"Because when you delve down you find the well of anger empty, and you find a profound sense of peace in the act of love you committed. You find too a wisdom from that peace, the wisdom that comes from the Holy Spirit."

"I cried afterwards though."

"Tears are the sign of the Holy Spirit. You cried from sadness, but also from a wisdom that was bestowed upon you that evening. And you cried for the end of a friendship. That is all natural, and healthy. Christ cried when the apostles denied him. He cried at the sadness of the people. He was human and reacted to profound sorrow in a human way. But the Holy Spirit was always with him, always guiding him, always giving him wisdom and growth during those periods.

"This episode was not just for your friend but also for you. It was a step toward the compassion you had been lacking in your life. You saw her as 'all are one' and felt a connection with her, and not a judgment of her. Not judging is one road toward compassion. Gaining compassion is the reason that you personally are on this particular journey."

"Thank you. You've made me feel better."

"No," he said, "it is not I. It is the comfort of the Holy Spirit and the love of God. You acted as God's arm, you did what you did in love and compassion, and that is God.

"Amen."

"Amen," I said. After he left I sat in the store and looked around. On one of the shelves was a book titled *Each Lesson Is For You*. I didn't even pick it up, because I finally understood that each lesson or event is a teacher for both parties.

That was a new one for me.

Fifty-Five

I pick a blue stone. It's rich in hue and smooth, the color of the ocean before a storm, dark yet somehow inviting.

I close my eyes in prayer, and the Archangel takes me to the beach. It is chilly, and the beach is deserted except for us and my German shepherd, who is playing in the sand. To my recollection, this is the first time my dog has ever been in one of these visitations.

"You walked your dog on the beach this weekend," the angel said.

"Yes," I said. "It was cold and pretty deserted, but I kept throwing a ball to give him exercise."

"We were with you," he said.

I shouldn't have been surprised, but I was. He has said that angels are always near us, with us, waiting to guide and help us. But somehow that always seems surprising to me.

"It was cold," I said, "not like today. "

"It is as cold today," he said, "but I have told you before, when you are listening to the messages and I take you to places, you are always protected."

I looked up, watching for my dog. "He too is protected when you are listening and writing the messages," the Archangel said, already answering my unasked question.

"We were proud of your progress on Saturday," he continued, "and you need to know that. All who progress need to have their achievements acknowledged. It allows them to continue to move ahead, to be encouraged that their path is unfolding as their soul needs and wants it to."

"What were you proud of?" I asked, but somehow I already knew. I looked to the left, where my dog was playing with a large rock, pawing it and digging it deeper into the sand. His black face looked up at me, covered with both snow and sand. I smiled at him.

"You were intent on exercising the dog, and you kept thinking of issues and problems in your life. You were all the way down this beautiful barren beach, trying to keep warm in the January cold, with the ocean wind blustering, and watching that your dog didn't eat a seashell or something, and then you stopped."

I looked down at my feet. I knew what he was going to say.

"And suddenly you realized that you were not in the moment. You were not accepting God's gifts."

I nodded. "I couldn't believe it," I said. "I walked the entire length of this beautiful beach and halfway back, and I still hadn't even looked at the ocean. I stopped dead, and even said to my dog, 'I have to stop, and inhale the sea air, and look at the magnificent ocean.'"

"And it was the color of the stone God gave to you today."

"Yes," I said.

"What does that mean to you?"

"That we have beauty all around us all the time, maybe not the beauty of the ocean, but always God's gifts are around us. But often I'm too busy, too wrapped up in my own world and thoughts, to see them, even when they are as large and as expansive as the ocean."

He smiled, but I didn't.

"When I stopped," I said, "I couldn't even believe that I hadn't looked at the sea, that I was so intent on keeping warm, watching the dog, exercising him, that the ocean didn't even get my attention."

"That is the situation with many of you. You walk through life so intent on what you think is important and so concerned with the comforts of life that God's magnificent gifts are there *right in front of you* and yet you do not even see them. You must look with new eyes, hear with new ears, and be open to the gifts of God and the Holy Spirit. When you do, suddenly the peace of the Lord will transform you. You will see the immensity of His gifts, you will breathe in the spirit of the Holy Spirit, and you will be grateful for God's presence in your life all the time.

"The lesson is an important one. Many of you think that God's gifts are obscure and difficult to find, that the peace of the Lord is difficult to obtain. But that is not true. It is all so simple. You need only to *look* and it is right in front of you. But many of you do not look and do not see what is apparent, because you see only what you think is important, and in many cases it is the least important view of the world.

"Take this blue stone today and hold it tightly in prayer, prayer to recognize and accept the gifts and the beauty which surround each of you. Someone suffering from an illness who is consumed with matters of health can step aside for a moment and try to see the beauty that God still sends, the help that God still sends, and the lessons that can be learned from the illness. Then God's gifts will become apparent."

"Amen," I said, because the words somehow seemed like a prayer to me.

"Amen," he answered.

Suddenly I was back home, my dog sleeping soundlessly in the family room, and the stone sitting in the middle of my desk.

"Thank you," I whispered. "Thank you."

Fifty-Six

I pick a gem and again it is blue, this time not as dark. It is more like the color of the ocean that surrounds the Caribbean islands, translucent, aqua, and calming. I feel the smooth gem in my hand and breathe out slowly, trying to take in the moment.

"Take in the calmness of the Holy Spirit," the Archangel says to me. His voice reverberates in the air, and I find myself sitting in the bookstore of the crystal arcade. "Many of you forget that the calmness and peace of the Holy Spirit surround you all the time. You need only to breathe in and accept it."

"It's not that simple," I said. "Many of us are very anxious; many of us worry. There is even medicine for it."

He nodded. "God gave humanity the resources it needs. Medicine saves lives and allows many people to function fully. It is a gift from God. But the peace of the Spirit that I am discussing is a different peace, a profound peace of serenity, the calm knowledge that regardless of what you may be suffering, what you may be experiencing, or what worries may engulf you, God is with you. It is a peace of the soul. Having that peace, you will understand your path."

"You mean you can still be anxious but at peace?"

He smiled, knowing that this was an ongoing issue with me.

"Your body can be anxious while your soul is still at peace. But the more your soul directs your life, the closer the humanity and the soul will mesh. Christ was anxious in the garden, dreading the death that faced him. His humanity was fearful, but still his soul had a profound peace from the Holy Spirit in knowing that his path was for the fulfillment of the Scriptures, for the example to humanity of true love, true compassion. Therefore his humanity had only moments of fear, because he was able to connect with his soul's peace."

"I'm not sure I understand this fully."

"Your soul can direct your humanity. Your soul is the life-giving aspect of your body. When your soul decides to leave this earth, your human body dies. When you can pray and get in touch with your soul, the anxiety of life will still be there but you will see it from a different perspective. You will see it more objectively and be able to understand it for what it is—fear for the body. The most important concern in this life is for your soul's destination. The more you begin to see and understand this, the more you will have peace and will understand the futility of anxiety, because anxiety serves no purpose."

"Fear serves a purpose. True fear—fear of evil, fear of bodily harm—allows you to survive. But when fear stays within your body too long, it becomes anxiety. It becomes toxic, and such toxicity drains energy from your soul. It envelops you so that you cannot concentrate on your spiritual path. Pray, pray, pray. With prayer the Holy Spirit will pour wisdom upon you, and with this wisdom you will distinguish the important tasks of the soul from the unimportant tasks of humanity."

"Humanity is important, though," I stated. "Or else why would we be in bodies?"

"Of course. Humanity teaches you the lessons you need to learn. It teaches you to direct your energy to the soul, and to make decisions for the soul. Without a body and the concerns of the earthly, you would not have the choices to make, the impetus to grow and develop that is so necessary. Your free will is essential to your personalities, but as you grow you will listen to the free and wise will of your spirit. Then your choices will be choices for God and of God.

"Amen."

"Amen," I said, sitting at my computer. I don't think I truly understood what he was talking about today. But perhaps as I pray, I'll get some of that "wisdom."

Fifty-Seven

I have been slacking off in my prayer life. I write these pages, and I pray silently during the day for people and for intentions, but I have not been setting aside real time to listen to the Lord, which the Archangel continually tells all of us we must do. I sit quietly for a moment and take a gem. I am surprised that it is white.

White—pure, a new beginning.

I hold the smooth glass stone in my fingers and rub it. It is cold and yet comforting. I hold the stone up to the light, and it is dense; only whiteness is given to me.

I have asked for a gift that will help me, and I am given a blank slate. I ponder that.

"Each day is a new beginning with God," the Archangel says at the bookstore in the crystal arcade. I find myself sitting on a leather ottoman, surrounded by books, and he is standing in front of me, his hands tucked inside his flowing sleeves. His robes today are cranberry red with golden threads throughout the fabric, and I see characters and letters embroidered around the bottom in a language I cannot understand.

"Hello," I say, still turning my stone over in my hands.

"Do you truly understand what I just said?" he asked.

"Yes," I answered. "Each day God gives us a new beginning."

"It is easy for you to repeat the words, but I want you to understand them deep within your heart. I want you, and the others, to truly believe this."

I looked up at him. This angel, this celestial being, this messenger of God, understood me more than I understood myself. "I'll repeat it," I said, somewhat defensively. "Each day God gives us a new beginning."

He wouldn't let me stop there. "And what does that truly mean to you?'

"That God forgives us, and lets us begin with a clean slate?"

He nodded slightly. "He loves you. All of you. That is what many of you still do not understand. You do not truly understand that this love of His for each of you is profound, deep, and everlasting, a love that

214

reaches far beyond your imagination. You do not understand this in the depths of your heart. You do not truly believe this, or you would give all your cares and concerns to Him."

"Help me understand it."

"Each day is a gift from God. Each day is a new beginning. Begin the day giving your works, deeds, thoughts and love to God. Ask Him to help you to forgive yourself for your own deeds. God always will forgive you. It is you who will not forgive yourselves. Because of this, either you carry your guilt with you each day, allowing it to grow larger, or you squelch it into your bodies and you become ill.

"Today you must work on forgiving yourselves. You must work on having a clean slate, a slate of purity, each new day. Remember, God's love for you is unending. His forgiveness for you is always there. Only turn toward Him, and He will shed his light upon you.

"But this is difficult for many of you, because you cannot—and will not—forgive yourselves. I have told you before that all of your imperfections become perfections in your life's journey. You grow from mistakes, and those mistakes become lessons and aids to you. God knows this and understands this. It is when you dwell on those mistakes, allowing them to grow and fester, that you block out forgiveness for yourselves. When you block out the forgiveness of Christ, evil slowly creeps into your lives. Evil is insidious. Its power is not in its strength but in its perseverance and subtlety.

"Remember to forgive yourselves and each other every day. Each night ask God to give you the gift of love for yourselves, not an egotistic love but a love based on understanding your divine connection to the Lord. If you truly grasp this, you will understand the peace of the Lord, and you will begin each day as if newly born. Each day you will be born again into the Lord. Your slate will be clean and your opportunities endless.

"Rejoice. Behold, the Lord is with you, and you are with the Lord. The connection of love is unbroken. Hold tightly to it, and the divinity within each of you will perform miracles in His name.

"Amen."

"Amen," I answered, suddenly reading the characters written on his robe. But as I write this I do not remember what they said.

Fifty-Eight

I pick a vibrant orange stone. Parts of it are clear glass and the rest just swirls of orange. Usually orange is not a color that I enjoy or wear, but today the stone seems to bring an energy into my hands, an energy into my body. I think of the warmth of a fire, the beating of a heart, the sun setting on a hot July day, and the color brings me warmth and delight.

"Take each day and delight in it," the Archangel says to me. I find myself sitting by the small stream with the snow-capped mountains in the background. The day is warm and the sun shines down on my body.

I sigh. "I don't think you realize that this life isn't as easy as you portray it, that just delighting in the day isn't as simple as the words imply. We have worries, concerns, illness, jobs, and so on, that often deplete us of joy, of this delight."

He is dressed in luminous silver and white robes, and an aura of bright light extends around his body. "Each day is a gift from God. Your soul has requested this gift, and it has been given lovingly to each of you. When your soul, in conjunction with God, decides that this earthly life is no longer where you need to be, you will return. But in the meantime, each day is a gift."

"How can you say that when I just read about someone who's paralyzed from the neck down? How can you still say that is a gift?"

He shook his head and looked at me, and for the first time seemed almost to chastise me. "Each life has a wonderful, fulfilling destiny. Each soul is here to grow and move closer to God, and with each breath you take you have the opportunity to do this. This is a gift more magnificent that you can imagine. The shape, the size, the condition of the body does not matter. The soul is here to move closer to God. If someone is paralyzed, brain-damaged, even in a coma, the soul has still made the decision to stay on earth for a purpose. The soul has still chosen life for a purpose. That is why each day is such a gift, because each day is an opportunity to bring you—or someone else—closer to God."

"Let's talk about the coma victim then."

"Yes. Even though the body is not awake and moving, the soul is still vibrant and still celebrating each day, and the growth of the soul may lie in helping others. The people around the sick person may learn compassion and tenderness, and learn that with unconditional love. Unconditional love and wisdom are all that you can take with you when you return to God. Therefore what a gift that comatose person is giving to another's life. You see from only a small, narrow perspective. You must broaden your perspective and learn to see with the divine guidance of God.

"God's divine guidance sees all and understands the purpose for your journey here, and delights in each opportunity. Whether you perceive it as negative or positive, it is always an opportunity to grow closer to God, and thus help others grow closer to God.

"Remember these words and heed them. Each day, regardless of how you feel in the morning, begin by giving thanks to God for the day, and rejoice in the opportunity that your soul has to return and become one with God. Ask for God's strength and wisdom to follow the soul's pathway home. Thus it shall be given, and you will find delight in the smallest of deeds.

"Amen."

Fifty-Nine

The stone I pick today is lovely, opaque with a stripe of aqua through it. Holding it, rubbing it, I have no idea of the gift this gem signifies.

The Archangel's voice booms from the heavens. I look up and I'm at the beach, and he is descending from the clouds. A bevy of smaller angels is around him, singing in Latin, their voices smooth and clear through the sky. It sounds like Gregorian chant, but lighter, more joyous.

"Each day, each hour, each moment, the gifts are abundant and everlasting. When you ask for a gift and are able to receive it, take the gift God wants you to have," the Archangel said quietly, sitting on the rock by my side. The other angels had disappeared into the sky.

"But I don't know what this gift means," I said quietly.

He looked at me, his dark blue eyes boring into mine. "You always need to know the answers," he said. "Tell the others that the answers are God-given, that it is not always important to understand them, or even to understand the subtlety of the gifts God gives you. But what is important is to open yourselves to being led by God. His gifts to you are the ones that are important to both you and your soul. Your soul understands each and every gift God gives you, and urges you each day to accept them. Many times your humanity gets in the way and you block your soul from accepting God's gifts. You have your own agenda, you have your own plans, and you seek only methods to accomplish those. Listen to these words and heed them: Open your hearts to the Lord. Your soul wants this, and needs this. Your soul can lead you, but your free will can change the course of your lives. If you open your hearts to the Lord, you will choose the path of the soul, and when God gives you a gift, even if you do not know what it is or what it is meant to do, your soul, aided by divine knowledge, will allow you to access the gift and grow from it. You will move forward in God's love and move closer to home."

"So I can accept gifts and not even know it?"

"If, and only if, you are open to having God lead you. This is important for everyone to remember. You must be *open*. You accomplish this through meditation and prayer. When you pray you open yourself and allow your soul to communicate with the Lord and lead you in the correct direction."

"I saw a man on TV last night who said that there are no tragedies. You've talked so much about how the soul decides when to leave, and so on. Do you agree with that?"

The angel sighed. "You see tragedies and you see sorrow. On the human level, yes, of course there are tragedies. A woman's child dies—how can you not grieve? How can you not see the young death as a tragedy? But on the soul level it is not a tragedy. It has a purpose. Everything can turn toward God, and everything can have a purpose—if you choose it, and only if you choose it."

"Well, then we get to evil, evil that you yourself talk about. Evil can make tragedies occur. Someone becomes a robber, a killer. Is that not a tragedy?"

The angel looked at me and said quietly, "Every time anyone turns to evil it is a human tragedy. It is a tragedy of the soul. But what we are saying is that with God, and with your soul's divine wisdom, that tragedy can become a learning tool. It can become a way to move closer to God. But it is the free will of the human being that makes it a tragedy or a triumph."

"So tragedy does exist?"

"Yes," he said. "It exists because evil exists. Let us return to Christ in the desert. He was tempted by Evil Incarnate. Had he used his free will to choose to yield to evil, it would have been a tragedy of huge proportions. But even then, God would have given him the ability, using his human free will, to turn it into something that heads toward Him."

"So you're saying that there are second chances for everyone?"

"Yes," he said. "The chances are infinite. That is what you do not realize. You are all one, yet you are not all learning and moving at the same pace. Christ was evolving as a human and as a divine partaker in God's love, and he chose to give up his life to show others unconditional love. But not all of you are yet capable of that choice. You must open your soul to God's word. Christ opened his heart and soul to God each moment. When he was tempted he turned toward God, not away from Him. That is the essential difference with many of your choices. When faced with suffering and temptation, many of you choose to look away from God. You need only to look at Him, and then the choice you make will be a choice for your soul, and thus a choice for everyone's soul.

"It is a progressive growth of love. It is a divine knowledge that moves through the earth each day, each moment. You need only to grasp it. When Christ cried out, 'Abba, Abba, why have you forsaken me?' he was tempted. His free will was being tested by evil. Satan still wanted Christ to turn from God. But Christ, even in his incredible suffering, knew what many of you do not yet understand: Turn toward God and the suffering becomes a triumph. The tragedy becomes a triumph. If you do not turn toward God, the tragedy takes over.

"But, yes, you will still have other opportunities, because God never abandons you. He is with you each and every moment, always trying to lead you with the conscious agreement of your soul. Listen to your soul each day and you will hear the word of God. Ask your soul to open up to the gifts. Ask the Holy Spirit to bestow knowledge and love upon you, and She will, and the knowledge will be abundant and will change the course of your life, and thus the course of others' lives. Each of you has all of you nearby. Each of your journeys is all of your journeys. The knowledge one has learned can be transferred to another by connecting the souls.

"That is what we will discuss next time: learning from each other's souls, communicating with each other's souls. This has been enough for today."

I heard the angels singing again and was awestruck by the beauty of their voices. They disappeared with him into the clouds.

Sixty

I've picked a white gem again. I keep being reminded that each day is a new day. Each day is a gift from God with opportunities that we must take or we lose them. Yesterday I had a friend on my TV show who spoke about a charity that feeds babies in Bosnia. The strife and chaos there are so rampant that people don't have homes. Families have been separated, and children are in orphanages but can't be adopted because no one knows if their parents are still alive. We have problems here in the United States, but most of us don't have to worry about the basic issues of food, shelter, electricity and heat. Those are daily struggles for many people in other parts of the world.

I look at my white stone again and give thanks to God for letting me understand today that it is a gift from Him.

At the inspirational book club I lead at a local bookstore, I get a variety of participants of all ages. This week I got the youngest one yet. She was 15 but going on 30. She asked the most profound and thought-provoking questions. She was searching and hurt, and yet was still looking toward God for the peace that resides with Him. She gave me so much hope for the future. I thought of the gift of the blank white stone and realized that she had it—whether she realized it or not. I could tell she was from a lower-class minority background, and I thought of other young people with so many more advantages who don't take the time to look for the gifts, to take hold of the gems.

The Archangel greets me on top of a snow-covered mountain. The air is thin, but I no longer worry about earthly illness when I am with him. I breathe deeply, and the air is refreshing, not at all cold as it should be.

"You are learning," he said. "You are learning that to do God's work brings pleasure and confidence."

"Confidence?"

"Yes. Self-esteem comes from loving yourself in a healthy way. That love can arise only when you understand that it is the same love that God gives to you. You can release this love and build your confidence when you tap into God's energy, God's love. When you begin to feel that, and do His work, praying and communicating with Him, you are tapping into a pure and healthy energy, one that revitalizes you and allows you to become the person you want to be.

"Many of the problems of the world are from lack of self-esteem. Wars over land and property are all because people think that having more land and more of what is material makes them more powerful, more confident. Many people who have mental disease have poor self-images from birth. These self-images, reinforced again and again, actually change the chemicals in the body, and then depression and worry set in. Feelings of worthlessness can lead to thoughts of suicide and harm. A large part of this is due to not connecting with the self and realizing that the self is a part of God. When you realize it, confidence and love for self grow and nourish you, and thus you co-partner with God. You work in conjunction with God to spread God's goodness and love. As more and more of your actions spring from love, you begin to see yourself as a vehicle for love—and what could be more wonderful than that?

"Then your self-esteem builds. Not only do you realize that God loves you unconditionally, but you also begin to love yourself unconditionally. You see that you are an instrument of God's work, and in seeing that you begin to understand that no instrument of God's work could possibly be inferior. This concept allows both your body and mind to relax, and allows you to have the peace of accomplishment in knowing that you are doing God's will. After that everything else becomes secondary."

"Where's the line between self esteem and pride?"

"Pride crosses the line," he said with a smile. "But it is a simple line. Pride looks at the accomplishment as solely of your own doing. Self-esteem connects you with your soul and with God. Self-esteem believes you need God; pride forgets that. So pride goeth before the fall, because without God there will be only failure."

"I know men who are successful and boastful and are filled with pride."

"Do not judge them, but remember what I just said. Without God there will be only failure."

"Without God there will be only failure," I repeat.

I'm brought back to my living room, still holding the clean white stone, thanking God for His gifts. From above I hear the angel's voice.

"And with God, there will be only success."

I repeat those words. They bring me comfort.

Sixty-One

I had dreams all night long, odd dreams. I heard somewhere that each person in your dream is actually you. Last night I dreamed of a rather plain woman buying a $17,000 ivory brooch. I stood next to her, first appalled at her buying ivory and then thinking it was unattractive. I asked her what she was doing. She said that her therapist told her to buy something expensive and then she would have better self-esteem.

I told her that in order to have true self-esteem you needed to do something each day that brought you and others closer to God.

She shook her head. She told me she was my age and hadn't achieved anything, but with this brooch people would recognize her and know she was worthwhile.

When I woke up I was very disturbed. I thought of my own struggle each day with the successes of the world versus spiritual successes. I oftentimes seek recognition, not necessarily monetary, but in our society of course recognition is frequently tied in with money. I thought about the inspirational book club I lead, and about filming my little community TV show last Thursday and realizing how many people could be touched by my guests' words. These things are not special and they don't bring me fame, but perhaps they make an impact on others' spiritual lives.

I realized I was the woman with the ivory brooch in the dream. I don't even like ivory, because it comes from killing elephants, yet I bought something I didn't like just to have people pay attention to me. I realized too, in and out of the dream, how unimportant that desire really is.

Usually my dreams are just silly or disturbing, but this one last night truly spoke to me. Thank you, God, for allowing me to listen to Your words. Amen.

Sixty-Two

I usually write and pray in the morning, but somehow the days got away from me this week. When I finally do sit down it's late Friday afternoon, and I wonder if the Archangel comes only in the morning.

I pick a black stone and I cringe, just as people in my audiences do. Black seems to speak of death and evil. But actually, as I've mentioned before, black is the combination of all gifts.

The Archangel is in the bookstore at the arcade. "You worry needlessly," he said.

"Tell me something new," I answered flippantly.

He shook his head. "No, it is not humorous. You worry needlessly about many things, but I am here especially to tell you about your worry concerning God's work. This is true for you, and for others."

My ears perked up, because he was right. I had been worrying. I was worried that I was being lazy, not marketing the second book to publishers—and here I was with a third book. I wondered where he was going with this.

"You worry that these words will not be heard," he said, sitting down next to me on a hunter-green leather ottoman. Today his robes were that color, and his blond hair glinted against the deep green.

"God's words will always be heard and read and understood," he said. "Do not worry about that. You are in a period of cocooning."

"Cocooning?" I queried. I had been feeling as if I were trying to escape, and not doing worthwhile work. People all around me seemed to be "advancing" and I wasn't. I just wrote, prayed, and thought a lot.

"Christ went to the desert for forty days, but remember, for thirty years he did not spread the good news. He did not perform miracles, did not preach, did not tell others of God. He learned, as a human, the feelings of others; he learned as a human the trials and tribulations of dealing with his own feelings; he learned what it was like to face the dark."

"What are you saying?"

"I am saying that many of you who know and listen to God's word go through periods of reflection, of learning to understand your own human nature and that of others. You cannot always go and preach, because you need time to understand who it is that is preaching and to whom you are preaching."

"What?"

"Many of you do not understand yourselves or each other, and without this necessary knowledge you cannot further God's message throughout the world. You need to understand your own human frailties. Christ learned and understood his frailties in those first thirty years, contemplating his humanity and learning from others. He was prepared for his next step—which was the fulfillment of the Scriptures.

"Each of you must take time in your lives and prepare for your next step. For some of you it may be forty years, for some forty days, for some two years. But no one can continue to grow spiritually without stepping back and understanding their own growth, and thus understanding others better. Are you beginning to see what I'm saying?"

"Yes, I think so. I shouldn't feel guilty about stepping back, not always working full throttle at delivering God's message. Rather it is a time to sit back and contemplate, to understand where I've been, what I've learned and what I need to do with it."

He nodded. "This is true for you, and for others. Sometimes you are overwhelmed with these messages and feel compelled to get them out immediately. Immediately has no meaning in the kingdom of God. The disciples described Christ's return as imminent, but for the world it does not seem imminent. Yet in the scheme of time it is."

"Well," I said, still thinking all of this over, "how do I know the difference between sitting and contemplating and learning where to go next, or just being lazy and not doing God's work?"

"You will not have that dilemma if you pray and keep in touch with the Lord. If you don't, evil will step in and laziness will override meditation. But that is not the case here, because you continue to search for God. We want you, and everyone reading this, to think back on something that has occurred this year, something upsetting or disturbing. Now think how you reacted to it this year, and then think how you would have reacted to it three years ago."

I thought of my friend whose car keys I took away when she had had a few too many drinks. I pray for her each day, and yet she still won't talk to me.

"And three years ago?" he asked.

"I would have been angry."

"Would you have been praying for her?"

225

"I doubt it."

"Then you have grown. Give this task to everyone who reads this, and those who have been touched by the messages, touched by God's word, will see advancement in their spiritual life. That is the only important task you are to achieve here on earth: to advance toward God in prayer and love."

"So I'm not lazy?"

"No," he laughed. "It is your cocooning time. But rest assured, the Lord has plans that are mighty for you and for these messages. Enjoy this time growing because soon you will be out in the world again—as will each of you who progresses.

"Amen."

"Thank you," I said.

"Do not thank me. Thank the One who sent me. Let the others realize that time spent with God, time growing, time resting in the spirit and nourishing your body and soul, is time that gives you strength to move closer to the Lord."

Sixty-Three

Today's stone is clear. Feeling it, looking at it, I realize—for some unknown reason—that I'm approaching a change in my life, that the view of the road will be getting clearer.

"You are," the Archangel said softly. We were sitting on a log near a stream. It was early morning, before the sun had fully risen. I looked up at the large trees surrounding us. Staring down at me was a white owl.

He was beautiful, and I stared back.

"You have been surrounded with owls from the time you were a young girl," the Archangel said. "Even as a child you knew that it was important to see in the darkness. You knew that the darkness held answers, and if you could see in the darkness you would find your own light.

"That is what people do not understand. If you do not get stuck in the darkness, it too serves a purpose, because when you are faced with the darkness and you allow yourself to see in it, you access your own light. The light of God shines within you and around you, the Christ-Light. Thus the darkness becomes light, and you learn and grow and see your spirit moving toward the Lord.

"Do not fear the darkness. Only be afraid of staying in it. The darkness is fear, anxiety, and alienation from God. For some it is suffering and not being able to escape that suffering. But when you use your inner light, which all of you have access to through your soul, you will see in the darkness. You will bring your own light to the darkness, and you will not be lost. You will head onto the pathway home."

"Can you explain that in simple terms?" I requested, still staring at the white owl. It had moved its head, almost all around, apparently at a rustle or noise that was inaudible to me.

"In suffering you see only darkness. Many of you do not understand that this suffering may bring you to growth."

"What about people terribly sick with cancer?"

"Yes, that is a darkness, a difficult period in their lives. They face suffering, and for some perhaps death. Yet instead of being frightened of this dark place, if you access the light in your soul, if you access your connection with God, you will lighten the darkness. You will be able to understand the darkness and thus it cannot conquer you. You will shine light upon the depths of darkness, and you will learn, and understand, and you will know the spiritual purpose for visiting that place."

"And this light is God?"

"This light is your own light, accessed from God. God will not light the darkness for you unless you ask, unless you want to learn, unless you access your own spirit in conjunction with the Lord's. When you do you will grow. What many of you still do not understand is that your soul each day searches for a way to fulfill its mission. Many times you stop it, or others stop it, and the soul has to keep trying. When it is faced with darkness, whether through evil or isolation or sickness, the soul can grow by shining the light and understanding its pathway, understanding the reason it has met the unknown. But unless you communicate with your soul, and thus with God, the light will not shine in the darkness. Many of you find yourself stuck in a dark, terrifying, isolated place, a place alienated from the light of the Lord.

"Do you understand that?"

"If I do, what I understand is that we hold the power to change the course of our lives, the power to overcome the darkness as if we have a built-in flashlight, but most of the time we don't even turn it on."

He nodded. "You hold the power, in conjunction with the strength of the Lord. You access God's strength and you are a co-creator with Him, and thus you find love and learning in all opportunities. Christ was faced with the darkness, with temptation, with Satan, many times. But in each case he did not stay in the darkness. Instead he prayed, accessed the strength of his Father, and connected that strength with his own soul. Thus he brought light to the world. That is why he is called the Light of the World, because he came into a dark place and was not consumed with it. He found it, faced it, and brought the light of the Lord and the light of his soul with him to the earth.

"Since he was also human, he was tempted, as you all are, and struggled with not getting caught up in a dark, isolated place. But he knew that he had the ability to shine a light, to learn and grow, and to bring others to God.

"Not only is he the light of the world, but all of you, too, are the lights of the world. But you need to access this light from the Father. Then you will overcome the evil and alienation from God by conquering the fear of the unknown.

"Amen."

Sixty-Four

I pick a rough yellow stone. Feeling its texture I lift it up to the light, and I see it's all marred with scratches, and has a large indentation in the middle.

The Archangel and I meet at the beach. It is deserted and cold and the sand drifts are snowy. Bundling up, although I am not chilled, I climb the rock to meet him and settle down next to him. He is dressed in magnificent hues of purple and blue, his robes not even moving in the wind. He looks at me and says, "Why do you not like the gift God has given you?"

"The stone?" I ask, my fingers still rubbing it. "I don't know. It's not as pretty as the others. It has imperfections. It's not clear. Usually when I get yellow, I think of hope, of happiness, of sunshine. But this seems muted."

"You have made it muted," he says, in the closest to a stern voice I have ever heard from him.

"What do you mean?"

"Many of you are given the gifts of God. But you don't see them for what they are. You choose to take only the ones you think you need. We have gone over this again and again, but it is important for all of you to realize it, to learn it, and to understand it deeply in your soul. The stone you received today is perfect for you."

"No, it's not perfect."

"It is perfect for *you*," he said quietly.

"What do you mean?"

"You, and many others, try to have control over every aspect of your lives, and when you don't have control, you feel helpless and lacking in self-esteem. You want a clear, bright yellow stone that signifies happiness to you. But God has given you a stone that is perfect in itself. It is not clear, and it has imperfections, but those are what you need in order to learn and grow. You have made it even more muted by not being able to clearly see the gift's purpose, the purpose of getting past your judgments, getting past your own blockages and moving on toward the gift itself."

I held the stone to the sun. "But look—you can't see clearly through it. It has all these dark dots in it, and a crack inside."

"And you think the gift of happiness is always just given clearly?"

"What do you mean?"

"I mean that you ask for happiness, or some other gift from God, and expect it to drop upon you freely and completely. Many of you still do not understand that you are co-creators with God, co-creators in your life. Happiness does not just happen. It occurs because you take action, because you move toward God and toward others and find that happiness. You cannot expect that God will just bestow happiness upon you. It is you and God together who find happiness and fulfillment in your life.

"Do you understand this?"

"I'm not sure. I've been given gifts of happiness before."

"And those gifts were given and available to you because you took action. You accepted them, and allowed the happiness to come into your life because of the actions you had taken to achieve that happiness."

"You're telling me that this stone with all its imperfections brings happiness?"

"I'm telling you that having imperfections in life *is* life, that this earth is a learning tool for you. Those imperfections you find in your life every day are lessons to help you grow and change and move toward God. The key is how you face those imperfections. You can face them and think of them as imperfections. Or you can face them and realize that without them you would not be able to embrace the gift, and thus the imperfections become perfections.

"What we are saying is that much of your life is in your attitude toward it, in how you perceive the obstacles. If you see them as learning opportunities, you and God create wonderful pathways toward paradise, wonderful opportunities to help others. You see the 'imperfections' as necessary, as important for your growth. Therefore when you receive a gift from God and it is 'not perfect' in your eyes, realize that all gifts from God are perfect. It is how you accept and work with them, how you embrace and learn from them that is the important part. God's plan is perfect, as are His gifts. So embrace each one. When you see 'an imperfection' realize that it is not what it appears to be. Rather it is a gift for growing and moving toward God.

"When you accept this, in conjunction with the Lord, you will be able to access the gift in its entirety. You will be able to move and grow toward God."

I looked at the stone. Suddenly the imperfections took on a new light. I didn't necessarily want or need a stone that was clear and beautiful and smooth. One that was rough had lessons for me to learn. I realized happiness could not just be taken—it had to be achieved through my own works and attitude too.

"Amen," the angel said, smiling. "You are beginning to take responsibility, to understand the need for growth, the reason to grow. The more you understand this, the more you will be able to become one with the gifts. Accept them, and learn from them. Remember each gift from God is perfect. It is your viewing of the gift that stops you from accepting it.

"You may pray for one particular gift—say, strength—and God sends you compassion. But if you do not access the compassion, you will never learn the strength. God, in conjunction with your soul, sends what you need.

"Please, please," he implored, "realize this and accept each gift from God each day.

"Amen."

Sixty-Five

I'm home sick with a cold and the congested headache that goes along with it, and what I used to term as a child a draggy feeling. I prayed this afternoon, but even that was not whole-hearted. I had to keep stopping myself from falling asleep.

Although I usually do it in the morning, this evening I pick a gem. It's a Caribbean blue that reminds me of Bermuda, where we were lucky enough to go on our honeymoon. (I ended up with coral burns down my thigh from a moped accident, and in a separate bed for the rest of our stay, but that's another story.) The gem's color is like the ocean there, a beautiful clear blue, warm and comforting and inviting, not deep and dark like the Atlantic portion that comes onto the beaches of Rhode Island.

The Archangel arrives, dressed in a golden robe, and extends his hand to me. I take it and find myself in the bookstore of the arcade.

"When you are physically low," he said, "when you are ill or sad, your body's memories take over. You remember, unknowingly, other times of illness or sadness or fear, and those emotions—whether you are cognizant of them or not—begin to filter through your body, and to affect your immune system."

"I just have a cold," I said, trying to be light-hearted about it. "But of course I'm afraid of anything that might go into my chest and trigger my asthma. After last winter I don't want to take antibiotics ever again if I don't have to, so even a cold triggers some fear for me."

"It doesn't matter if it's a cold or something more serious," he said. "Your body in its deepest cells remembers fear. Fear comes with illness or depression, or any time that your body is not functioning at its healthiest."

"So what do we do?" I asked.

He looked toward the stone I was holding in my hand. "God gave you this stone today for a variety of reasons. Each of you must accept the gifts God gives you. What does that blue gem mean to you?" he asked.

"It reminds me of the warm ocean."

"Tell me."

"The ocean in Bermuda that day was so warm it was as if we were walking into bathwater. The sun shined down on us, and the saltiness of the water buoyed us, and I could have stayed there all day. I was peaceful and content and nothing else seemed important."

"You were grateful?"

"Yes, very."

"Remember this—you were grateful for the moment. How many times can you remember being grateful and enjoying the moment?"

He knew me too well. I was grateful a lot, but I didn't always enjoy the moment. When I was resting I'd feel guilty. When I was working with a cold and should be getting rest, I'd feel guilty. I struggled to enjoy the moments of life.

"Not many," I said sadly. "But I am grateful."

"Yes," he said, "but you rush through the moments. You rush through the minutes that are there only for the day.

"This stone was given to you for a variety of reasons, but the most important today is to access memories of gratitude and happiness. When you are ill your body remembers fear, and thus your immune system is affected. When you access memories of happiness, gratitude and contentment, your body believes that. The chemicals of such feelings run through your body and help to fight disease and fear."

"That sounds just a little New Age-y or something," I said.

"Why?" he asked. "Many of you still do not realize Christ's words: Heaven is on earth. You think heaven is in the beyond, but heaven is obtainable each day. You hold the keys to the kingdom of God, and you don't even realize it. It is such a gift, but it goes unused. You have all the knowledge you need but you have locked it up and submerged yourselves in the material. When you access the emotions of gratitude, love, happiness, they generate into the material. Your body feels it and responds positively, and your immune system becomes stronger."

"So I'm supposed to think of happy things?"

"Think of that ocean. Think of the feeling of safety and warmth. Remember your gratitude for being there that day, and understand that. Take it into your soul, and your body too will change.

"Take hold of each moment, good or bad, and realize that it is the only moment that you have. Relish it and understand that the experience is for your growth. When you are ill, you can rest, replenish yourself, pray and learn to access the positive memories of your body.

"Tell everyone to list positive, heartwarming, grateful times in their lives. List them now, before you need them, so you can access them when necessary. Just listing them will change your body, your mood, and your spirit. When you tap into the divine creation, when you tap into the memories of happiness, of love, you become one with them. You take energy from them. The same is true of memories of fear and anxiety and hatred. When you tap into these memories, you become one with them. Your body becomes one with them. The fear runs through your body, and it begins to break down not only your spirit but also your physical body.

"Understand that you are a co-creator with God, and when you access the divine creation, you access the gifts of God. You access God's energy and love. This can also be done through memory techniques."

"What if someone doesn't have wonderful memories? What if a child has been ignored or molested, and as they grow they can't access memories of love and kindness? Then how do they ever connect with the Divine Creator?"

"That is where the circle of souls is of utmost importance. You are your brother's keeper. Christ came to earth to save each of you, and you came to earth to save each of you. You are all on the same mission of love. If someone is immersed in the darkness so deeply that it becomes evil, only the love and prayers of his neighbors can allow him to find new experiences, to make new memories. Do you understand this?"

"What about you? Can't you help? You're an angel."

"Angels are messengers of God. We cannot interfere with free will without the person's consent, conscious or unconscious. Therefore, although we can aid a person in darkness, we need the prayers of his neighbors to allow him to let us into his life, to let the Lord into his life. Do you understand this?"

"I think so. What you're saying is that some people are in such darkness they can't see the light, and it is for us to pray for them to see light so that they can make the right choices with their free will."

"Yes, and it is not some people, it is all people. Each of you in your lifetime has been in darkness or will be faced with darkness, and some of you will not be able, on your own, to turn toward the light. The prayers of your brothers and sisters return you to the light. Christ is your brother, and he too is praying for you. He sacrificed his life to teach you true love, true compassion. Compassion is God. And you are Christ's sister. You are God's child. This love and compassion is accessible to you if you only reach out for it. When you do, it will be like an everlasting well. It will never run dry, and the water will be fresh and clear and nourishing to your soul.

"Go now. Hold your stone and think grateful, kind, happy thoughts. Allow your body to remember the goodness and allow your body to heal. By remembering moments of wonder, you are remembering God's gifts to you and accessing them. Then those gifts change your body.

"Amen."

Sixty-Six

I haven't sat down and meditated in a while. This is the Lenten season and I've been praying novenas, but of course I realize that's a different form of prayer. It's more "listing" than listening. I need to listen. I know that.

I sit down, pray and pick a gem. Initially I'm very disappointed. It's dark, deep blue and rough, with a chip out of it. As I hold it in my hand it seems depressing, as if sea waves have battered and cracked it and made it old. Lifting it to the light I see it in a new perspective. The color lightens and it's much prettier. When I hold it vertically it looks like an Easter egg, changing from dark blue to almost powder blue.

The Archangel returns. We are at the beach.

"We have gone through this before, but many of you do not grasp it," he said.

"Grasp what?" I asked, but I almost knew what he was going to say.

"You are given a gift from God, and you don't accept it. You don't take the time to savor it and understand it, and so you judge it automatically. Because it does not seem to be what you've prayed for, what you've imagined, you dismiss it. None of you even see it as a gift from God. There is beauty all around you and yet you do not see it. There is heaven on earth, and yet in your limited view you are blind to it."

I looked down, holding my stone.

"That gift represents many things today. For you it represents a new perspective. God wants you to have a new perspective on His world. When you picked that gem you thought it looked sea-worn and chipped and dark. You do not yet understand that all of you requested this voyage. All of you requested the dark and turbulent times of this life in order to grow and to learn. You have been tumbled about in the sea of life, been chipped and cracked, and yet you never look beyond that. You never hold yourselves up to the light and see the beauty of what you are and the beauty of what you have learned."

"You mean I'm the gem?"

"The gem today is a metaphor for you and for many of the others. You do not remember choosing this journey, but you did because at that time you could see the larger picture and you realized the need for growth and moving back to God. But now when you think you're battered and bruised, and are perhaps in a dark place, you no longer see the beauty of the journey. You get caught in the tumbling of the sea of life and forget that when you arrive at the shore, and are held up to the light, you are radiant from God's love and light. You forget that the lessons you have learned, although you perceive them as difficult, are truly lessons that you need in order to understand and have compassion for yourselves and your neighbors. You have grown through being tossed about on the sea of life. Do you understand that?"

I looked at my stone and held it up to the heavens. It looked even more radiant here by the beach than it had in my home. I no longer noticed the chip, or the roughness. It appeared smooth and beautiful. The light shone through it and the color was iridescent.

"I'm sorry," I said. "Is that how God sees us?"

"When you have finished with this sea of life and have returned home to His shore, you will be held up to the light. You will absorb the light and become a conduit for it. You can do this now, on earth, but many of you do not realize it. You are a co-creator with God of beauty, love and compassion. You need only to access God's strength and energy for wondrous things to occur. But in this material world you often forget to look toward the light. You are immersed in the storm of the sea, not realizing that the storm serves a purpose, that the yin and yang of life is the reason you are here. You are here to choose light. You are here to grow into love. God is love, and you are His children. Therefore you are love. But you have buried that love, and forgotten it, and have become immersed in small and petty things.

"God wants you each to receive a gift of perspective. He wants each of you to look at yourselves in His light, not in the critical, judgmental way that you usually see yourselves. You must start this today, and wondrous things will happen.

"You will see yourself for what you are: a child of God, loved unconditionally and without judgment. When you understand this deep in your soul, you will be able to teach it to others. You will be able to impart God's wisdom to others, and they will be able to help you. When you see it in yourselves, seeing it in others comes easily. You often say that you are less judgmental with others than you are with yourself. But if you can see that God loves you wholly and totally, you will find it even easier to love others with that same mindset. It will become like breathing. You will separate the deed from the soul, and see only the beauty of the soul.

"Go. Take the stone. Remember your first impression of it, and realize that for many of you that is your impression of yourselves. Then hold the stone to the light, and hold yourself to the light, and you will see the beauty God created in each of you. This beauty shows itself only through the journey of learning, through understanding the lessons you have chosen. It can be learned and absorbed only from the tumbling of life, like the tumbling of a stone in the sea.

"Go, blessing yourself and blessing the world, understanding that God is with you all the time. Pray. Pray. Pray.

"Amen."

Sixty-Seven

I was up half the night with horrendous cramps and am exhausted this morning. I was supposed to have a lunch with a friend but I was nauseated too, so I cancelled. Really, the last thing I feel like doing is sitting at my desk and praying, but somehow I feel that's when I need to do it the most. I pick a clear gem this morning. Because I feel so tired and beaten down, I don't know, or even honestly try to find out, what it means.

I close my eyes in prayer and find myself in a busy mall, with stores everywhere. It is a typical American mall, not the arcade where I'm used to meeting the Archangel, where we have the entire building and all of the stores to ourselves.

I stand still in the midst of mothers pushing strollers, people jostling past me, and I feel lost. What am I doing here? I'm not even much of a shopper; ordering from catalogs or online is more my style. Why would I ever be sent here during a meditation? I walk alone through the crowds and sit quietly on a bench outside a young-teen dress shop.

I feel a presence next to me and I'm somewhat startled to see the Archangel has joined me. "Can they see you?" I ask.

"No," he said. "Many of them could if they were receptive to it. But in a place such as this people are rarely receptive to the unknown. They are concerned with schedules, material things, their own agendas, so they bypass all the beauty of the world as they hurry along on a human treadmill of life."

"A human treadmill of life?" I liked the sound of it—not the meaning, but the sound. So often, I think, many of us feel we're on a treadmill, going nowhere but hurrying faster and faster.

"Do they see me?"

"Not right now," he said, "because you are with me, and it would seem odd to them that you were talking to air. So you are invisible to them."

"Oh, thanks," I said, thinking that would be all I need, to have people recognize me at the mall, sitting alone and talking intently to a blank seat. He nodded.

"Why are we here?" I asked.

"You picked a clear stone today, and you didn't even have the energy to pray for its meaning. You didn't even understand that God has given you another gift for the day. You put it aside, concerned only with your tiredness, your pain."

I rolled my eyes. I knew it wasn't polite, but sometimes I really thought he just didn't understand. "You don't get it even yet," I said. "After all these years talking to me, you still are dense about this human body. It gets tired, it gets sick, and when it does people lose interest in other things. They need to rest. The body is connected to the mind, you know." My voice was rising and I stopped. Even though he had told me that no one in the mall saw us, I felt I was speaking too loudly.

"Yes, I know that the body is connected to the mind. I have told you that before. But what you are missing is that the mind is connected to the body."

I must have looked puzzled.

"You are telling me that if your body is tired, your mind becomes tired. Change it!" he said, as if finally giving me an order rather than just continuing to make suggestions.

"Change what?"

"Change your mind. Take it and use it conversely. If your body can make your mind uninterested, your mind can make your body interested. Sexuality is an example of this. Oftentimes your body wants to be close to another person, but it is your mind that makes that decision. Your mind can also stop that decision, and then your body loses interest. This is a very animalistic example, but it works on all levels.

"If your body is tired, you—and you alone—make your mind tired.

"Conversely, if you decide to keep your mind enlightened, alive and energetic, that power will move toward your body."

My shoulders slumped. I knew my words would sound like whining, but I had to say them. "But I was physically ill last night. The cramps were so bad I was doubled up. I'm exhausted from being up all night, and of course my mind just wants to let my body rest. What's so wrong with that?"

"Nothing," he said softly. "But you must also see clearly. Take the gem that was given to you today and understand that your mind can control your body. Your mind can control your pain and your tiredness. We are not saying that when your body is tired or ill you should not rest. That is far from what we are saying. We are saying that many of you live by your body's actions and reactions to life, and allow your mind to follow your body. You must learn to allow your mind to lead your body in many instances. When you have done this you will understand that there is a balance, and the balance is a trinity: your soul, your mind, and your body. Each of them should balance the others for this earthly journey. Your physical needs are important—sleep, food, exercise. Your intellectual needs are important, being able to thrive and grow and understand. Your spiritual needs, your soul work, is the third element in this journey. On other planes you will have your soul, which will have taken the knowledge of the body and the mind and incorporated it, and moved on. But here on this earth you need to integrate all three.

"Go. See clearly and understand this. Amen."

"Amen," I said, not yet seeing it clearly, and definitely not understanding it.

Sixty-Eight

I pick a white gem. This morning a friend came over and I read aloud from this book to her. It always amazes me that even though I've transcribed it, it sounds new to me each time I reread it, as if I hadn't heard the words and concepts before. My friend agreed. It seems we need to hear the instructions from the Lord again and again. Otherwise they don't become part of our lives.

I look at the white stone that sits on top of my computer. It always reminds me of new beginnings, a clean slate.

"Each day is a new beginning," the Archangel says quietly. We are sitting in the bookstore in the glass arcade, surrounded by leather-bound books. I am sitting on an ottoman and he is in a large wing-backed chair. His burgundy and gold robes match the leather of the chair.

"We have told you that before, but many of you forget it. You carry your worries, your concerns, and your mistakes from yesterday into today. Thus you become overburdened with unnecessary luggage, and your souls are buried in the midst of it."

"It's hard to just start each day new," I said. "There are uncompleted things from the day before. Life doesn't start new each day. We still have to follow through and make plans for the future. You don't understand that because you don't have to do it."

"Not only is each day new," he said, seeming to ignoring my comment, "but each moment is new. Each second is new, a gift from God. That is the only moment of life you have, the one that is now. God said that He is the alpha and the omega. He is the circle of life. The moment you are living in is also the beginning and the end. Each moment is a moment unto itself. If you waste it, it is gone forever. But each moment holds an incredible potential. It is a microcosm of your day, of your week, your month, year, and life. Each has a beginning and an end. When you realize this, you begin to understand that each moment is precious and a gift from God. A moment is not to waste."

"That puts a lot of pressure on us," I said, "because if you haven't noticed already, people are running around like chickens with their heads cut off. People are stressed out and packing everything into the day and night, trying to do too many jobs. Women are mothers, workers, wives; they leave a workday job to come home to another job. Each moment is too filled."

The Archangel shook his head. "There is a difference between filling the moments and grasping the moments. Grasping the moments means savoring each one. That is where many of you lose your lives. You fill each day, hurrying on to the next moment, never truly in the moment that is NOW. In filling them up with things of the world, you lose the value of the gift of life. You lose your lives by always looking ahead to the future. 'Next year, when I have a baby...next year, when we buy a house...next month when I get a raise,' —always humanity is thinking of the future. We are not saying that you should not plan for the future, because that is important. But what we are saying is that too many of you are planning the future and losing the present. You live in the future, which may or may not come. If it does it may not hold the happiness you thought it would, and so you have to plan again for the future. Each time you do this, you lose the moment, you lose the hour, you lose the gift of the present that God has given you.

"Pray to live and understand God's gift of life. Do not fill it up with busywork and think you are living in the moment. At the end of the day you need to know that day was a gift from God. How did you move closer to God and your fellow humanity? If you did not do that you wasted your day. You lost your gift.

"That is the test. If you have moved closer to God or helped someone else move closer to God, you have used the gift of the present day the way it was meant to be used.

"Amen."

"Amen," I said, thinking of all my wasted days.

"Do not berate yourself," he said. "Each day is a new beginning. Do not carry the guilt of what you did not understand over to the present and into the future, because you understand it now. Leave it behind and begin again."

Looking down at the white stone I am so grateful that each day, each moment, is a blank slate that God gives us to start anew.

Sixty-Nine

I don't particularly like the colored gem I picked today. It's large and metallic-looking, somewhere between coral and orange. It means nothing to me and doesn't seem to give me any comfort.

The Archangel appears in the bookstore in the crystal arcade. He is sitting behind a large mahogany desk, his hands folded on top of it. Today he is wearing a dark red robe with golden threads running through it. His golden hair, which falls past his shoulders, is the same color as the threads. He looks at me, almost sternly.

"Have I not told you before that every gift from God is needed?"

I shrugged my shoulders. "Yes, but I don't even know what this means. It's not particularly pretty and it holds no meaning for me."

"In lectures across the country you tell people to pray in order to listen to God and understand the meaning of the gem, understand the gifts He wants to give you, and yet today you do not listen to that advice yourself."

I looked away, not wanting to admit he was right.

"Each gift from God is a beautiful one. What many of you do not understand, nor see, is that a gift may not appear to be a gift. Some of you have asked for learning experiences that are difficult and hard, but knowing this you will grow and your soul will move toward God."

"We asked for difficult experiences?"

"Someone who studies in school and continues to pursue an education continues to move onward, taking courses that are difficult and challenging. Sometimes these courses are pleasant and sometimes they are not. But they are essential for what you need to learn for your goal. Such is this course of life. Before your earthly birth you chose lessons, and although sometimes those lessons are not exactly the 'courses' you chose, because your free will and that of others have changed matters, your soul will attach itself to the 'course' most needed at the time, the course that most fits your original learning objective. Oftentimes it is difficult, yet you need to understand that each course, each gift, is a life-giving experience, and by embracing it with joy will move you toward God. That is the entire objective of being on earth."

"I went to a lecture the other night," I interrupted. "It was about the

Garden of Eden and how God didn't want us to eat of the Tree of Knowledge. After we did He said, 'Now you will be like us.' What did He mean? The professor said perhaps He meant that with knowledge we would know about good and evil and be like the serpent and God. Or does it mean more than that? And why did he put the Tree of Knowledge there if He knew us so well?"

Rising from his chair, the angel moved from behind the desk and stood near a floor-to- ceiling bookshelf.

"When God created you, humanity, He wanted you to be co-creators of the world with Him. He wanted to be able to give His love to you and have you understand it and appreciate it. The only way to do this was through free will. The only way to truly be like God is to have the wisdom of the Holy Spirit, because, as we have said many times, wisdom brings compassion, love and understanding. It also brings the ability to distinguish evil from goodness, and fear from love. Therefore the Tree of Knowledge was imperative for your free will. God knew that Eve would eat from the fruit, just as He knows all of His children. The Scriptures seem to imply that God was surprised, but He was not. He knew, just as a loving mother knows a child, what humanity would do when tempted by evil. Once humanity succumbed to evil, it also learned that evil existed. Thus it became aware of fear and evil, love and hate. The road to wisdom must start with the knowledge that you need to embrace and learn. And so your journey began.

"If you did not have the opportunity to choose, as God chooses, you would not be co- creators with Him. As He sent Christ to the earth to do His work, He sends you to the earth to do his work. Each of you is here to do His work, to create with Him a learning-filled and wisdom-filled earth, an earth that embraces love and forgoes fear.

"Do you understand this?"

"I'm not sure."

"As you learn, you learn to move away from fear and evil and move closer to God. You move closer to your initial state of paradise, but this time it's because you have chosen it! You have chosen it with knowledge and wisdom, and therefore can be partners with God in helping to bring others along to Him, on many different levels."

"Isn't it sacrilegious to say we're co-creators with God?"

"When Christ said, 'You will do this and much more than I,' was he being sacrilegious? No. He was telling you that when you are with God, you take in His energy and can perform His miracles. It is opening yourselves up to this energy that is essential, through lessons you have chosen and petitions you pray, and meditation when you listen to God speaking to you."

"Thank you," I said, wondering what exactly I was thanking him for. It seemed to me that he was talking about a life before our birth, where we chose our birth and our lessons. That seemed very difficult to understand.

"You are all one. When Adam and Eve chose the Tree of Knowledge, you chose the Tree of Knowledge. You were there in the garden. And God knew of each choice. It was planned, only because He loves you so. He wanted you to understand and reap the rewards of wisdom."

"But you—you have wisdom, don't you?"

"Yes," he said. "But ours is not the same kind of wisdom that you will acquire. Christ's wisdom is beyond us. Because we chose to stay with God we understand some of His plan. But humanity will have profound wisdom because of the experiences they have chosen to bring into their souls. What you have learned through experience becomes richer.

"Amen."

What you have learned through experience becomes richer, I repeated in my mind. I liked that line; it seemed to say so much, so simply. Somehow it gave me comfort because it made me think that experiences, no matter how difficult, are always rich, if we so choose.

I found myself back at the computer, repeating the line again. My prayer today is that I embrace the experiences, and become rich with wisdom. And that is my prayer for all of us. Amen.

Seventy

I was lucky enough to go on a cruise from New York to the Caribbean and back. Each time the large cruise ship docked or left a port, I watched from the deck as a small tugboat, barely discernible in the sea, came up and pushed or pulled us in the direction the captain needed to go. When it left us, its job done, it signaled three times, and our large ship then did the same. In response the tugboat signaled once, and we signaled once. I have no idea what the signals meant in navigational terms, but to me, leaning over the rails to see the little boat, they had their own meaning. The three signals from the tiny boat seemed to say, "I've done my job. Everything's okay at this end." Our ship's deep bellowing return meant, "Yes, all set on this end too." Then tugboat's single signal said, "Bye," and our response was, "Thanks for the help!"

Every time I saw this scene it had a profound effect on me. Here we were on one of the largest cruise ships in the world, maybe twelve stories high, and we desperately needed a tiny little tugboat to push or pull us. It seems almost miraculous that such a small boat can lead a giant ship to the sea. Yet it does.

As I watched the tiny tugboat disappear from view, I would say a silent prayer. Many times in our lives we struggle to be the glittering cruise ship, the biggest, the best, the one that can be seen from afar. But without this small tugboat the cruise ship would never be able to dock or head out to sea. I think this has a message for us. Oftentimes we berate ourselves, thinking we're not good enough, not smart enough, not producing enough. Yet the tiny, almost comical-looking tugboat is essential to the grand ship.

I thanked God for the realization that came upon me. In life I no longer wanted to be the glittering star. I wanted—and needed—to be the tugboat, small, efficient, knowing its job and doing it each day with joy. I thought of the teaching in *Songs of the Soul* that the ripple effect of our daily actions is so important that one tiny deed can have profound effects on people we don't even know.

So with humility I accept this lesson I have needed to learn, that I would be honored to be a tugboat in life. No longer longing for accolades, I want simply to do my best, to do what God has asked me to do with my life, and continue to do it, regardless of where I am led. Lord, allow me to be your tugboat.

Seventy-One

Today I pick a sunny yellow stone. It means nothing to me except to remind me that today is sunny and very hot for May, over ninety degrees. I've already decided I've had enough of summer and want to snuggle up in the house with a fire going. But I'm sure if I looked back to January, I was complaining about the cold days when I had to walk the dog.

I close my eyes and find myself sitting on top of a warm rock on the familiar beach, which today is more crowded than I've ever seen it. It's packed with people, but of course I know they cannot see either the Archangel or me.

The Archangel, in a light orange robe, sits next to me. I don't recall ever having seen that color on him before, and I wonder if it means anything.

"No," he answers, reading my thoughts. "Nothing except that all colors are gifts from God, and are beautiful. Enjoy them and relish their beauty. Many of you are always questioning, always wanting to know what something means, always asking, what is the real meaning of this? During all this pondering you often miss the meaning of it—to just enjoy it and the moment.

"We have told you many times to bless the oatmeal, and what that really means is to take time with each task and give thanks for it, being grateful for that moment, asking God to let it bring you closer to Him. All of this is so important. You all hurry and worry about the future, expecting it to be there for you. God has given you this moment, nothing more, nothing less. You harp on past mistakes and worry about future concerns, and forget to be in the moment, which is all you have. Rejoice in the moment."

I sighed. He had told me this before, and of course I remembered it for a minute or two but then forgot it. He was right, at least in my case. I often hurried through the moment in order to get to the next moment. I had forgotten to feel pleasure and gratitude in making my husband's oatmeal in the morning. Then I heard of a woman so stricken with MS she could not even lift a spoon to her mouth, and I bowed my head in humility, so grateful was I to be able to get out of bed and make oatmeal.

"Why do we forget some of these lessons?" I asked. "When I was so sick with my liver problem, I vowed that when I got better I would never take anything for granted again. Going to the grocery store would become a joy, because for months I couldn't do it. And at first it was, but gradually I began to forget."

"You are hard on yourself," the Archangel said. "You have progressed. You may forget the lessons sometimes, but on the whole you have changed since that illness. You are much more grateful for your health. But it is a human condition. You progress and then you move backwards somewhat when you forget. But still, when you face God, you are always moving forward, as if a silent conveyor belt is moving beneath your feet, bringing you closer to God. You may step back, but still the belt moves forward."

I nodded. "So what do we do?"

"Pray in thanksgiving, pray in adoration, pray to understand your lessons. We have heard many of you question: How do I know if I'm going in the right direction, if I don't know my path?"

"Yes," I said, "a lot of people ask me that."

"They will know, because the path will continue to move toward God. They will discover, if they take the time to listen to their souls, a deep silence within them and a peace they did not have before. Many of their worries will be gone. It does not have to be an earth-shaking experience, which is what many of you are seeking. When you are aligned with God, in your heart you will know it. You will know you are doing your best in finding and fulfilling your path. It will speak to you in the depths of the night. You will listen to the Word in your dreams as you sleep. You will understand your neighbor more fully. When you receive this wisdom from the Holy Spirit you will be enveloped in love.

"Amen."

Seventy-Two

I've picked a yellow stone quite often recently, and as I reflect on it I think my attitude toward life is changing. I'm feeling better emotionally and more optimistic. (But I know myself—if something were to befall me, would I be so "sunny"?) I just finished reading C.S. Lewis' *Screwtape Letters*, letters from a Senior Devil, Screwtape, to Wormwood, his nephew and prodigy devil. The book was interesting because everything is backwards. "The Enemy" is God, and evil is good. The letters instruct the young devil how to entrap a soul and bring it to Hell. Oddly enough they say that bringing someone to evil is a slow, gradual, and subtle process. Screwtape chastises his nephew when he allows the "client" to take a walk in the woods, or read a book he enjoys—because it is the simple pleasures that bring him back to "The Enemy," to our God. Screwtape wants the client to read books he doesn't enjoy in order to impress others. He also talks of despair and encouraging the client to while away time doing nothing, because boredom offers evil such a quick entry.

The Archangel appears to me on the deserted beach. "You enjoyed the book, I understand," he said, as we watched the waves crash onto the sands. On this foggy day I loved sitting here with him admiring the view, which seemed even more expansive than usual. Even through the mist I could see a ship outlined in the far distance.

"Yes," I replied. "Sometimes we think evil is large and looming, and that we will realize it the minute we see it, but that doesn't seem to be the case."

He shook his head. "I have told you before that evil is insidious. It creeps up when you least expect it, and then you don't realize it."

"Even in boredom?" I asked.

"Especially in boredom," he replied. "Think of all the young teenagers who find themselves bored. Many are bored because their parents are not home when they return from school. They don't have the opportunity to discuss the day immediately, when it is fresh with them. They have no real instruction or direction, and instead of doing their work they let themselves be bored. So they call each other, and soon boredom leads to bad behaviors, to taking drugs and fighting and so

251

on. All of this is the Devil subtly walking in on families. When family communication breaks down, evil steps in. It is simple then for evil to make more inroads, paths that are not even recognized.

"Boredom is not an option. Tell the others that boredom is an opportunity for evil."

"What's the difference between boredom and resting?" I asked. "Is taking a nap boredom?"

"When you are tired your body needs to refuel. That is nourishing. When you are not tired but can think of nothing else to do, it becomes boredom. Boredom is unacceptable."

"To God?"

"To yourselves. Remember, as a soul before you arrived on earth, you had a plan, a destination and a path. All of this you wanted to follow so you could learn the lessons you needed for this road. When you do not follow your innate plan, you are missing opportunities and thus preventing your soul from doing its work. Therefore any type of boredom is really wasted soul time. You are going against what you wished to achieve before you arrived on earth."

"Well, the way you put it seems to create even more pressure for me. It seems to say that I, or all of us, planned to do certain things for our soul, and if we don't do them, there's more pressure. I like to read and hook rugs for relaxation, but now I'm beginning to think that's a waste of my soul time."

He shook his head and smiled. "We say in the heavens that you always take everything to the extreme."

I looked at him wonderingly. They talked about me in the heavens?

"What do you mean?"

"You are in an earthly body. You need to care for it, let it rest, let it relax and allow it to replenish itself. Activities to relax your body, as well as your mind, are necessary. Some will turn to sports, others to reading, and others to hobbies, all of which allow them to escape their worries for periods. They relax physically and mentally and refresh their bodies and minds, and thus allow their souls to continue the path. *That is not wasted.* Do not confuse those activities with unnecessary activities, or with boredom. Each of you knows when boredom arrives in your heart. When it does you must do something constructive. Perhaps for that day it is reading a book, which might not be true soul work but will allow the boredom to dissipate and your mind to relax. When your body and mind are relaxed your soul is refreshed and can do its work.

"Do you understand?"

"I think so, but I'm not sure."

"You will, because the peace of God will surround you when you do His work.

"Amen."

Seventy-Three

I think some days it's just hard to pray, or even to sit down and find the silence. Am I being lazy? Or even worse, do I not want to hear God's plan for me? That's just selfish.

The stone I pick is a different color than I've ever had. It's a mixture of blue and green, but not turquoise, and it's metallic in some places. I leave it on my computer while I type.

The Archangel arrives. He hands me the stone I received yesterday, when I gave a talk at a women's Communion breakfast. As I passed out the stones, I took an orange one with a shape of a fish inside it. It spoke to me, not the color but the fish, which is the symbol of Christ's ministry, the symbol of the disciples. As I held the stone it gave me confirmation to continue my studies on the universality of these messages. I feel that Christ's message is an old one, probably starting from the beginning of time, and that he wants all of us to live it and be fishermen of people.

The Archangel nodded.

"The stone you were given yesterday was a tremendous gift," he said softly. "It was a sign for you to continue to spread God's word and to learn and study more about the universal love God has for all mankind. Many religions have structured God's love to fit their own ideas, but God's love cannot be structured by only one religion, one dogma. He created all of you in His likeness and image. He wants all of you to return home to be with Him. The greatest message is love, love for God and love for one another. This was Christ's message, this was the Creator's message at the beginning of time, this will be the message of Eternity."

"It sounds so simple, doesn't it?" I said sadly. "But it isn't. I think of the wars all around the world, and then I think of my own pettiness. My neighbors asked to cut down some of our trees, which they had a right to do because they were leaning on their property, but they didn't remove the stumps. Silly, huh? But I think to myself, if something as small and petty as that bothers me, no wonder wars begin over huge territories and countries."

"The earth is yours only to care for," the angel said. "No one owns it. No one has boundaries on it. The earth will continue long after your earthly bodies have returned to dust. As the prayer says, 'world ever-lasting.'"

I wondered at his wording: "world everlasting." I had always heard "world without end," but I guess it meant the same thing. Everlasting world. Everlasting God.

"Everlasting souls," he added, as if he had read my thoughts.

"What?"

"Everlasting souls. Your souls are everlasting. God has created you to be with Him, and He wants that for all of eternity. You have a word for eternity, but you really cannot fathom the concept of it. Nor can you fathom the concept of infinity, but both are very real with God. Your souls will travel the infinite road of eternity. You will move to different levels in knowledge, as your soul always tries to move closer to God."

"I saw an Episcopal bishop on television last night," I said. "Many in his church say he is not even a Christian because he says he can't believe that God would sacrifice His only son and have to have him suffer and die for our sins, rather than just forgive us. What would you say to that?"

The angel shook his head. "God has forgiven all of you, and Christ knew that when he came onto this earth. He came to save you from your sins, and he was your savior by teaching you the true meaning of loving your neighbor, loving your neighbor as yourself. He brought that commandment with him and he lived it out.

"God forgave humanity at the moment when all of you turned from Him. God has always continued to love you. It is you who have put up barriers to accepting His love, because by accepting pure love you must understand and be able to give pure love. That is your journey of learning, to be a vessel of love. When you have learned that, you will have reunited with the Lord. Christ came to teach you to understand pure love and to be pure love. By teaching you that lesson he has saved you. He gave up his life for his brother. He spent his life teaching others true love and was crucified for it. But he rose again in joy, because you have been taught the lesson.

"Now learn it."

Seventy-Four

I pick a stone that has no meaning for me. It's orange, with a large petal-like design in the middle. I had picked one similar to it a few weeks ago, but the inside looked like a fish so I saw in it a symbol of Christ, and confirmation that I was on the right path. This doesn't look like a fish, or if it does it's a jellyfish—hardly symbolic of Christ.

The angel appears to me at the beach. I haven't prayed or picked a stone in a while, and I hope he's not angry.

"You must pray every day," he says, approaching me from near the large rock. He is dressed in navy blue, with yellow and gold piping on his sleeves. The threads shine in the sunlight.

"I do pray every day, but I just don't sit down and pray quietly all the time."

"We have told you the importance of listening to your soul. Listening is the key word. You have been praying with 'lists,' as you often do. God understands that, and no prayers are empty. Of course He listens to your petitions, but how will you understand His answer unless you take the time to listen to it?"

I shrugged. I was hoping I didn't have to "listen" to His answer, that it would appear right in front of me, such as someone praying for a job and suddenly getting one, or praying for healing and being healed. They didn't have to "listen" to the answer—they just got it.

"But," the Archangel challenged, "what if the answer is more complicated than what you see? What if the answer is no, or if the answer is not so easily apparent as yes or no? What if someone is sick and God answers her prayers, and although she is not cured she is healed on a spiritual level, and thus is changing and her soul moving closer to God?"

I dismissed his words. "I knew you'd say something like that, but you know I also like to see 'the answer.'"

"Well, the answer from God is not always apparent, but it can always be accessed by listening to Him. That is where quiet meditative prayer is so powerful, because you understand the answers and the reasons for them, and because God gives you comfort and strength when you listen."

I sighed. I wanted answers up front: Yes. No. Right away.

"But that was not always your choice. You chose to learn in the human form. In doing so you must continually understand the lessons and the reasons for the lessons."

"I've been looking into a doctoral program," I said. "Can you help me?"

"Help you get in?" He smiled, shaking his head. "No, I'm sorry. That is up to you. We do not intercede in your lives in that manner."

"No, I don't mean help me get in and you know that. I mean help me understand the topic I might be picking."

"Yes," he said somberly.

"I've been researching Origen." I didn't bother explaining who Origen was because I was sure the Archangel knew all about him; I wouldn't have been surprised if he'd met him personally. Origen was an early Christian theologian, a teacher who lived from 175 to 263 A.D. or something like that. He believed in interpreting the Scriptures through reasoning, using the intellect, to discover the divine meaning the Holy Spirit had placed there on different levels. Origen believed in the pre-existence of the soul, universal salvation (which could encompass even Satan and the fallen angels), and the rising of the incorporeal body at the resurrection. During his lifetime he was considered conservative, but in the mid-500s the church excommunicated him and declared him a heretic.

"Yes?" the angel asked.

"It seems to me that his message, from those early years so much closer to Christ's death, was one of eternal hope and love."

"Are you surprised?"

"Yes," I said. "I'm not surprised at the message itself, because it's the message you've been giving me for years, but I'm surprised that he was considered conservative and that later on the church excommunicated him for the very ideas—"

"—that we have given to you."

"Yes," I said. "They are so similar."

"There is a resurrection of faith and spirituality going on now. The Holy Spirit is touching many people in many ways. Although churches are the basis of Christ's foundation and message, over the years many have forgotten their true purpose. They became places of politics, not of holiness. Each of you, as we have said before, has God within you. Your soul knows the answers it needs, and it knows where to seek them. But because you have all forgotten your true origin, you lose

257

your ability to interpret the God Who resides within you. For many centuries this divine connection you have with God was hidden from the masses. Individuals were kept from going astray by the threat of eternal damnation. Also, many people at the time were not educated, and trying to interpret Scriptures on their own could easily have led them down a wrong path. The Bible must be read very carefully, not merely in the same fashion as any other book. It must be surrounded in prayer. When you do this and ask God and His angels to protect you, you will interpret the word of God in His sense, but if you do not, you may be led astray by other spirits. The early church knew this and acted upon it in the easiest way, by shutting down individual interpretation and keeping the people strictly in line. But times have changed. Many more people are educated and have free time, which they understand they can use to delve more deeply into their spiritual lives. Thus they begin to get in touch with the divine within them and outside of them. But as I have stated, when you do this, encircle yourself with God's protection, because even now, many who are educated but don't do this can interpret the Bible wrongly."

"What about Origen then? Did he interpret Scripture correctly? Did he surround himself with prayer?"

"Yes," the angel said. "He was a devout and learned Christian. He prayed often and constantly, and although he knew evil existed, he would not allow it to come into his interpretations of Christ's words or those of the Old Testament."

"What I'd like to do in my studies," I said, "is to understand why Origen's message is so similar to mine."

"Because it is the true message," the Archangel replied. "It is the message Christ gave to you all, in different forms and at different times. But it is the same message. You are one and none will be saved until all are saved. Origen believed in a loving and true God. His God could not send people to an eternal damnation, no more than my God can. It is the soul's choice to turn away. Both Christ and Origen believed that with prayer and with God's unconditional love and mercy, all can return to God."

"Origen said that even the fallen angels can return to God. Is that true?"

The angel looked at me directly, his blue eyes piercing into me. "It has been stated that we made our decision and it was a final decision. But God is love. If the fallen angels want to return to love, God would

258

accept them. But they are in such darkness that they cannot understand love."

"But you tell me that we're to pray for people who are in darkness so that they can understand that love beckons them. Is that true for the angels also?"

The Archangel nodded. "Yes, it is true, but it is more difficult. They understood at the beginning of time their choice. Humanity turned away, but more out of ignorance than malice. The angels turned away in malice, pride and greed. So they need to overcome all of those before they can even see the light shining.

"Just go do your research and do not be anxious. Did we not tell you that God has a magnificent plan for each of you? Do not worry about the plan. Just follow the signs and follow the love of the Lord and everything will be done to glorify His name.

"Amen."

Seventy-Five

Picking a yellow, oblong-shaped stone, I wonder at its meaning. I'm confused these days. I want to enter a doctoral program, but I feel inadequately prepared. I'd like to study Origen, but the professor who is helping me said that many people have studied him, people who know Aramaic and Greek, people who know far more than I do, and that I had to find a different topic.

I am relieved to see the Archangel when I meet him at the beach, which is swarming with people. But I know they don't see us. I climb hurriedly onto the top of the rock.

"Am I on the right path?" I ask. "I feel so inadequate. I've been reading about the beginnings of religions, and I know nothing about any of them."

"And what have you learned?" he asked.

I shook my head. "It's amazing. The three large religions—Judaism, Christianity and Islam—all started out with a loving God, and then politics and people took it from there and changed it. I also discovered that all mystics have similar worldviews—the One, the love of your neighbor, the Light, and so on. And I found that the mystical side of religion is really the true religion."

"You have learned much in a short time," he said. "Now what will you do with it?"

"I don't know," I said. "I may have learned much for me, but theologians already know all this. What can I discover that is new?"

"The old."

"What?"

"Discover what is old and show how it is resurrected in the new again. You have been thinking of this. Do it. Show the Resurrected Christianity. It is Christianity in its earliest form, before politics and the pettiness of humanity changed it. It is being resurrected now, among each of you."

"Well, I have a question then," I said. "Everything about religion seems to be either 'divine revelation' or 'reasoning.' How is it that people are learning the old Christianity? Are they taking these paths?"

"They are learning the buried Christianity by divine intervention, through angels or other mystical experiences or through mystical readings, and then they are using reasoning to understand it. A mystical revelation, as you have read, was often just for the educated. The Kabbalah had to be studied later in life, when one was mature enough to understand it. All of these were valid reasons because people on the whole were not educated. The mystical understandings of the churches would have frightened them or led them toward evil. Knowledge such as this had to be understood from an educated and grounded point of view. So now that more people are more educated than ever before in the history of the world, not only is divine revelation given to them, but also, even if they did not experience it themselves, they are able to understand it by using God's gift of divine reason.

"Divine reason is rarely spoken of. Theologians put 'reasoning' and 'divine revelation' into two separate categories, thus dividing intellectuals from the masses. But divine reason is the coming of the Christ into each person's heart. It is the mingling of the revelations and reason. It is the answer to many questions and the answer to many prayers. It is what this third millennium will bring. Christians are searching for answers within their churches, and they will bring the answers to their churches. They are not Christians in exile but Christians in action. They are the Resurrected Christians.

"Study the early Fathers, study the conservative meanings of Christianity and Christ's message and bring that knowledge into the forefront of today. People are reading Buddhist works, ancient works, to understand their own Christianity. Then they are being brought, divinely, back to Christianity. It is a movement of divine reason, neither reason nor divine revelation alone but a mixture of the two.

"You will see that Origen understood that, and now the people of this time are understanding it. They are not reading the Scriptures on only one level but seeing the stories on many levels. They are seeing that Christ's message is one of salvation for all. This is being shown to them through academics, through writings from different cultures, and it brings them to the true message of Christianity."

Seventy-Six

The next day I pick a black stone—all colors combined.

The Archangel and I meet again, this time by a small pond on a high mountain. I no longer worry about the altitude or if I can breathe. I know I'm safe with him.

"Tell me more," I implore. "Tell me more about Christianity and today."

"It is simple. Christ has said He will return, and He is returning. He has sent the Holy Spirit, but many of you have closed your eyes and hearts. Now you are suddenly beginning to realize that there is more to life. As a society America has much in material possessions, but is discovering that it is still lacking and hungry for joy. That joy comes only from knowing and understanding God and understanding that you have a divine purpose in this life. The early Christian Fathers understood this. They also understood that the spiritual, not the material, is the most important aspect of anyone's life. They passed on their teachings and their reasoning and the divine revelations to groups. That process is beginning again. People have readings in their homes; they have group prayer; they find the divine in the compassionate nurse at a hospital. Each of you has God with you all the time, but you have forgotten that. You have forgotten your true purpose on this earth: to learn the lessons you are lacking and to return home to God.

"Many of the Resurrected Christians are following the ways of the early church. They are gathering in small groups, in people's homes, and finding a solace that they lost when the bureaucracy overwhelmed them."

"It's too bad the bureaucracy started," I said.

"It was necessary. Order is necessary for education. If some order had not evolved in the early church, there would have been too many different ways of thought, too many differing opinions, and the message of Christ would have died completely. The Gnostics had many wonderful beliefs, but also some that were not valid. But because they had no organization, their beliefs died along with them. So initially the bureaucracy that brought order to the church was a good thing. But humanity got carried away with it and forgot the purpose of the church.

262

In the bureaucracy and the politics, Christ's message was lost.

"Go, read more, and understand that a resurrection of Christianity is occurring. It is happening through divine reason, which is a new view of the world of spirituality."

Seventy-Seven

I'm writing my proposal for postgraduate work today and I'm very anxious. It's only two pages, but it's an academic two pages and needs to be clear and concise and have a point. I pick out a gem. It's clear, and it gives me comfort. I wonder if I'm on the right path. My husband says I am, but oftentimes on this journey I've had signs and doors open and I think I'm heading in the right direction, and then suddenly the doors shut. A stranger called me the other day and told me she had watched my TV show. She said she had had seven miscarriages, and that on my show I had said it was okay to get angry with God, because God can take it. I do always say that. I say that when people don't get mad at God, then they've broken the communication. As long as you're still talking to God you are open to the divine communication from Him. She went on to say that she doesn't know the difference between false hope and facing reality.

And I know what she means. She said that she was finally going to give up and realize that she was never going to carry a pregnancy. She said that a negative attitude would at least protect her.

I'm no psychologist, so it's hard for me to give advice to people who are struggling. But I'm a struggler too, so I told her what I believe to be the truth, that we can never succumb to negativity because it will engulf us and we'll become negative people who expect negative things and we'll attract negative things. There is a difference between false hope and protecting yourself from hurt. I said it was important to say the prayer I read in a book somewhere: "Lord, this or something better." I love that prayer, because it allows us to ask for our wants and still hold out hope for them, but gives it to God's will for something better. I suppose it's very much like the Our Father, but instead of saying "Thy will be done" you're saying it in a different way, a way that shows we understand that the will of God will always be better.

It gave her comfort, and when I hung up the phone I reminded myself, as I do after many lectures, "*Listen* to this advice. Don't be negative. Be open."

I look at the clear stone and I find myself back on the mountain with the Archangel. Snow is everywhere, and we are looking at a snow-covered icy pond. I see that I do not have the heavy coat and boots that he often gives me for cold places, but I am perfectly comfortable, not even chilly.

"Your faith is bringing you that," he said softly.

"What?" I said.

"Faith that God will care for you and not put you in danger. Initially you needed the comforts of the world, the heavy coat and boots, because you were still drawn to the materialness of the world. But slowly you are evolving, and you realize that when we meet the messages are for your spirit and the spirit of others, and that the comforts of the earth are secondary to all of that so they no longer even come into play for you. Just as the sparrows and the daisies are taken care of by God, so are you."

"Gee," I said, "is that only because I'm with you?"

"Eventually, if all of you accessed the spirit within you, it would become an everyday occurrence. In the Garden of Eden none of you needed clothing, not necessarily because of shame but because you were not concerned with the body. You understood the Lord would care for it. You were neither cold nor hot. You were enveloped in the Spirit. Then, when you turned away, you realized that you had material and bodily needs—and they took over. The soul became secondary. So when all of you find the Christ within you, and stay in that place and live in that place, you will no longer be concerned with heat and cold, with material necessities. All will be provided to you, because your soul will be completely nourished, and therefore your body will be completely nourished as well.

"That is what the resurrection of the body will mean at the end of eternity. The body is only a shell, and you will understand that the body is not necessary, because you will be in the spirit, seeing and feeling your bodies but not needing them. Then you will discard them and rise up to the Lord in spirit. That is living and being with the One, living and being in the Spirit. You will return to your knowledge."

I felt selfish. Here he was talking about important matters, and I was still concerned about my school paper. "Can you help me?"

"We have helped you," he said. "We have brought to you the means to use your intelligence to structure what is necessary for your learning and the learning of others. You have seen much and now realize the importance of all being one, and all returning to being one with the One.

"Go in peace. Never be anxious, for if you follow God's path, your way is beautiful. Take joy in it. I repeat those words for you today: Take joy in it. That is a lesson you need to learn personally, because often you are too obsessed with the goal, and you are not in the present joy that knowledge, work, and life bring. Take joy in today. Rejoice in today and co-create with the Lord.

"Amen."

"Amen," I said, seeing him rise in his yellow robes into the cloudless sky and then disappear. Easy for him to say, I thought. Take joy. Well, perhaps I could try. After all, as I told the woman who called me, negativity only brings negativity. Joy must attract joy.

Wouldn't that be nice?

Seventy-Eight

I haven't sat down and meditated for a while and I feel guilty about it. Today I pick a pale green stone, a color I have never seen before. Turning it around and around, I feel no meaning from it. When I place it on my computer it gets brighter and darker against the plastic keyboard.

Within minutes I'm sitting on the rock at the beach. The Archangel is beside me, his blonde hair appearing almost white against the color of his robe, the same color as the stone I picked today.

"Hello," I said softly, casting my eyes downward, ashamed that I hadn't sat down and meditated or visited with him.

"Do not be concerned," he said. "You have been praying to the Lord Almighty in many ways. There is no one correct form of prayer. We are here to instruct you in God's word when you need guidance, but we are with you all the time. We are messengers of God. As long as you continue to talk and pray to God, His messengers are pleased."

"But you said before that I must pray every day."

"And I still say that. Prayer should be not be just daily but constant. Your life should be a prayer to God. When you pray you speak and communicate, and you *listen* to God's plan for you. When you are open to that at every moment of your life, you will be led and your soul will follow its path. You have been learning that in the last year. Before that you needed to sit and listen to the messages each day. Although you still need these messages, you have begun to learn an important lesson and are changing."

"What lesson? What change?" I asked. I was always surprised to think I was making any progress.

"You have been giving more to God. You have been listening to His plan for you. In prayer before, you always prayed for your plans, and rarely did you listen to God's plans for you. Now you are beginning to give more of your anxiety and worry to God, and allowing the plans to unfold."

In his hand he held a gem of the same color as the one I had picked out. "This green is vital. It is healthy. It is the color of new June grass. The grass grows just by listening to the seasons, following its intuition,

267

following God's plan for it. It does not worry about the timetable. It waits for God, and then moves as God instructs."

"It's grass, for heaven's sake," I said sarcastically. "It's supposed to just grow. This is ridiculous. You can't compare grass to humans."

He looked at me and smiled. "I am comparing the plans of God with the plans of your soul. Your soul's plan is God's plan, the divine plan, and if you keep in touch with God your soul's plan will evolve just as the grass grows. But when you step away from it, and bring in human anxiety and doubt and worry, your soul does not move in the natural direction at the time it is supposed to bloom. You move away from the light toward the darkness and do not listen to the divine timetable."

"Oh," I said. "That makes a little more sense. There's a divine time-table?"

"One that you have chosen on a prior level, one that your soul wants to fulfill. By keeping in touch with the divine you allow your soul to follow its timetable."

"Can you tell me what mine is?"

He shook his head. "Your timetable is yours alone. It is not for me to divulge. You have chosen what you need to learn and how to learn it. If you move from that path your soul will continue to try to bring you back to the correct one. You already know your plans. You have just blocked them out. Keep in touch with God, and your soul will bring them back to you.

"Amen."

"Amen," I said, confused and wondering. I held the green stone and hoped that I would grow like the grass.

Seventy-Nine

I pick a clear gem and I'm relieved. I've been confused about the "divine plan" God has for me, and the clear gem seems to say that it will all become clear. That's probably very elementary on my part, but it's comforting.

The Archangel greets me on the rock near the beach, which is deserted and cold. The fog is hanging lightly over us, and snow is beginning to fall onto the sand. It's not sticking, but still it's falling, and I am surprised because in reality it is fall, not winter.

"Why the snow?" I ask, raising my palm up to try to catch a flake. "It's only September. We don't get snow yet."

"There are times in your life when you are in the winter of your soul. Right now that winter has been with you for a couple of years. You have been listening, resting, and trying to understand God's plan. Recently you have been going with it, and we are proud of that. You are accepting an offer to publish the second book, even though it involves humility and acceptance on your part. God works in all kinds of ways. You must be open to His gifts, and finally you are seeing that.

"But this week you again seem to be stepping away from the silence within your soul and trying to consciously take control of your soul's life. Don't. The winter of your soul is a time of rest, growth, and rejuvenation for the spring of your soul. Each of you goes through cycles, like the seasons. Each of you needs time to burrow, to think, to contemplate, and to allow the seeds to rest. Then spring will come and bring the divine growth. Christ went to the desert and meditated and prayed for forty days. It was the winter of his soul. Each of you needs that winter; each of you needs each season. They will continue to repeat in cycles throughout your life. Some of your seasons may be longer than you expected, but they are always there. Seasons are for growth, rest, rejuvenation and moving on."

"Did you do that in order?"

"Fall, winter, spring and summer. Fall is growth."

I shook my head. "No, fall is death."

He smiled. "Is not death the ultimate growth? Is it not the ultimate stage of moving to another level, of opening another chapter, of putting behind the old and beginning to face the new?"

"I didn't think of it like that," I said. "You make it sound as if it's something to look forward to."

He smiled. "No. This life is a gift, and you are here to grow and appreciate the opportunity to grow. But when you are not capable of growth anymore, you are in the fall season of your soul. In life, you are in the fall of your life, and you move on to the next level. When the flowers have bloomed to their fullest, their cycle is over and fall arrives. So is it at each stage of your development, or chapters of your soul's journey. You complete phases, bury them, learn from them, and then move on. Like buds on a rose, you learn and move until the rose has bloomed.

"It is a beautiful cycle.

"I am here to tell you today, and to tell the others: Do Not Struggle. Learn and grow to your capacity, do the best you can and continue to persevere in your spiritual life, but do not struggle in it, because struggling is just a sign that your personality is trying to overcome your soul's path. Go with the flow of the current, go with the breath of God, go in peace and honor this gift of opportunity, this gift of life.

"Amen."

"Amen," I said, not quite sure I understood everything he had told me today, but sure that at some point at least a part of it would make some sense.

Eighty

It's been two years since this book started. It's been a tumultuous time and yet one of growth for me. I haven't talked with the Archangel in months, partly because of my own laziness at prayer but mostly because I didn't feel called to sit, meditate and listen to him. I felt the need to go out into the world and try to apply some of things he has taught me.

I'm leaving for England in a few weeks to go for a final interview at a British university to pursue a doctoral program there. I'd like to compare third-century Christianity to the Christianity that is reviving in the churches today. In the third century the Christian theologian Origen was considered one of the most conservative theologians of the time, and yet he believed in the preexistence of the soul, and that all will be saved, even Satan if he turns to God. I've also been exploring how Origen often wrote of God in the feminine, something that many women of today need to hear. Abused by fathers, boyfriends or other males, they find it difficult to pray to a male figure. I personally believe that God is neither male nor female, yet our language is so limited that it forces us to refer to God as gendered.

Today as I try to sit in prayer I am still extremely upset over a recent incident. Someone who has not, I know, had an easy life lashed out at me in anger, and because of the hurt I too had suffered, I didn't act with compassion and I returned that anger. I feel horrible about that, and extremely guilty for not practicing compassion as the Archangel has taught us to do.

I pick a green stone. Although to others it may mean something different, to me green has always meant health, healing and new growth, like the green grass of June.

The Archangel returns. He is sitting on the large rock overlooking the sea, which is turbulent today. We've had a big storm recently, and although there is little snow on the sands, the sea is roaring. I bundle up my collar.

Looking at me he says, "You do not need that with me. God will protect you from the elements."

At his words my overwrought emotions boil over. I begin to confess to him all my transgressions, not to receive absolution but to get it off my chest. I cry and feel guilty, wondering why he has given me all these lessons, for it seems I have learned none of them.

He takes my hand, pats it, and smiles at me. "For years you did not even understand that you needed to learn lessons for the advancement of your soul. Now you do. And now, when you see that you are struggling with these lessons, you are even more torn—because knowledge brings wisdom. When you were ignorant you did not know what you were not learning. But you do now. That is a monumental step for all of you, to realize that you are here to learn lessons. You personally are here to learn compassion, but do not be so difficult on yourself. You too become hurt, and that is human. That is why Christ was both God and man. He was hurt when his disciple Peter denied him three times, but he forgave him and loved him. That is the example of God/man. This is the example that you, as a people, must try to embrace. You will not do it all the time, because at this stage you are not yet able to. Many of you think of yourselves as 'enlightened,' and in some cases you are. But still, when it truly hits home, such as when someone denies you three times, you cannot find forgiveness in your heart.

"But the step is in knowing that you need to forgive, to give it to God and forgive yourselves. The Our Father says, 'forgive us our transgressions as we forgive others.' The 'others' include not only your neighbor but also yourself. If you do not forgive yourself, how can you forgive your neighbor? When you hold all this anger or guilt within, you are not ready to give it to God, or to turn to God so that you can accept God's forgiveness. Remember, you must turn and give your transgressions to God. This is for all of you to remember and hold fast to. When you do this you are given the strength of God within you. You are given the light to follow on your spiritual path. You are given love and understanding from the One Who radiates it."

I bowed my head. The words were lovely but I felt like an emotional mess. And I wasn't sure I was even "getting" the words.

"These visits are ending now," he said.

I began to cry loudly. The sobs shook my shoulders. "How can you leave me now? I thought I was just beginning to 'get it' after two years of these conversations, and when I falter and fall, like this week, you tell me you're leaving? At one of my darkest hours? Don't do that to me!"

He took my hand. "We never leave you. It is just that these visits are ending for now. None of you yet realize that with change, whether it

272

appears chaotic or not, growth arrives. This is a period of growth for you. I have come to you today because God has sent me. He has sent me to tell you that each of you needs to work toward wholeness, not perfection. Being whole does not mean being perfect in human terms. Being whole for God means that you have returned to Him, and with that you have joined His perfection."

"I don't quite understand."

"Remember that this journey is not always one of understanding here on earth. Sometimes it is, and other times it is not. But we are here to tell everyone that in each situation you have the opportunity to grow. So take each wondrous time, and each difficult time, and realize that it is the soul heading you in the direction you picked before your birth. Realize that through prayer and joining with God, you will follow the path your soul wants to be on. But you must join with God. You must not lament and ruminate on your errors or the errors of others, because then forgiveness will never happen. Even if mental illness is involved, do the best you can and then give it to God, because the mentally ill are also learning and teaching lessons, just as you are.

"My words to you, to all of you, are to join with God. Give God your worries, your fears, your failures, but in doing this always ask for guidance and compassion and love from Him from Whom all wondrous things flow. Tap into that Power, knowing it is a power beyond your understanding. It is the strongest power in infinity, stronger than evil, stronger than anything you can imagine. Call to us. We are messengers of God who surround each of you all the time. We cannot interfere in your lives without your soul's consent. So each day talk to your soul, asking it to lead you and to allow you to be open to its path.

"Go. Forgive yourself, forgive others, and turn to the Lord. Then you will feel the forgiveness He always has for you. But you cannot find that forgiveness without finding love and compassion, finding God, within yourselves and within your neighbors. When you unite yourself with this energy of the Lord, your lives will be empowered.

"Go now. Take these lessons to heart and learn from them, always at the pace you need to. Remember this is infinity. God does not limit you to a timetable. He waits patiently until 'all are saved.' He waits for all to learn wisdom and love. And it will be.

"Amen."

He took his hand from mine and disappeared into the dark cloudy sky. I heard angels singing from the heavens, their voices a variety—

high and sweet, low and strong. I kept my eyes on the sky. It looked as if it might snow again, and I wanted to see my friend—one last time.

It seemed he was leaving me just when I needed him most.

I heard his voice. "Go. Learn the lessons, follow your soul, and each of you will change the world. Christ's prophecy will become reality: Heaven will be on earth for everyone. Amen."

The skies filled with the voices of the angels singing "Amen" over and over again.

I stood up, somehow more fortified yet still tired and drained. Looking up to the sky again I saw nothing but dark clouds. I thanked the Lord for these visits, and silently thanked my friend the Archangel for his patience with me. He was more patient with me than I was with myself.

"That is the lesson of compassion." The words echoed again and again in my head.

I turned, climbed down from the rock, and walked the lonely stretch of beach. The sands blew, the snow drifted slightly, but I felt no chill. Oddly enough, in a time of turbulence I was starting to find peace.

Lead me, Lord. Allow me to follow my soul's destination, the path I chose before I was born to help me come closer to You. Help me to learn wisdom, compassion and love. And please help me, even when I falter, to pick up again, and turn toward the light.

I walked slowly on the deserted beach, trying to understand the words of the angels, and knowing that I wouldn't be on this beach again for a long time, if ever.

Thank you for this journey, I prayed, and help me to continue it. Amen.

Dear Reader,

Gems are readily available at a number of easily accessible shops: arts & craft stores, flower supply stores (many times these gems are used in a glass vase before filling with silk or real flowers) and toy stores (I used the gems from a game called Mancala and there are often replacement stones available without buying the game); if you can't find these particular gems, try marbles at a toy store, or even pieces of sea glass found on the beach.

To order books, the easiest way is through the Internet site of Amazon.com or others. But if you would rather order through the mail, for each book please send a check for $14.95 plus $2.00 for shipping and handling to Veritas Press, P.O. Box 270735, West Hartford, CT 06127-0735. (Connecticut residents please add 6% sales tax.)

Thanks!

Anne